THE RULE OF LAW
IN ENGLAND

Dr. Harris has written an exceptionally lucid study
of an intricate period and assessed its unique impact
upon the history of England. The Parliamentary victories of the late seventeenth century came to fruition
in the eighteenth century, in the period that has since
become known as the classical age of the constitution.

*The king no longer wielded despotic power, and
statesmen such as Walpole and the younger Pitt had
as large a control in the affairs of state as the Crown.
The triumph of legal administration was accompanied by gigantic economic expansion. The accumulation of capital, the advance of industry and trade,
a new colonial empire, an expanding population and
growing cities—all combined to make eighteenth-
century England a nation of vigorous power.*

*The author also evaluates the period's cultural ad-
vance. Its writers were Dryden, Defoe, Dr. Johnson, Pope . . . its craftsmen Chippendale, Sheraton,
Wedgwood, Spode. The eighteenth-century country
houses such as Blenheim, built by "Capability"
Brown, have never been equaled. But most important, there was a new spirit of humanitarianism, an
awareness of social justice and the rule of law, that
was to become the conscience of ensuing centuries.*

The text includes illustrations and a bibliography
of sugges

Other MENTOR Books on English History

A Short History of 16th Century England: 1485-1603 *by G. W. O. Woodward*

How the Tudor monarchs from Henry VII to Elizabeth I suppressed the medieval church; brought order to a politically chaotic land, and launched overseas exploration that was to result in the far-reaching power of the British Empire. Includes brief bibliographies of notable personalities of the era, reading lists, and eight pages of photographs.
(#MT511—75¢)

A Short History of 17th Century England: 1603-1689 *by G. E. Aylmer*

A study of the most crucial period in English political history: the struggle between Crown and Parliament during the eighty-six years between the accession to the throne of James I and that of William and Mary. Includes full comparative date chart, maps, and eight pages of photographs.
(#MT512—75¢)

A Short History of 19th Century England: 1793-1868 *by John W. Derry*

A study of England under the impact of the Industrial Revolution, which transformed her from a rural to an urban nation, brought about heated debates on reforms, and posed new questions in areas of politics, philosophy and religion. Includes chronological table of events, comprehensive bibliography and eight pages of photographs. (#MT516—75¢)

A Short History of 20th Century England: 1868-1962 *by T. L. Jarman*

England's most catastrophic years, as she passed from a position of unrivaled strength through two wars that threatened her existence and led to the emergence of Russia and the United States as greater powers. Includes chronological table of events, comprehensive bibliography of suggested reading, and eight pages of photographs. (#MT517—75¢)

To Our Readers

A Short History
of
Eighteenth-Century
England

by R. W. HARRIS

A MENTOR BOOK

PUBLISHED BY THE NEW AMERICAN LIBRARY

*Published as a MENTOR BOOK
by arrangement with Blandford Press Ltd.,
who have authorized this softcover edition.*

FIRST PRINTING, JULY, 1963

This book is published in England under the title
England in the Eighteenth Century, 1689—1793

MENTOR TRADEMARK REG. U.S. PAT. OFF. AND FOREIGN COUNTRIES
REGISTERED TRADEMARK——MARCA REGISTRADA
HECHO EN CHICAGO, U.S.A.

*MENTOR BOOKS are published by
The New American Library of World Literature, Inc.
501 Madison Avenue, New York 22, New York*

PRINTED IN THE UNITED STATES OF AMERICA

Contents

List of Illustrations

Plates will be found between pp. 120–121

Acknowledgments

The illustrations have been reproduced by permission of the following:

1 The Duke of Bedford
2 Pat Maxwell
3 The Trustees of the British Museum
4, 5, 6, 7 and 11 The Trustees of the National Portrait Gallery
8, 9, 10 The United States Information Service

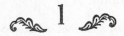

Preview: The Eighteenth Century

IT IS CONVENIENT to regard "the eighteenth century" in England as extending from the Revolution of 1688 to the outbreak of the great French Wars in 1793. If we ask what there is of special importance in this period, we may single out three aspects for special mention.

First, it is the classical age of the constitution. Before 1688, government was very much the personal affair of the monarch; after 1830 it rapidly became the business of ministers and the House of Commons. Between these two dates there was a subtle balance between the powers of the Crown, its ministers, the Lords and Commons, which contemporaries thought to be one of the special virtues of the English system of government. The king was head of the executive; he chose ministers and was directly concerned with policy-making; yet ministers such as Walpole, Newcastle and the Younger Pitt clearly pursued policies of their own. The Commons did not choose ministers for the Crown, but they could make it impossible for the Crown to retain for long a minister they did not want. In such subtleties lay the nature of the eighteenth-century constitution. But too much attention need not be paid to the intricacies of the political machine in order to discover the virtues of that constitution. Perhaps the two most praiseworthy were:

1. The triumph of the rule of law: equality before the law was rightly prized, and both judges and juries put the principle into practice. No minister was above the law.

9

2. Religious toleration: this was by no means complete; the Roman Catholics of Ireland certainly still suffered from legal disabilities, and Roman Catholics anywhere might occasionally be the victims of the mob. Yet toleration was widely practised in the eighteenth century, and the dissenters flourished.

Second, the economic expansion of this period was without parallel in English history. The growth of population, the speed of capital formation, industrial expansion, the growth of overseas markets and of Empire, all combined to make Britain for the first time a great world Power.

Third, it was an age of great cultural achievement. It is customary to refer to this age as the age of Enlightenment. This phrase covers a good many things. It meant that men and women were much concerned with the business of living, with the comforts and enjoyment which this life could offer, and with the achievements of the human mind. It meant deep interest in the new science, in ethics, in moral discussions, in prose works. It meant that the poet, the controversialist, the architect, the painter, the landscape gardener, had wider recognition than hitherto. It meant a reading public: writers and poets made more money from literature than ever before. It meant a close connection between literature and politics, with the great controversies of Dryden, Swift and Addison at the beginning of the period, and the writings of Burke at the end. It was an age which revelled in the new-found freedom of the press, subject only to a savage law of libel.

In one sense it was the age of aristocracy, the age of refinement. This was the ideal of the third Earl of Shaftesbury (d. 1713) and of the Earl of Chesterfield; it was the ideal reflected in Richardson's Sir Charles Grandison, the hero of the novel of that name. The eighteenth century survives for us especially in the superb country houses, now often maintained with the help of the half-crowns of a visiting public: Blenheim, created by Sir John Vanbrugh as a national monument to England's greatest soldier, with a lake specially provided by "Capability" Brown; Wentworth Woodhouse, built by Henry Flitcroft for the Marquis of Rockingham, the largest house in England, but architecturally less satisfactory than many others; Woburn, also by Flitcroft, built for the Duke of Bedford; Stowe, built for Lord Cobham; Houghton

Hall, Norfolk, the splendid home of Sir Robert Walpole; Chiswick House, built by Lord Burlington. Such houses were built for the glorification of their owners and still seem to reflect the aristocratic ostentation of their age. Yet it was an aristocracy of wealth as much as of birth. Many noble houses were built from the proceeds of trade. Many a tasteful town house was built for a prosperous merchant. But the aristocracy set high standards of taste, and had a discerning eye for the able artist and craftsman. The secret of the success of eighteenth-century styles lies partly in the homogeneity of all the arts: the furniture of Chippendale, Sheraton, Hepplewhite, the interior decoration of Robert Adam, the china of Wedgwood, even the silverware and the book-bindings, were chosen with the same object of harmony.

In another sense the great achievements of the age were those of the middle class, the merchant, the craftsman, the adventurer, the industrialist. The great literary names of the period, Defoe, Addison, Pope, Dr Johnson, Goldsmith, Cowper, were of humble origin. So were the great pioneers of invention, Kay, Hargreaves, Arkwright, Crompton, the Darbys, John Wilkinson, James Brindley, Wedgwood and Spode. But the aristocracy were ready patrons of literature, the arts and industry, and thus again the homogeneity of eighteenth-century society was preserved.

The eighteenth century was a vigorous, individualistic age, of growing wealth and civilisation. It had its dark side, its dirt, disease, brutality; these were part of all past ages. The great achievement of the eighteenth century was to begin to look at them with new eyes, and to begin their elimination. To these things we shall return in the course of this book.

The Wealth of England

THE ENGLAND OF the century following the Revolution of 1688 was one of very remarkable economic expansion and social change. The first remarkable fact is that the population doubled between 1688 and 1801, rising from about five millions to over ten millions. The reasons for so rapid an increase, without parallel in previous history, are perhaps not fully understood, but they must be closely related to a fundamental improvement in economic and social life. Before the eighteenth century the size of a population was largely determined by its food supplies, for in times of famine people starved, and disease took a heavy toll, especially of the young. During the eighteenth century there was usually an abundant supply of good food, meat and fresh vegetables for those able to buy them. The birth-rate appears to have risen slightly after the middle of the century, probably through earlier marriages consequent upon greater freedom and prosperity. But more important was the fall in the death-rate. At first the fall was slow, and in fact in London, up to the middle of the century, deaths exceeded births, and the rapid growth of the capital is to be explained by the steady influx of people from the countryside. But after 1750 the death-rate in London fell rapidly, so that whereas it was one in twenty-one in 1750, it was only one in thirty-five by the end of the century. There was greater care of the young and old with the new spirit of humanitarianism. There was improved medical knowledge, consequent upon the discoveries of Smellie, the Hunters and Jenner. There was greater cleanliness, both in city streets and the disposal of sewage, and in personal habits, such as in the washing of clothes. With all its imperfections, life in the eighteenth century was in some ways more secure than in previous centuries.

It is difficult to present an accurate picture of eighteenth-century life without suggesting contrast, and even paradox. For there are few statements which can be made about the period which cannot be countered by an apparent contradiction. Thus the eighteenth century can be thought of as the age of hard materialism, cruelty, public hangings and floggings, gin-drinking and early death, but also as the age of gracious living, prosperity, growing humanitarianism and greater security of life. There is much truth in both sides of the picture.

The later seventeenth century saw a rapid growth of national wealth and prosperity. England's total foreign trade, which in 1662–3 was valued at £7,750,000, had increased by 1688 to £11,500,000, and capital accumulation had increased by £70,000,000. The main source of this new wealth was foreign trade. The English had learnt much from the Dutch about seamanship, shipbuilding and the organisation of trade. London was ousting Amsterdam, as Amsterdam had ousted Antwerp, as the greatest commercial city of the west. In the age of Mercantilism state power was closely allied with national wealth, and the great chartered companies were seen as the spearhead of both. The three most important were the East India, the Royal African and the Hudson's Bay Companies. All three prospered in spite of the French wars after 1689; East India stock varied between 122½ and 500 in the reigns of William III and Anne. By 1700 total foreign trade was £13,500,000, and by 1717 £15,500,000.

London

The bulk of the new wealth flowed into London. London dominated England more completely in the eighteenth century than it was ever to do again. Between 1688 and 1800 London about doubled in size, from about half a million to nearly a million, and was thus much the largest city in Europe. Its rapid growth was a powerful stimulus to economic and social change. It constantly sucked in people from the countryside. Its enormous demands in food and manufactures were a stimulus to both an agricultural and an industrial revolution, the effects of which radiated throughout the country. Dr Johnson and Boswell speculated in 1763 upon the importance of London:

> I have often amused myself with thinking how different a place London is to different people. . . . A politician thinks of it merely as the seat of government in its different departments; a grazier, as a vast market for cattle; a mercantile man, as a place where a prodigious deal of business is done upon 'Change; a dramatic enthusiast, as the grand scene of theatrical entertainments; a man of pleasure, as an assemblage of taverns, and the great emporium for ladies of easy virtue. But the intellectual man is struck with it, as comprehending the whole of human life in all its variety, the contemplation of which is inexhaustible.

Much of this we can reconstruct in our imaginations today. There was the Whitehall, Westminster, St James' Street, St James' Square and Mayfair of Walpole, Pitt, Burke and Fox; there was the world of literature and art, Covent Garden, the Strand, Fleet Street and Vauxhall Gardens, the world of Reynolds, Dr Johnson, Goldsmith and Garrick; and finally there was the world of which we know much less, the world of courts and alleys, gin-shops and poverty such as we glimpse in Hogarth's prints. At one end of the scale was the tasteful magnificence of William Kent's No. 44, Berkeley Square, with its staircase, the finest in London; and at the other the spectacle of Newgate, Tyburn, the pillory, the press-gangs and the workhouse.

After 1688 London became less industrial and more commercial. There were still important textiles, metallurgical and shipbuilding industries around London, but these became less important than the great business of finance and commerce. The growth of a new monied interest soon burst the bounds of the old "City of London" both geographically and figuratively. The City in the sense of the ancient corporation consisted of some twelve or fifteen thousand freemen, who elected the Common Council, the four members of Parliament and the city officers. There was a vigorous corporate spirit, and the City usually found itself in the eighteenth century in opposition to the government. It was so hostile to Walpole that in 1725 he had to pass an Act curbing the activities of the Common Council. London was always the centre of many rebellious spirits who rejoiced in opposing the government. Some were merchants who had financial interests in maritime and colonial war, some were artisans or unemployed, the victims of periodic trade recessions. They found ready leaders among the parliamentary Opposition. During the eighteenth century William Pulteney, the elder Pitt and Charles James Fox successively drew much strength from being the idol of the London malcontents. Sometimes historians have referred to them simply as "the mob", but that is to do them an injustice. It is true that from time to time we see the London coal-heavers a turbulent and brutalised crowd of rioters. But in 1761 Alderman William Beckford, a Lord Mayor, Member of Parliament, and devoted follower of Pitt, explicitly denied that his followers were a "mob":

> The sense of the people, Sir, is a great matter. I don't mean the mob. . . . When I talk of the sense of the people I mean the middling people of England, the manufacturer, the yeoman, the merchant, the country gentleman, they who bear the heat of the day. . . . They have a right, Sir, to interfere in the condition and conduct of the nation which makes them easy or uneasy who feel most of it, and, Sir, the people of England, taken in this limitation are a good-natured, well-intentioned and very sensible people, who know better perhaps than any other nation under the sun whether they are well governed or not.[1]

"They who bear the heat of the day" is a fine phrase, and the whole is a manly statement of the new liberalism.

More research is needed before we can speak with certainty about the condition of the lower classes in eighteenth-century London. There were many gradations: masters, journeymen, artisans, labourers, street-sellers and casual workers, Some skilled men, such as instrument-makers, could earn as much as four pounds a week. Defoe said that journeymen and artisans could earn from fifteen shillings to fifty shillings a week. Yet it is certain that many were not so well off. Silk-workers, framework knitters and stocking-weavers were particularly badly off, and many were earning no more than nine shillings a week at a time like the 1770s, when it was estimated that the minimum cost of keeping a man, his

[1] See the brilliant paper by Miss Sutherland in *Essays Presented to Sir Lewis Namier* (Macmillan).

wife and three children was about one pound. It followed that women and children were expected to work. There were times of comparative prosperity, but also times of great hardship, as in the years after 1777 when the price of food rose, and the price of labour fell. Silk-weaving was particularly affected by trade fluctuations, and Mrs. George writes:

> The history of the parishes of Christchurch and Bethnal Green in the eighteenth century is one of a continual struggle with poverty and debt, their workhouses repeatedly swamped with destitute weavers.[2]

It was certainly a century of trade fluctuations and periodic hardship, but the picture was by no means entirely dark. Men worked hard, though irregularly. The chief anxiety of employers was that their workers, with a few shillings in their pockets, would not turn up for work until it was spent. No master expected to see his workers on a "hanging day", that is to say, a public execution, which became also a public holiday. There were trade-clubs by which workers bargained with their employers, and Francis Place commented upon their activity in the years after 1770:

> I have before me now tables of the weekly wages of journeymen tradesmen in London, who, in their different trades, may amount to about 100,000 men, all of whom had separate trade-clubs for many years, and, in spite of the Combination Laws, did, from time to time, raise their wages by means of strikes.

He showed that the average wage in 1777 was from eighteen shillings to twenty shillings a week; that a strike among the tailors pushed them up to twenty-five shillings in 1795, and that succeeding strikes pushed them to thirty-six shillings by 1813. These wages were in part offset by the extremely high price of food, yet there was still a margin which permitted an improved standard of living.

The housing of the poor was certainly shockingly bad: many families occupied a single room, and indeed slept in a single bed. Clothes were rarely if ever washed. The poor lived in crowded courtyards; drains were open, and water

---

[2] On the subject of London see M. D. George: *London Life in the XVIII Century* (London School of Economics).

supplies contaminated. Yet the century saw a steady improvement in conditions. The Great Fire of London had gutted some of the worst slums, and they were never quite so bad again. Brick houses replaced the old lath-and-plaster and timber buildings of the Middle Ages. Some main thoroughfares and fine squares were laid out, streets were widened. Westminster Bridge and Blackfriars Bridge were built about the middle of the century. In 1762 an Act was passed providing for street-paving in Westminster. Previously each householder was supposed to pave and repair the street in front of his house; now commissioners were appointed to pave and repair the streets. Other Acts provided for scavenging and sewage disposal. In the seventeenth century street-lighting hardly existed, and the streets were extremely dangerous after dark. During the eighteenth century London received the best street-lighting in Europe. It is said, indeed, that when the Prince of Monaco came to London at the invitation of George III, he arrived in the evening and was flattered to find the streets magnificently illuminated in his honour; what he saw was in fact only the normal street-lighting.

The sports of the time were always full-blooded, often brutal and degrading. The tavern, the alehouse, the gambling den, cock-fighting, bull-baiting, annual fairs, the theatres, the tea-gardens, Bedlam, Tyburn, were all part of the riotous London scene.

After 1715 the price of corn was low, spirits were cheap, and there was a great outburst of gin-drinking. Spirit-shops opened everywhere; the Westminster justices reported that every tenth house sold liquor. In St Giles in 1750 it was said that every fourth house was a gin-shop. The death-rate rose rapidly, but the government was slow to act, for distilling was said to be a needful buttress to the agricultural interest. The Gin Act of 1736 imposed heavy restrictions, but it was so unpopular that it could not be enforced, and gin drinking not merely continued, but increased. It was not until the Act of 1751, which was moderate and enforceable, that drinking was really curbed. Consumption then fell steadily during the following decades, and the death-rate declined accordingly. Mrs George comments: "It would be hardly possible to exaggerate the cumulatively disastrous effects of the orgy of spirit-drinking between 1720 and 1751".

Commercial Revolution

To understand the eighteenth century we must set all these facts of contemporary conditions in a wider perspective. Every century from the twelfth century onwards can be thought of, in England, as in some way or another enlarging the scope of human activity. Often this was connected with the growth of towns, of trade and new industries. It was accompanied by the slow disintegration of feudal society, the disappearance of villeinage, and the rapid changes of land-ownership in the sixteenth and seventeenth centuries. It was marked by the growth of the powers of Parliament, and by the idea of the rule of law. The period after 1688 must be seen as one of the periods in which this evolution takes a great leap forward. The triumph of parliamentary government and the rule of law, the growth of population, the expansion of foreign trade, the accumulation of capital, the growth of industry, the expansion of London, all these things are both the cause and the consequence of greatly increased productive capacity and ingenuity. The whole amounts to a commercial revolution. There are abundant facts to illustrate this. By 1700 there were more than a hundred joint-stock companies in existence, with a nominal capital of £4,000,000. Stocks and shares were beginning to be regarded as an excellent form of investment. Many of these companies were for the development of patents, of which 236 were taken out between 1660 and 1700. There were water companies, postal companies, street-lighting companies, companies for the manufacture of white paper (for which the patent is dated 1685), silk, linen, glass, vegetable oil, soap, textiles and salt-petre. There were banking companies, fire insurance and life insurance companies, a company for the development of the Greenland fisheries, and even a company for the recovery of treasure from wrecks. Hence the growth of stock-jobbery, and the whole business of Exchange Alley. The governments of William III and Queen Anne soon learnt the importance of the great new engine of credit. Before 1688 men lent money to the government at great risk, and therefore at extortionate rates of interest which were sometimes unpaid. After 1693 government loans were guaranteed by Parliament. Men lent money with a new confidence, and the government learnt how to make a National Debt a form of strength instead of weakness. The connection between the government and the new monied interest became very close. Thus in the reign of Queen Anne a City syndicate headed by Sir Gilbert Heathcote invested heavily in government stock. Heathcote was a wine merchant, a shrewd financier, one of the founders of the Bank of England, and the model for Addison's Sir Andrew Freeport in *The Spectator*. These financiers usually found it wise to be close allies of the succeeding governments of the eighteenth century.[3]

At the centre of the financial system was the Bank of England. The idea of the Bank had been borrowed from the Dutch, for it was believed that the Bank of Amsterdam was the secret of Dutch financial strength. It was probably suggested by the Scotsman, William Paterson, to the great financiers of the time, Heathcote, the three Houblon brothers (French Huguenot immigrants) and Theodore Janssen. The Bank of England was established by the Ways and Means Act of 1694, by which it was to raise £1,200,000 at eight per cent., the subscribers to become a corporation entitled the Governor and Company of the Bank of England. It was greatly aided by the enormous stock of bullion which had piled up in England, and the loan was subscribed in twelve days. The Bank made its profits not only from the £100,000 from the government, but also from discounting bills and tallies, and from interest on further loans. Its issue of bank notes has been called by Sir John Clapham "England's main contribution to the evolution of European banking". It was a great financial success, and after the first half-year it was able to pay a six per cent. dividend. It was useful to the government, not only by its loans, but also by facilitating the transference of large sums to the Continent for the wars against Louis XIV. The close relations between the Bank and the government has much to do with the success of Marlborough's wars. England was fortunate in having a number of able financiers among her ministers. Charles Montagu, the father of the Bank, was First Lord of the Treasury until 1699, and a financial genius. Godolphin (an excellent financier) was Lord Treasurer from 1702 until 1710. Walpole was Chancellor of the Exchequer in 1715, and later First Lord

---

[3] But Heathcote overplayed his hand when he took it upon himself to lecture Queen Anne on the dangers of accepting a tory government in 1710. The Queen ignored his advice. See Ch. 5.

of the Treasury. Important also was the fact that behind the scenes William Lowndes was Secretary of the Treasury from 1695 until his death in 1724. He and Pepys are the first great civil servants in the modern sense in our history.

With all its great national importance, the Bank of England had become involved in politics. It was thought of as a whig institution, and many of the great financiers of London were whigs. The tories attempted to gain their own engine of credit, first by a National Land Bank in 1696, and then by the South Sea Company in 1711. The latter was a masterstroke of Harley. In May 1711 he proposed to incorporate the holders of the £9,000,000 unsecured debt of the time into a South Sea Company. The Company would receive from the government six per cent. on the debt, secured against indirect taxes, and the Company would gain the right to trade with Spanish South America when concessions were obtained from Spain at the end of the war. From Harley's point of view it was a brilliant stroke. The tories had gained an important footing in the City (where the news of the Company was received with bonfires of rejoicing). It sweetened the tory proposal to make peace by offering merchants the opportunity of new profits in the Spanish market. The new journalism of the time was beginning to make itself felt. There poured from the press stories of the unimaginable wealth to be gained from new markets overseas, and men gathered in the coffee-houses, not for entertainment, but to hear the latest news, and to do business.

By the Asiento Treaty with Spain in March 1713 the Company gained the right to supply 4,800 Negroes a year for thirty years to Spanish South America, and in addition to send one ship of not more than 500 tons for other trade. But the Company was never much more than a sham. It was ill-organised, there was dreadful inefficiency, and its profits were few. It might indeed have sunk into an early insignificance if John Law had not been performing his financial miracles in France. Something of the fever which was gripping France spread to London in 1720. In January Parliament approved the government's plan to transfer the debt to the South Sea Company at four per cent., thus saving the government £400,000 a year. At the end of the year the Company would make an outright gift of £3,000,000 to the government for the extinction of the debt. The project was thoroughly unsound, for the Company must have known that it could not possibly provide the £3,000,000 at the end of the year. Yet by March South Sea stock started to rise sharply. Isaac Newton, who said that he could calculate the motions of the heavenly bodies, but not the madness of people, sold out in April when his profit was a hundred per cent. A wave of speculation followed. Many other companies were floated, insurance companies, pawnbrokers' companies, manufacturing companies. Some newspapers published as jokes mythical companies with fantastic objectives (such as we might see in *Punch* today). They were only to amuse, but unfortunately some historians have taken them seriously! Some, however, were intended to defraud, such as the company to import broomsticks from Germany. But there is no evidence there was ever a "company for a project which shall hereafter be revealed", as some textbooks aver.[4] By June South Sea stock was being offered at one thousand per cent. Great fortunes were made. One director is said to have made £3,000,000 in three months. The shrewd old Duchess of Marlborough sold at just the right time for an enormous profit. On the other hand Walpole's investments in South Sea stock seem to have been unspectacular and ill-timed. By September the tide had turned; prices toppled from 700 to 250. Disaster faced many. A Jacobite coup d'état was freely talked about; George I was urged to hurry back from Hanover and summon Parliament.

For some it was a disaster. The Duke of Portland was nearly bankrupt. Isaac Newton, who had gambled again, lost £20,000. The whole credit system received a severe shock. Many banks failed, work stopped on many projects, such as shipbuilding, with consequent unemployment and food riots. We shall see[5] how the subsequent enquiry broke up the government. But these were all temporary misfortunes, and the real importance of the bursting of the South Sea Bubble lies in another direction. It is important not to think of it as an isolated event. In fact it was a culmination of the great development of commercial activity and capital formation which we have traced since 1688. In some ways it was a price to be paid for a better understanding of the mysteries of credit. It was not merely an English event; the events in

---

[4] By far the best book on the whole subject is John Carswell: *The South Sea Bubble*.

[5] See Ch. 6.

England were closely linked with the collapse of Law's schemes in France. An unfortunate consequence was perhaps that for some decades the experience made men over-cautious. A brake was placed on economic expansion for the next twenty years. The economic activity of the period 1688–1720 is not again equalled until after 1760.

Agricultural Revolution

Turning from the London of the eighteenth century to the rest of England, the first impression is that it is overwhelmingly rural. The two greatest provincial towns were Norwich and Bristol, each with a population of about 30,000. York and Exeter came next with about 10,000, and it is doubtful whether any other town in England had as many as 10,000 inhabitants. Many of the so-called towns had less than 5,000 inhabitants and were at best small market towns living in the heart of the countryside. Even so, about 1750, only twenty per cent. of the population lived in towns.

We know too little about the social conditions in the country in the seventeenth century, but what we know suggests that life was hard. Gregory King, at the end of the seventeenth century, estimated that half the population were either on poor relief or charity, or lived by some form of plunder. He estimated that there were about 2,500,000 labourers, cottagers and paupers. Above these he estimated that there were about 750,000 farmers with their families, and about 180,000 superior farmers. Even for the better-off farmers, life was simple, and even grim. One contemporary pamphleteer wrote:

> He is a rich man that can afford to eat a joint of fresh meat once a month or fortnight. . . . They cannot afford to eat the eggs that their hens lay, nor the apples or pears that grow on their trees, but must make money of all.

Gregory King estimated that a farmer could just manage on eight pounds, ten shillings a year and that cottagers and paupers had to manage on about two pounds, ten shillings a year. Those farmers who lived near London fared better, for there was a large market for their produce; and many farmers and labourers near towns supplemented their incomes with weaving, or the manufacture of scythes, chains or nails (as in the Birmingham district, for instance). But for the most part, if Gregory King is right, it appears that in the late seventeenth century half the nation lived in conditions of poverty. Many even of the more substantial farmers and squires managed on an income of a hundred or two a year. Dr Plumb [6] has shown how frugal a life was that of Sir Robert Walpole's father even though he was a Member of Parliament and a squire.

The picture presented by the eighteenth century is on the whole a good deal better than this. It was a time of prosperity. The population was growing; above all, London was growing. The problem of feeding so vast a city was a powerful stimulus to agriculture in the home counties, and as far away as East Anglia. Thus East Anglia began to specialise in turkeys, and Wiltshire in cheese for the London market. With the growing profits of trade, wealthy merchants invested in land. The combined result was the increase in land values. In 1700 at least one-quarter of England was waste- and moor-land. During the eighteenth century there was a steady encroachment upon this waste; much of the Fens, for instance, was drained, and parts of Exmoor were brought under cultivation. The Napoleonic Wars were a great stimulus to this process because by that time England had difficulty in feeding itself, and land values shot up.

The new stimulus to agriculture hastened the practice of enclosure which had been going on since at least the sixteenth century. The process was so complicated that it is difficult to make accurate generalisations about it. In some parts of the country, such as Wales, Cheshire and Lancashire, there never had been open fields. In some areas, such as Somerset, Cornwall, Hereford, Shropshire, Kent, Sussex, Surrey and Essex, enclosure was already complete long before the eighteenth century. Yet great areas of the Midlands were still unenclosed as late as 1750. Enclosure is in fact the general name given to three distinct developments: (1) the enclosure of the open fields by the gathering together of the scattered strips and the fencing off of each man's holding; (2) the enclosure of the Commons, which had formerly been for the use of the villagers; (3) enclosure of land which had formerly been waste- or moor-land. Economically there was everything to be said for enclosure. It enabled more efficient agriculture, greater experimentation with crops, and scientific

[6] In his biography *Sir Robert Walpole* (Cresset Press).

breeding of animals.[7] Professor Trevor Roper has shown that few great families were able in the sixteenth or seventeenth century to maintain themselves from generation to generation by the profits of the land alone. But in the eighteenth century it was different. Great profits awaited the large landowner who was an efficient farmer; the rent rolls of Coke of Holkham, in Norfolk, ran into thousands of pounds. The tenant-farmer on the whole prospered, and certainly the yield of land substantially increased.

It used to be argued, however, that enclosure led to rural depopulation; that smallholders were driven from the land to swell the army of cheap labour which gathered in the new industrial towns. There certainly was a drift into the towns, but the charge of rural depopulation cannot on the whole be maintained, and still less be associated with enclosure. A careful study of statistics in some areas where enclosure took place (e.g. Lincolnshire) has shown that the population increased rather than declined, that sometimes new villages actually emerged, and that the number of small owners did not decline, but often increased. The farmer who could maintain himself on his land certainly prospered and could enjoy a higher standard of living as the century progressed. The people who suffered from enclosure were the squatters, casual labourers and cottage-labourers, who were dependent upon the Commons for the maintenance of a pig or two, or some geese or chickens, and who with enclosure lost the use of the Commons and could not substantiate a claim to a share in the enclosed land. On the other hand, small owners who could substantiate a legal claim found it easy to satisfy the enclosure commissioners as to their claim, and they received their share of the enclosed lands. In such a period of rapid change there must needs have been personal hardships and dislocation, but the old view that enclosure destroyed the English peasantry cannot any longer be maintained. It is wrong to think of a nation of large farmers; even as late as 1831 the ratio of farmer to labourer was only 1:2½, and it was certainly less in the eighteenth century. The real flight from the land in English history came in the nineteenth, not the eighteenth century.

Enclosure was accompanied by improvements in agricul-

---

[7] Not that the old open field system was as rigid or backward as is sometimes supposed.

tural technique. Every century revealed some new discovery or other, and they became more frequent after 1660. The main weaknesses of the old system of agriculture were: (1) the low yield of crops per acre; (2) the waste involved in leaving fields fallow by rotation; (3) the absence of scientific breeding of cattle; (4) the inability to feed more than the minimum number of cattle through the winter, so that surplus stock had to be slaughtered in the autumn and salted for winter meat. All these difficulties were largely overcome during the eighteenth century. In Norfolk such men as Coke of Holkham revealed the principles of estate management. Jethro Tull (1674–1740) showed how, by planting in rows and careful weeding, the grain yield could be increased. Viscount Townshend (1674–1738) showed that with a rotation of crops in which clover, vetches and a root crop alternated with wheat, barley and oats, the fallow field could be eliminated altogether; and the clover, vetches and turnips would provide ample food for the cattle during winter. Robert Bakewell (1725–95) developed scientific breeds of sheep and horses and made enormous profits from them. All this does amount to a revolution in agriculture, but the new methods spread slowly. Those who adopted them made huge profits, but many farmers preferred the old methods. The wars against the French after 1793 were a great stimulus to change. Food prices were high, there were fortunes to be made by those farmers who could increase their production. Arthur Young (1741–1820), a journalist, was a notable publicist of the new agriculture and did much with his pen to spread the new ideas. Enclosure went on with increased rapidity. After 1760 there were some 5,000 enclosure Acts, affecting 6,000,000 acres, and by the General Enclosure Act of 1801 the whole process was made much simpler.

In spite of the hardships which enclosure inflicted on many a labourer and his family, the agricultural revolution was an essential and beneficial part of the economic expansion of the eighteenth century. Without improvements in agriculture it is difficult to see how large towns could have been adequately fed. The rapid growth of population was certainly related to increased food supplies and a healthier diet. Some writers have regarded the eighteenth century as "the golden age of the agricultural labourer". Foreigners when they visited England were impressed equally with English liberty and with the good food of poorer classes, and they deduced that the two were connected. The Englishman thought so too, and sang of the roast beef of old England as an aspect of the national character. In that they were right.

Industrial Revolution

The term "Industrial Revolution" is a convenient short-hand way of referring to certain fundamental changes which took place during the century after 1750. These may be briefly summarised as:

1. a rapid growth of overseas trade;
2. scientific inventions which were applied to industry;
3. the consequent concentration of industry in factories and works in large towns;
4. a vast increase in industrial production.

Yet the phrase "Industrial Revolution" must not be over-worked, and the greatest economic historian of the period, Sir John Clapham, preferred not to employ it at all. For nothing really began in 1760, or ended in 1850. Industry had for centuries been organised on a capitalist basis of increasing complexity, and there was already a high degree of specialisation by the sixteenth century. Inventions did not begin in the 1760s with Arkwright and Crompton. A hand-driven knitting machine was invented in 1589, and frequently improved during the seventeenth century. The Dutch loom, which could weave a dozen tapes or ribbons at once, was widely used in the seventeenth century, and by 1660 the "inkle" loom was used in Manchester for the weaving of linen. Thomas Lombe brought the secret of water-power in the manufacture of silk from Italy in 1719 and employed it in his throwing-mill at Derby. Water-power in the rolling and slit mills of the metal industry was in use in the sixteenth century. As the forests were diminished, and charcoal became scarce, open workings of coal were developed in many parts during the sixteenth century. The difficulty was to transport it except where water transport could be used. London was already supplied with Newcastle coal in Queen Elizabeth's day.

The developments of the eighteenth century must be seen therefore as a speeding up of an intricate process which had been going on from the sixteenth century. With the growth of foreign trade, the increasing population and growing refinements of the age, there was a steadily increasing demand for manufactures. The oldest and most widespread industry was the woollen, and by the eighteenth century it was highly organised and specialised. Traditionally spinning might be done almost anywhere, but each area tended to specialise in the finished product, so that one place would concentrate upon stocking weaving, another upon shalloons (a light worsted), another upon bombazines (a light worsted with a silk or cotton weft) and so forth. The three great areas of woollen manufacture were (1) the eastern counties from Norwich to London; (2) the West country—Wiltshire, Somerset, Gloucester, Dorset and Devon; (3) the West Riding of Yorkshire. By the eighteenth century the eastern counties tended to concentrate upon worsteds; in some areas such as Kent the industry had already died out. The West country industry was still flourishing in towns such as Salisbury, Exeter, Frome, Trowbridge and Bradford-on-Avon. In Yorkshire, Leeds had been an important woollen town as early as the thirteenth century, and there was an important woollen cloth industry in the West Riding long before 1500. But for years the Yorkshire industry could not compete with the fine West of England cloths, and had to concentrate upon rough woollens such as kerseys. In all areas the clothier or manufacturer lived in the market town, and put out his work to the spinners, weavers, combers, carders, dyers in the neighbourhood. Defoe said that on a weekday a town like Norwich seemed "a town without inhabitants, they being all in their garrets at their looms, and in their combing-shops, twisting-mills and other work-houses". The whole formed a national industry, and woollen cloth was the largest English export.

Technical changes came rapidly in the eighteenth century. In 1733 Kay invented his flying shuttle, enabling one person to work a much broader loom. In the 1760s Hargreaves invented his Spinning Jenny, enabling a worker to spin at first a dozen, and later a hundred threads at once. Arkwright invented a new spinning machine which was worked by water-power. Samuel Crompton combined the inventions of Hargreaves and Arkwright into his famous "mule", which produced a fine thread stronger than had ever been produced before. About 1790 Cartwright developed a loom which was worked by steam-power. Steam-power was now readily available, because in 1776 James Watt began the manufacture of steam-engines in the Soho Works at Birmingham and with the help of the great iron-master, John Wilkinson, greatly improved its design in the 1780s. These inventions meant a fundamental change of organisation for the textiles. They must now be concentrated in factories, where expensive machinery run by steam-power was available. The domestic system of industry found it increasingly difficult to withstand the advance of the new technology.

Yet the change-over to the factory system in the woollen industry was slow. Even the flying shuttle was not in general use much before 1800; the "mule" was coming into use in Gloucester only about 1828. Hand-spinning was killed by the competition of the mills fairly quickly, but with weaving it was different. There were perhaps half a million hand looms still in use about 1830, and only about 20,000 or 30,000 power looms. It is true that the output of the power looms was vastly greater, and the hand-loom weavers found it increasingly difficult to make a living, but they persisted at least until 1850.

So far as the period covered by this book is concerned, we can say, therefore, that the domestic system of industry was still general in the woollen industry, and by 1793 had only begun to give way to the factory system. In cotton the change-over was more rapid, for it was a "new" industry. In 1700 there was little manufacture of cotton in England, firstly because the quality was much inferior to the imported Indian calicoes, and because the government frowned on it as competing with the native woollen and linen industries. But the inventions of Crompton and Cartwright enabled Lancashire to equal, and even surpass, the Eastern products. In most instances the cotton industry began as a factory industry, and this explains why the first legislation on factory conditions applied to the cotton industry. The average cotton factory in Manchester in 1816 employed about 300 workers, and some employed 1,000. One Glasgow factory employed 7,000 men in 1816.

The bases of the industrial revolution were the twin raw materials, coal and iron. By the beginning of the eighteenth century the search for coal required deeper mines. But these were possible only if the mines could be drained. About 1711 Newcomen invented a steam pump which served the purpose, and this was the main use to which steam-power was put until the time of Cartwright and Watt, when it was applied to machinery in the iron industry and textiles. Some of the worst industrial conditions in the eighteenth century were to be found in the mines, where conditions were primitive, life was extremely dangerous, and labour retained at all only by a harsh bond system which prevented workers from going elsewhere. Harsh also were the conditions in the iron industry. At the beginning of the century the supplies of charcoal from the local forests were all but exhausted in England, and coal was unsuitable for the smelting of iron. In 1709 the Quaker, Abraham Darby of Coalbrookdale in Shropshire, invented the process of coking the coal, but he kept his discovery quiet, and it was largely confined to his neighbourhood for the next forty years. For one thing, coke iron was still inferior to charcoal iron, and remained so until a stronger blast furnace was invented. But three generations of Darby made Coalbrookdale one of the great iron centres in the country, and it was the third Abraham Darby who joined with John Wilkinson to build the first iron bridge over the Severn in 1787. John Wilkinson (1728–1808) was the greatest iron-master of his day, and a most inventive man. He was the first to develop a new blast furnace with the use of steam, and to use steam to work the forge-hammer and for the processes of slitting and rolling. He combined with Boulton and Watt to produce the greatly improved steam engine in the 1780s, and he made important discoveries in the boring of cannon which were put to good use in the Peninsular War. It was largely due to Wilkinson that British iron production trebled in the twenty years after 1788. Meanwhile about 1740 Benjamin Huntsman, a Sheffield clockmaker, invented a superior type of steel by re-melting pig iron in crucibles and mixing with it a little carbon, but steel was not widely used in the eighteenth century.

In the textile industries the factory system was certainly a marked feature of organisation after 1780, and the iron industry was mostly organised into large-scale capitalist units. So were the potteries. But in many industries, such as nail-making in the Birmingham area, small workshop organisation remained far into the nineteenth century. As it disappeared in industry after industry it was natural that workers and writers alike should tend to romanticise the old domestic system of industry which had passed away. But there was little to regret in its passing, for it often took the form of sweated labour at cut prices for long hours of the day and night. With all the grim realities of the new industrial towns, it is probable that the standard of living of the new industrial workers was higher than that of their domestic predecessors.

Revolution in Transport

An Industrial Revolution could not have developed far without an accompanying revolution in transport. Until the second half of the eighteenth century the only satisfactory mode of transport over great distances was by sea. As late as 1750 it took nearly a fortnight to reach Edinburgh from London by road, and the journey to Manchester took about four days. Coaching was an exhausting and hazardous venture over the dust- and mud-tracks which passed for roads before the turnpike trusts began their improvement after 1748. These trusts made great improvements. They began scientific road- and bridge-building. They employed expert road engineers such as the blind John Metcalfe (1717–1810), Thomas Telford (1754–1834) and John McAdam (1756–1836), and the latter invented the first satisfactory road-surface since the Romans. The trusts were established only on some of the most important roads, where the toll-charges would make a profit, and never extended throughout the country. They were, moreover, unpopular, and sometimes the subject of riots. But within their limits they were of great value. Regular coach services between the main cities were organised; mail coaches were organised by Palmer in 1784, and travellers found themselves bowling along through the countryside at as much as twelve miles an hour.

Water, however, was still thought of as the best method of transport for bulky industrial goods. About 1760 the canal era opened with the construction of the famous Bridgwater Canal from the Duke of Bridgwater's collieries at Worsley to Manchester. His engineer, James Brindley, opened the way for a whole network of canals built in the next forty years, such as the Grand Junction Canal, linking London with the Midlands, the Grand Trunk Canal linking the Mersey, Trent and Severn, the Kennet and Avon Canal and the Forth–Clyde Canal. The great advantages of canal transport were that it was suitable for bulky goods such as coal, clay or china, and was cheap. Canals had much to do with the opening up of the Industrial Midlands and the North, and between 1760 and 1830 was the most important form of internal transport in England.

* * * * *

We have seen that the period 1688–1720 was one of remarkable economic activity; the same is true of the years after 1750. British overseas trade increased under the impact of war; indeed it expanded more rapidly after the loss of the American colonies than it had done before. The most important export was woollen cloth, though by 1800 it was surpassed by cottons. The export of iron and coal increased rapidly after 1780, and the United States became one of the best markets for English goods. After 1720 the formation of new joint-stock companies was hampered by the "Bubble Act" by which companies could be formed only by Act of Parliament or by Crown Charter, though lawyers found a way round the Act in certain cases. Dealers in stocks and shares became a feature of eighteenth-century life. At first they dealt mainly in government stock and in insurance, at first in coffee-houses, and after 1773 at the Stock Exchange. There was little dealing in industrial stock in the eighteenth century, for most industrial investment was personal, often on a partnership basis; and industry relied more on the ploughing back of profits than upon further investments.

In the new era London retained its importance in its political and financial aspects, but in other respects it lost its enormous preponderance. Cities such as Liverpool, Manchester and Birmingham increased between five- and tenfold during the eighteenth century; Bristol and Glasgow grew rich on the proceeds of colonial trade. By the end of the century there were over four hundred country banks, many of them short-lived. It was at Birmingham that the ironmaster Sampson Lloyd and his partner started Lloyds Bank, and it was at Norwich that the Gurney family founded Barclays Bank. The centre of gravity of England's economic life moved steadily northwards.

The period after 1750 was the great age of private enterprise. Men of enterprise and determination were accustomed to stake their all on the pursuit of an idea. When Crompton invented his "mule" he was too poor to patent it. Richard Arkwright was the son of a poor labourer, became a barber's apprentice, and died a millionaire and the greatest cotton magnate of his time. John Kay's flying shuttle brought him nothing but disaster, and he was forced eventually to flee abroad. James Brindley's father was a labourer who could not afford an education for his son. John Wilkinson rose from humble origins to be the greatest iron-master of his day. It was such men of ideas and industry who increasingly made the England of their day.

3

The Revolution Settlement
(1689-1702)

The Nature of the Revolution

IN 1688 THERE WAS a strong feeling in England that there was a constitution, both in church and state, and that James II was seeking to overthrow it. When, on June 30th, four whigs and three tories invited William of Orange to England, they declared that the government of James II threatened the people in "their religion, liberties and properties", and they added that the discontent was so general that nineteen-twentieths of the nation would welcome the invasion. When on September 30th William issued his declaration, he enumerated the offences of the last Stuart king. He declared that James had "overturned Religion, Laws and Liberties", used the dispensing power, tampered with the judges, threatened to supplant the Anglican by the Roman Church, confiscated the charters of towns, and finally that he had gathered a large standing army with which to overawe his people. William declared that he came for no other reason than to ensure the meeting of "a free and lawful Parliament".

The Revolution of 1688 was therefore conservative in intention. It did not at all attempt to establish a new form of government, but merely to safeguard the religion and liberties of the nation. The instrument of the Revolution was Parliament, which proceeded to pass a series of laws intended as practical safeguards against the abuses of the reigns of

Charles II and James II. But farther than that no one wished
to go. This was why it was so difficult to find a suitable
formula to cover the deposition of James II. For if he was the
legitimate monarch, how could he be overthrown without
tearing up the very roots of the constitution? This was what
the tory Earl of Nottingham meant when he warned the
Lords in February 1689 that whatever they did with regard
to the monarchy must be "upon the foot of our ancient
laws and fundamental constitution", lest they should "over-
turn all our legal foundations". Hence the desire of some
high tories that, failing the return of James II under guaran-
tees, or the proclamation of his infant son, Mary should rule,
as the next legitimate heir. But William himself scotched
that suggestion by letting it be known that "he would not
like to be his wife's gentleman usher". Thus, by the Bill of
Rights (1689), "the said late King James the Second having
abdicated the government, and the throne being thereby vacant", William and Mary became joint sovereigns by Act of
Parliament. Before, however, that vital clause was reached
in the Bill, Parliament laid down a charter of practical liberties. The suspending and the dispensing powers, the ecclesiastical commission, taxation without a parliamentary grant,
the maintenance of a standing army in time of peace, and
all arbitrary fines and forfeitures, were all declared illegal.
The Act declared, vaguely, "that the election of members
ought to be free", that there should be freedom of speech
in Parliament, and that "Parliaments ought to be held frequently". In the interests of the liberty of the subject, the
Act laid down that excessive bail ought not to be required,
that jurors ought not to be tampered with, that they should
be freeholders, and that all subjects had the right to petition
the king. These rights were claimed, not as innovations, but
as the "true, ancient and indubitable rights and liberties of
the people of this kingdom". Finally, it enacted that no
king or queen of England could be a Roman Catholic, and
that this should be "the law of this realm for ever".

As a necessary corollary of the clause making illegal a
standing army in time of peace without consent of Parliament, the Mutiny Act (1689) gave legal existence to the
army for one year only. In this way Parliament secured its
control of the armed forces which it has always subsequently
maintained; and, incidentally, it ensured that Parliament itself must meet at least once a year.

The Revolution of 1688 had had the united support of the Dissenters, who had regarded James II's offer of toleration as no more than a bribe. It was felt in 1689 that a Protestant Parliament could not offer them less than the Catholic monarch had done. On the other hand, none of the high tories wished to admit the dissenters to political equality by repealing the Test and Corporation Acts. The result was the somewhat grudging Toleration Act (1689), which granted dissenters freedom of worship, so long as it did not take place behind locked doors, and so long as the consent of the bishop of the diocese could be obtained; but it was silent on the subject of the political disabilities. The dissenters, however, were glad enough for the freedom thus obtained, and they soon found ways, by "occasional conformity", to avoid the political disabilities. Many of them prospered, became good whigs and valued citizens in the new world of trade and industry which was opening before them.

Before 1688 there were two complaints about the meeting of Parliament. One was that Charles II had violated the Triennial Act of 1664 by failing, during the last four years of his reign, to summon Parliament. The second was that Parliament, once summoned, was kept in being much too long. Charles II's Long Parliament had lasted from 1661–79. The Mutiny Act and the financial needs of government would ensure that Parliament would in future meet every year. The Triennial Act of 1694 laid down, somewhat archaically, that Parliament should meet at least once in three years, but also that no Parliament should remain in being for longer than three years.

Perhaps the most important aspect of the Revolution settlement lay in finance. The Restoration of 1660 had failed to hit on a satisfactory financial arrangement. It had given the king his revenue for life, thereby forfeiting the chance to control policy. On the other hand, in practice the royal revenues had varied during Charles II's reign between £800,000 and £1,200,000, and this was often insufficient to provide for the needs of state. James II had been better off than his brother, and his revenue for life had enabled him to maintain a large standing army and thus threaten the liberties of the state. Parliament in William III's reign sought wisely to avoid both these errors of the past, and in doing so they made one of the most important constitutional advances in our history. For the first time a clear distinction was drawn between the private expenditure of the king (the Civil List) and the National Expenditure. The former was fixed at £600,000 (increased in 1698 to £700,000), and was set against the Excise. The Customs, which traditionally had been assigned to the support of the army and navy, were voted for only four years at a time. Moreover, as their yield was quite inadequate to support a great war, William III was entirely dependent upon his parliaments for the continuance of his foreign policy. This fact was of far more practical importance to him than any of the limitations imposed by the Bill of Rights (which he had little incentive ever to break). William often found this dependence upon Parliament exasperating, yet in one sense, as he well knew, it was the foundation of his power. For Charles II had been in the eyes of Europe a feeble monarch, the mere pensionary of France. William III on the other hand was one of the most powerful monarchs in Europe. Charles II's revenues were rarely much above a million pounds a year. William III had a revenue which averaged over the course of his reign more than five millions a year. Why should Parliament have entrusted Dutch William with a revenue five times that which Charles had had? The answer is that once Parliament had a government it could trust, and the knowledge that they were in control, they were usually not grudging in the sums they granted. William III never disputed their right to examine accounts. His Dutch mercantile training had taught him that a government, to be strong, must be trusted, and to be trusted it must be honest, and be known to be honest. Men lent to the government of William III with a confidence they had never had in any previous reign. A simple balance-sheet of the thirteen and a half years of William's reign, given on page 37, will repay study.

The following points are worth noting: (1) trade carried a good deal more of the tax burden than did the land; (2) the cost of the war of William's reign far exceeded that of any previous war in English history; (3) debt charges far exceeded those of any previous reign; there was now an organised National Debt.

The truth was that the Revolution of 1688 brought with it a profound change in the relationship between the government and the financiers. Firstly, the latter were growing richer and more numerous; they had ample capital to in-

REVENUES 1688–1702		EXPENDITURE 1688–1702	
	£		£
Customs	13 millions	Navy	20 millions
Excise	14 millions	Army	22 millions
Hearth Money, etc.	2 millions	Ordnance	3 millions
Land Taxes	19 millions	Civil List	9 millions
Poll Tax	3 millions	Interest Charges, etc.	13 millions
Various Taxes	8 millions	Recoinage, etc.	5 millions
	59 millions		
Borrowings	13 millions		
Total	72 millions		72 millions

vest if they had confidence in the project. Financiers had lent money to kings all through the ages, but they were personal loans, they were at the mercy of the impecunious monarch, interest rates were often ruinous, and many of them never saw their money back. Charles I had seized the bullion deposits in the Mint at the outbreak of the Civil War. Charles II incurred heavy debts, and his Stop of the Exchequer in 1672 ruined Sir Robert Vyner and many another financier. Charles II died leaving a debt of £1,000,-000, which his successors did not see fit to honour until 1704, and then only in part. In William's reign loans were differently managed. They were now loans not personally to the king, but to the state, and their interest rates were guaranteed by the taxes. Thus in 1694 a Tonnage Act was passed to guarantee the £100,000 annual interest upon the £1,200,-000 raised by the new Bank of England, and lent to the government. In future a man could invest in government stock with a new confidence.

This is why the founding of the Bank of England in 1694 is regarded as so important an event, though the sum involved was at first so modest. It marks, indeed, the beginning of the National Debt; for the first time a government loan was guaranteed by Parliament. Moreover, the transaction was a clever one. When Gilbert Heathcote, the Houblon brothers, Theodore Janssen and others lent the government £1,200,000, and in return were constituted the Governors of the Bank of England, it was not cash, but credit, which they put at the disposal of the government. They received their eight per cent on the banknotes which they created, and they reserved their cash for banking transactions. In fact therefore they had created £1,200,000 worth of credit; and the Bank of England has gone on creating it ever since. The great wars against Louis XIV, Louis XV and Napoleon could not have been fought successfully without this great system of credit; and credit would have been impossible without the confidence engendered in the Revolution government.

To sum up the Revolution of 1688, we may say that it deserved the epithet granted to it by history of "Glorious" because it was effected so easily, because it was bloodless, because it had in 1688 the support of the great mass of the politically conscious part of the nation, and because it inaugurated a healthier period of national development than that of the reigns of Charles II and James II. It was a conservative revolution. The only spectacular change appeared to be the change of monarch from James II to William and Mary. Parliament made a few practical provisions for the future, but made no attempt to define a new constitutional system. Such was not necessary, for it was already certain that Parliament could not be dispensed with, and future problems could always find a parliamentary solution. It is a mistake to think that there was some new whig constitutional theory waiting to be effected in 1688, and that it was inimical to monarchy. The Bill of Rights did impose a few limitations upon the Crown; the monarchy after 1688 was always a "parliamentary monarchy" in two senses of the phrase, both because after 1688 the monarch owed his Crown to an Act of Parliament, and because parliamentary control of finance made it impossible that the king could ever again dispense with Parliament. In future, government would be most successful when king and Parliament worked in harmony. But this did not at all mean, and was not intended by anyone in 1688 to mean, that in future Parliament would *control* policy. The king was still head of the executive; the appointment of ministers was his alone; he and his ministers determined policy, especially foreign policy. Parliament always expected such a lead from the king, but reserved to themselves the right to sit in judgment upon the policy pursued.

The practical and conservative character of the Revolution of 1688 did not exclude a measure of political theory, although its importance might easily be over-estimated. In some ways it invoked the shades of Shaftesbury, with his opposition to royal despotism, his defence of parliamentary and personal liberties, religious toleration and the Protestant succession. It was his secretary, John Locke, who composed the *Two Treatises of Government*. This great work was published in 1689, and was thus formerly thought to be a justification of the Revolution of 1688. But in fact it was written about 1681, in answer to Robert Filmer's justification of the theory of Divine Right of Kings, the *Patriarcha*. It was written therefore not to justify revolution, but to promote it. Locke entirely denied the divine origin of monarchy. Government was the result of a social contract made by free men for the prime purpose of defending their property. The ruler was, in a sense, a steward. If he gave good government, and respected the rights of property, he deserved to be obeyed. But whenever he tried "to take away and destroy the property of the people, or to reduce them to slavery", he put himself into a state of war with his people, and rebellion was justified. In 1689 also Locke published his great essay on Toleration, though it too was written much earlier. In it he declared that the commonwealth was formed for the protection of "life, liberty, health and indolency of body, and the possession of outward things". The business of government was to secure such things, but a man's conscience and his beliefs were no part of that business. Locke regarded the sphere of government as strictly limited, and a man's beliefs were his own concern.

Locke is the most important philosopher in the history of English thought. He provided the whigs with such political philosophy as they needed in the eighteenth century, and he laid the basis of liberal thought of the nineteenth century. His influence throughout Europe and America during the eighteenth century was profound. It is clear that he was not in any sense the author of the Revolution settlement after 1688; rather he was the genius who distilled and articulated the ideas which were inherent in the political development of his day. It was because his thought was so closely related to the facts of the time that it proved so powerful and so enduring.

The Revolution of 1688 had had the general support of the nation because England and Scotland were overwhelmingly Protestant, and James II had forced people to choose between their loyalty to the Stuarts and their loyalty to their church. But once the Revolution was over, there was much heart-searching, and many, albeit sentimental, regrets. The basis of the old toryism of loyalty to Anglicanism and Divine-Right monarchy was shattered. Many tories accepted the Revolution, but grudgingly, and they found it difficult to adapt themselves to the new order of things. They resented the whig assumption that the Revolution was *their* revolution, and too often the whigs delighted in embarrassing them with their oaths of allegiance to the new king. They were bewildered at the vast increase of government expenditure, at the Land Tax of four shillings in the pound, and at a foreign war which, as it progressed, seemed more in Dutch than English interests. They resented the toleration extended to dissenters; they disliked the Calvinism of William III, and they feared the movement for Comprehension,[1] which would have brought the dissenters within the church. Comprehension was killed in Convocation in 1689, and William III, resenting its intolerance, did not summon Convocation again for ten years. The Toleration Act of 1689 was therefore all that the high church tories would concede. Locke commented:

> Toleration has indeed been granted, but not with that latitude which true Christians without ambition or envy would desire. But it is something to have got thus far.

The tenderest consciences of the age were those of the Non-Jurors. Both the Bill of Rights and the Toleration Act laid down the form of oaths of Supremacy and Allegiance, and, to do justice to their authors, it must be said that the oaths were worded as inoffensively as possible. Thus for instance, they made no mention of the nature of William and Mary's right to the throne. The offending words were simply:

> I do sincerely promise and swear that I will be faithful and bear true allegiance to their Majesties King William and Queen Mary. So help me God.

Archbishop Sancroft, and eight other bishops, those of Bath and Wells, Gloucester, Ely, Chichester, Norwich, Peterborough, Worcester and Chester, refused to take the oath. Sancroft was suspended, and retired quietly to the village of Freshingfield in Essex. Only Turner of Ely became a Jacobite, and involved in plots which eventually forced him to flee.

---

[1] Comprehension was an attempt to bring all Protestants within a single church.

Some four hundred clergy also surrendered their benefices rather than take the oath. For most of them the motive was simply one of conscience; having already taken an oath of allegiance to James II, they felt they could not break their word, so long as that monarch lived. Many of them faced poverty for the sake of their consciences. Politically they were insignificant, but they left the church the poorer in piety and integrity, though not perhaps in political capacity and tolerance.

The new leaders of the church were men like Archbishop Tillotson, and Burnet, Bishop of Salisbury. Tillotson was much influenced by the Cambridge Platonists, to whom reason was the true guide in religion. They felt that religious controversies need no longer arouse heat. Anglicanism should be reasonable and seemly. Burnet was a whig, to whom the decision of the Non-Jurors seemed incomprehensible, since some of them had actually been persecuted under James II. Fleetwood, Bishop of Ely, was also a whig, and a noted preacher. Sharp, Archbishop of York, was a tory, but a moderate one, and was always on excellent terms with the dissenters. William III preferred to advance whigs to bishoprics, with the result that the episcopal bench was a good deal more latitudinarian and politically moderate than the great mass of the clergy.

William III's task in governing England was extremely difficult. He had come to England with the fixed intention of committing England to war with France. For this purpose he was determined to assert the royal prerogative to the full. He believed in prerogative government, and had little patience with turbulence and factions which seemed the mark of parliamentary government. The House of Orange had long stood opposed to the republican party in Holland, and he instinctively equated the English whigs with republicanism. He made too little effort to conceal his hostility. The Commons, he declared to Halifax, "used him like a dog. Their coarse usage boiled so upon his stomach that he could not hinder himself from breaking out sometimes against them", and on another occasion he declared that "he was so weary of them, he could not bear them". This was understandable exasperation in a man who saw more clearly than most people in England the great European issues which were at stake, but it was not tactful to make his feelings so apparent.

When Bishop Burnet came to write his great history of this

period, he declared that, although he had always hated the terms "whig" and "tory", he could not avoid using them, "they being now become as common as if they had been words of our language". In modern times some historians have sought to dispense with them, but the experiment has not been a success. The fact is that there was a whig and a tory point of view on most of the great questions of the day between 1679 and 1714. The Revolution of 1688 itself was too big an issue to be a party matter; it had the support of the great majority of the nation. But the settlement which followed it often raised party issues. Thus the high tories, members of the Hyde faction, were at first extremely reluctant to desert James entirely. Bishop Compton proposed that William might be Regent for James' infant son. When this was narrowly defeated in the Lords in January 1689 by 49 votes to 51, the high tories favoured Mary alone as monarch. Only when William himself rejected this solution, did they reluctantly accept the inevitable, and recognise William and Mary as joint sovereigns. For tender consciences among the high tories, the distinction between a king "de jure" and "de facto" was bandied about.

William III was inclined to believe that, in spite of this initial reluctance to accept him, once the tories had taken the oath of allegiance (as the great majority of them did), they were more to be trusted than the whigs. Once, when Sunderland was trying to persuade him to rely more upon the whigs, the King said "he believed the whigs loved him best, but they did not love monarchy". Sunderland replied that "though it was very true that the tories were better friends to monarchy", yet he must consider "that *he* was not *their* monarch". The Revolution settlement was not in fact exclusively the work of either party, for whereas some of the clauses of the Bill of Rights were an obvious vindication of the policy of the Earl of Shaftesbury, yet the Triennial Act was always accounted a tory measure; the Toleration Act was largely moulded to the tory wishes, and for this reason Comprehension was omitted; finally the Act of Settlement (1701) was passed by a tory House of Commons. William's early preference for the tories proved to be mistaken, for they proved unable to provide good government, and when he turned to rely on the whigs, he found tory opposition both effective and intensely frustrating to the monarchy. On the other hand the whigs, though effective administrators and

financiers, were often individually intensely grasping and
self-seeking, and they too often failed to keep their support either in the Commons or in the country.

The student of the period will have a confused and inaccurate picture if he imagines that there existed anything
like the two-party system of the nineteenth and twentieth
centuries. For the unit of political organisation of the time
was not the party, but the group, built up by the political,
social and perhaps moral influence of the great men of the
day. These groups can well be labelled whig or tory, but it
did not always follow that the group took the whig or tory
line upon any particular question. For much depended
whether the group was in office or out of it, anxious to
force an entry into office, or content for the moment to hold
aloof from it.

William at first determined to choose his ministers without reference to party labels; his first government included
both whigs and tories. The man who perhaps had most reason
to expect to head that government was Danby. He had been
the virtual saviour of the monarchy in the period 1674–8.
He had been the leading tory to sign the letter of invitation to
William, and he had raised Yorkshire on his behalf. He
was a strong man, with wide administrative experience. But,
to his intense annoyance, William failed to appoint him
Lord Treasurer, but made him Lord President of the Council instead. William preferred to give his confidence to the
Marquis of Halifax. Perhaps he sensed that Danby was chiefly
interested in power, was too concerned to gain appointments
for his friends and relatives, and was intensely unpopular
with the whigs. On the other hand, Danby was a master of
political organisation, and had built up great political influence in the country. He could not be alienated without
danger.

The second political group was the Finch–Nottingham
faction. Daniel Finch, Earl of Nottingham, was a simple,
limited man whose distinguishing mark was devotion to the
Anglican church. His tall, thin, dark and solemn appearance
had earned him the name of "Don Dismal", and he was easy
sport for the satirists of the day. But his singleness of purpose had made him the natural leader of the high church
party. He had been gravely embarrassed by James II's Roman
Catholic policy, but in 1688 was slow in bringing himself to
accept William. On the other hand, having once done so, he

was completely loyal, and in December he was appointed Secretary of State. It was he who introduced the Toleration Act, and he also supported Comprehension, which was thus one of the many issues on which there is no clear party division (for the whig Burnet, in company with his fellow-bishops, opposed it). Politically he was of the first importance, for he was related to no less than fourteen members of the House of Lords, himself nominated some twenty members of the Commons, and his group numbered thirty-one in that House. His devotion to the church endeared him to the Queen, who preferred him to any other of the early ministers of the reign. But he was no administrator; he was held responsible by the whigs for the naval muddles of the time, and in 1693 he was driven to resign.

William showed a marked preference for independent men of moderation, and quiet administrators, who would get on with the business of government. He was to be disappointed in two of them. The first was Halifax the Trimmer. He had shown great wisdom and moderation since the stormy days of Exclusion, but he had built up no following, and his point of view was too individual to be widely understood. He had taken no active part in bringing about the Revolution, but in the absence of a Chancellor he became Speaker of the Lords in January 1689, and in the following month Lord Privy Seal, and in these capacities, exercised much influence in working out a Revolution settlement. But he was hated by both whigs and tories for his past record of trimming; Danby hated him, and he himself was characteristically full of doubts about the future. In 1690 he insisted on resigning. The second was the Earl of Shrewsbury, who had been one of the seven to invite William to England. He was accounted a whig, though there were constant rumours that he was in close touch with the Jacobites. He strongly supported William and Mary, and became Secretary of State in 1689, though aged only twenty-eight. William showed him more real affection than anyone else in England. But he soon showed himself to be a broken reed. He complained of his health, he disliked the hurly-burly of politics, and in June 1690 he, too, insisted on resigning. More satisfactory were the men of business, of whom we may take Sidney Godolphin as the leading example. He had been one of the "Chits", governing England in the last years of Charles II, and he had, as Chamberlain to the Queen, been one of an intimate circle of advisers during the reign of James II. But he was a man of business, not a politician. He was not implicated in James' foolish policies. His business acumen appealed to William, and in 1689 he was appointed head of the Commission of the Treasury (William preferring not to appoint a Lord Treasurer). He was closely concerned with the great work of financial reconstruction of the reign.

William's attempt to rule with a mixed ministry of whigs and tories proved a failure. It hampered the attempt of Danby (now Marquis of Carmarthen) and Nottingham to reconstruct a new tory party which would take account of the Revolution of 1688. At the same time, the whigs who were omitted from the government were furious that "their" Revolution had given them so little of the sweets of office. They therefore attacked the government at every point. They refused to grant the King his revenues for life. They sought to raise the whole question of the responsibility for the past, for the executions in the Rye House Plot, for the disfranchisement of the Corporations, and for James II's Catholic policies. William, on the other hand, wanted only to draw a veil over the past. He was not interested in English party squabbles; he believed that all English politicians were equally corrupt. To stir up the past would cause only bitterness at a time when national unity was needed in the face of the French war and the Jacobite menace.

Perhaps the fundamental reason for the political confusion of the time was that, although the Revolution had taken place, and some specific curbs had been placed on the monarchy, yet Parliament had not yet established effective control over the executive. The King was still head of the executive; ministers were still his; Parliament met only a few months in each year, and could not possibly control the day-to-day business of government. Moreover, Clarendon, Danby and Sunderland had all shown in the previous reigns how votes in the Commons could be organised, and thus the freedom of the House curtailed. It was these considerations which gave rise in the early years of William's reign to a new "Country" party, sometimes called "Old Whig" or "New Tory" party, distrustful of the executive and its policy, and distinct both from the whig "Junto" and the old doctrinaire high church party of Nottingham, Rochester and Clarendon. Its two leading figures were Paul Foley and Robert Harley. Neither of them was interested in the religious fanaticism of the high tories, for both of them had active sympathy for the dissenters. Both were anxious for greater parliamentary control of finance; both felt that too much was being spent on a continental war in Dutch interests and too little on the maintenance of the navy and the fostering of trade. In 1692 they carried a Place Bill through the Commons (that is to say a Bill for the exclusion from the Commons of men who held offices of profit under the Crown), though it was defeated in the Lords. It was carried through both Houses in 1693, and they were furious that this time the King used his veto. In 1693 they carried a Triennial Bill, which William also vetoed, though he accepted the Bill, however grudgingly, in the following year. Finally the new opposition drew strength from the mishandling of the war, and above all from the loss of the Smyrna convoy in 1693, the result, it was said, of the incompetence of the tory admirals Killigrew and Delaval.

Before this new opposition, combined with the attacks of the whig junto, the government of Camarthen, Nottingham and Godolphin went down. The King had begun to take private advice from that great enigma of the period, the Earl of Sunderland. Sunderland had been Secretary of State during the last three years of Charles II's reign, and he had been the powerful adviser of James II throughout his reign. There was therefore good reason for regarding him as a principal instrument of Stuart despotism. In December 1688 he had fled to Holland, and might well have been brought to justice in the new reign if William had not intervened to save him. Instead he had returned quietly to England, and it is a mark of the statesmanship of William III that the latter saw that the political sagacity of Sunderland could still be of use to the monarchy. It is a mark also of the ability of Sunderland that he saw that William could no longer afford to ignore the party divisions of the time. His advice was that the King should take the whig junto into his service. He saw that their "republicanism" was a myth, that they were (as the high tories were not) men of considerable administrative ability, and that it would be dangerous to leave them any longer in opposition. He argued that:

> whenever the government has leaned to the whigs it has been strong; whenever the other has prevailed, it has been despised.

Reluctantly the King took his advice. One by one during
1693–4 the tories (though not Camarthen) were dropped
from the government, and the whigs came in, John Somers as
Lord Keeper, Sir John Trenchard as Secretary of State, Russell
to the Admiralty, Charles Montagu as Chancellor of the
Exchequer. Four of the whig leaders were given dukedoms.
Behind the scenes Sunderland directed the activities of the
able Sir John Trenchard and the venal Speaker of the Commons, Sir John Trevor, in building up a Court party in
the Commons by every means of bribery and influence open
to them.

The leading members of the whig junto were Somers,
Montagu, Orford and Wharton. John Somers was a lawyer
who first made his name as counsel for the famous Seven
Bishops. He was a passionate defender of the Revolution of
1688, and Sunderland called him "the life, the soul, the spirit
of his party". In 1693 he became Lord Keeper of the Great
Seal, in 1697 Lord Chancellor. He built up a great reputation as a lawyer, and also as a patron of Literature. Charles
Montagu was the son of the Earl of Manchester, and one
of the signatories of the letter of invitation to William III. He
became a lord of the Treasury in 1692, and Chancellor of
the Exchequer in 1694. He was an able debater, a financial
genius, and like Somers a great patron of Literature. But his
ambition, vanity and arrogance made him a difficult and
unpopular figure. For a time he was First Lord of the Treasury, but he resigned in 1699, and did not hold important
office again until the accession of George I, when for a
few months he again headed the Treasury. Edward Russell,
Earl of Orford, was a brother of the Duke of Bedford. His
cousin had been executed after the Rye House Plot, and he
himself had accompanied William to England in 1688. He
was trained to the sea, but he owed his command mainly to
political intrigues. He was the victor of La Hogue, but thereafter turned solely to politics, and in 1694 became First
Lord of the Admiralty. Lord Wharton came of a Puritan
family, but he had the reputation of being the greatest
rake in England, and was certainly a connoisseur of horse-
flesh. He was an enthusiastic supporter of William III, but
with all his zeal for whig principles, he never succeeded in
winning the confidence of the King, and, to his bitter disappointment, he gained no office higher than that of Comp-
troller of the Household and a seat on the Admiralty Board.

The main achievement of the whigs in office was the organisation of the system of credit which enabled England to bear the burdens of a war far greater than she had ever before experienced. We have already mentioned the founding of the Bank of England. This was merely one aspect of a new financial system. Between 1695 and 1699 Montagu and Somers, with the aid of Isaac Newton, the Master of the Mint, called in the old, clipped and debased coinage, which made transactions so difficult, and issued England with a new coinage. Montagu also began the issue of exchequer bills which readily circulated as paper money. Montagu's work of sound finance was continued in the reign of Queen Anne by Godolphin, and the two contributed enormously to England's success and prestige in the period, particularly in winning the war which ended in 1697.

Yet their difficulties were great. The Commons greatly resented the influence of Sunderland behind the scenes, and the whigs saw no reason why they should defend him. Speaker Trevor was expelled from the Commons for bribery in 1695. The Commons also relentlessly pursued Camarthen (now Duke of Leeds), who clung on grimly to office until 1699. There were constant rumours of Jacobite plots, and in 1696, in revealing a plot to assassinate the King, Sir John Fenwick made a confession which implicated some of the greatest names of the day, Shrewsbury, Marlborough and Godolphin. The high tories always found it effective to raise the cry of "the church in danger", for they could point to the growing power of the dissenters, the latitudinarianism of bishops such as Tillotson and Burnet, and the growth of scepticism. The country rapidly wearied of the war; taxes were high, and fell heavily on the small gentry, while it seemed that the London financiers made profits out of the war by investments in government stock. Thus it was that in the election of 1698 the whig junto entirely failed to retain control of the Commons; the tories were triumphantly returned.

They now had their revenge. They set about cutting down William's fine army of 87,000 men to a mere 7,000 men. It was in vain that the King pointed out that so long as Louis XIV remained in strength this was a disastrous move. William well knew that the death of the King of Spain could not be long delayed, and that the only hope of negotiating successfully with Louis XIV was to speak from strength.

The Commons would not look so far, and slashed his forces. As an added insult, they refused any longer to pay for William's favourite Dutch Guards, and he had to disband them. William was deeply hurt, and for the moment seriously thought of abandoning England. Henceforth he spent much of his time abroad. Sunderland had taken fright and insisted on resigning. The only Englishmen in whom William now had any confidence were Somers, Shrewsbury, Godolphin and Marlborough, but they were quite unable to stem the tide of the Commons' hostility. The Irish forfeitures and the Partition Treaties gave them their opportunity.

In the question of the Irish lands, William was certainly much to blame. After the suppression of the Irish rebellion, great tracts of land had been forfeit to the Crown. William III, in spite of a promise to the Commons to the contrary, had been most prodigal in giving away some 1,700,000 acres to his Dutch favourites, Portland, Albemarle, Athlone and Galway. In 1698 the Commons instituted an enquiry, and when they were in possession of the facts, they introduced a Bill for the resumption of the lands. Moreover, to ensure its passage, they "tacked" it to the Land Tax Bill. The government was thus faced with the alternative of accepting the greatest insult to the Crown since 1660, or being deprived of the revenues. The King decided to accept the Act, with all its indignity.

It is impossible to read the correspondence of William III during these years without feeling the greatness of the man, and the sureness of his grasp of essentials in foreign policy. He had to resort to duplicity. Portland, his Dutch adviser, was instructed to send the King two letters, the genuine one, and one to be shown to ministers. William wrote in 1698 that Somers was "the only minister who remains to me". The French government noted that in England:

> The councils meet only for form's sake, and important affairs are not discussed in them. Thus all centres in the King of England alone.

Instructions to the French Ambassador, 1698

Never for a moment did William relax his complete control of foreign affairs. To maintain this power, he was prepared

to put up with insults in domestic affairs. Thus he instructed
Somers to send him a blank commission under the Great
Seal for the conclusion of the Partition Treaties, so that in
fact they would be negotiated without even consultation
with the English ministers. Somers merely learnt of their
contents subsequently. William's attitude to Parliament was
contemptuous. For instance, he wrote in May 1699:

> I calculate that towards the middle of next week this miser-
> able session of Parliament will terminate: not to speak of
> their having inflicted on me a mass of impertinences, and of
> their having, so to speak, despoiled the kingdom of its entire
> military force, they have not even voted the wherewithal to
> supply the taxes that were granted, nor a single farthing to
> discharge any kind of debt; so that credit is gone. Hence you
> can fancy what confusion must prevail in all this. (*He was
> writing to the Dutch Pensionary, Heinsius.*)

In 1700 the Commons proceeded to attempt the impeach-
ment of Somers, and the other whigs, for their part in the
Partition Treaties. Somers' defence was that what he had done
had been at the express command of the King, and that that
was his justification. The trials collapsed, and thus for the time
being the royal control of foreign policy was vindicated. The
King was aided by Louis XIV's recognition of the Old Pretender as James III of England in 1701, and he was thus able
to bring a comparatively united nation into the war of 1702.

Before this, however, the Commons had inflicted a final
insult upon the much-tried monarch. In 1700 the only son of
the Princess Anne, the Duke of Gloucester, had died, and
the whole question of the succession was re-opened. William
III, well knowing the dangers of war, and the Jacobite threat,
was anxious that the succession should be settled with all
speed in the Hanoverians. The Commons were ready enough
to agree, but they appended to the Act of Settlement (1701)
a series of clauses which amounted to a list of tory grievances.
With the accession of the Hanoverians, England would not
go to war in defence of any foreign territory without the
consent of Parliament; the ruler could not leave England
without consent of Parliament; all government business
should be transacted in full Privy Council; no foreigner was to
sit in the Privy Council or hold any office under the Crown;
no person holding an office of profit under the Crown should
sit in the House of Commons; judges should not be removable

at the will of the executive; and finally, the Crown could not grant a pardon which would deprive the Commons of their right to impeach. These clauses read like a commentary on the history of the previous twenty years. William had no alternative but to accept them.

In February 1702 William III, riding his favourite horse Sorrel at Hampton Court, fell and broke his collar-bone. He was exhausted, the shock was too much for his frail constitution, and he died, two weeks later, at the age of fifty-two. It was a critical time; England stood on the verge of a great war. But the Grand Alliance had been made, and he left the military future in the safe hands of Marlborough, the greatest soldier of the age.

William III was the greatest monarch to have sat on the English throne since Queen Elizabeth. His whole life had been spent in the giant task of resisting the power of France. His difficulties, both in the Netherlands and in England, were enormous; his statesmanship was of the highest order. His occasional errors were often the result of sheer fatigue. Perhaps he was mistaken to have spent so much of his time in the field, for, though he was dogged and persistent, he was not a great commander. He lacked the power to win popularity, although he did sometimes, painfully, make the attempt. He defended his prerogative to a remarkable extent (for the limitations imposed by the Act of Settlement were mainly stillborn), particularly in the field of foreign affairs. Yet the turbulence of Parliament in his last years was such as to give the Venetian envoy the impression that England was already virtually a republic. It was an understandable, but an inaccurate, observation.

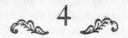

4

The Continent and Sea-Power (1688-1713): A New Era in Foreign Policy

The French Wars and the New Strategy

THE REVOLUTION OF 1688 meant a revolution in England's foreign policy. Under the Stuarts, England had played a subordinate, and at times humiliating, part in the affairs of Europe. Charles II was a pensionary of France; James II was less pliable, but no more independent of Louis XIV than his brother. William III on the other hand came to England with the fixed intention of bringing England into the continental alliance against France. Without England, the League of Augsburg could hardly hope to succeed. It is easy to see why William should have thought it worth while to risk everything on the English venture. To his great relief, he found English opinion ready for the reversal of the foreign policy it entailed.

For the fear of France had been growing during the twenty years since Arlington first gave expression to it by making the Triple Alliance of 1668. It had become a common fear that Louis XIV and the Stuarts were parties to a joint conspiracy to establish both despotism and Roman Catholicism in England. When James II fled to France, Louis at once agreed to aid him in an expedition to Ireland. The English could feel that in going to war with France they were defending both their parliamentary liberties and the Protestant Succession. William's curt dismissal of the French ambassador was therefore generally approved.

There was a further reason. Under the influence of the Navigation Laws, England was rapidly becoming a commercial nation, and commercial motives had much to do with all England's wars of the next half-century. But commercial expansion depended upon sea-power. Twenty years before the Revolution France was a negligible factor in European sea-power; now, thanks to the care of Colbert, France had the third largest fleet in Europe, in 1688 some eighty ships of the line. If France overwhelmed the Dutch, and added Dutch wealth and naval skill to her own, the danger to England would be immense. Moreover, the French, in invading Flanders, was attacking the Spanish Empire. England was more concerned with the survival of Spanish independence than with that of any other people in Europe except the Dutch, for not only was trade with Spain itself important, but the Spanish South American Empire had aroused English cupidity ever since the days of Drake. The two great enemies of England's former wars had been the Spanish and the Dutch. The old enmities were now submerged in the new menace of France, but the commercial interests remained.

England was now required, for the first time since the fifteenth century, to fight a major continental war. Her wars against Spain and the Dutch had been almost entirely naval wars, in which the prime objects had been to cut the trade routes, and capture the shipping of the enemy. It was natural that many Englishmen should continue to feel that this was how England should fight her enemies. As the years passed, and England poured 90,000 men and £6,000,000 a year into a continental war (the figures are Defoe's) it was natural that many should feel that English blood and treasure were being squandered for Dutch, rather than English interests. But this was to misunderstand the character of the new enemy. France was a continental power, she did not rely on her overseas trade routes; Louis XIV could not be defeated by sea-power alone. The focal point of the war was in the Netherlands. But sea-power had nonetheless a vital part still to play in war; just what that part was England had to work out during the wars between 1689 and 1713.

The war in the Netherlands need not detain us long. The geography of the area provided no natural frontier, for the land was flat, and the rivers to the west of the Rhine tended to run from south-west to north-east. In the course of time, therefore, successive rulers had studded the area with great fortresses to serve as formidable barriers to French invaders. As the menace of Louis XIV to Europe grew, the Dutch, the Emperor, Sweden, Spain, the Palatinate, Saxony and Bavaria, formed the League of Augsburg, in 1686, for the preservation of the *status quo*. War began in 1688 when Louis invaded the Palatinate and occupied Cologne. In 1689 William III changed the entire situation by bringing England into the war. Savoy was a member of the alliance and French troops overran Piedmont, but Louis' main war effort was in the Netherlands. Here his object was to seize a defensible line of major fortresses which might serve as a permanent frontier for France. In 1691 he laid siege to Mons with an enormous army. William III hastened to relieve it, but it fell in April. In 1692 Louis captured the great fortress of Namur. In 1693 he attempted to turn the allied flank by capturing Liège. He failed. William was defeated by Luxemburg at Neerwinden in 1693, but he had his greatest success in 1695 with his recapture of Namur. Although in 1696 Savoy deserted the allies and joined Louis, thus releasing 30,000 men to fight in the Netherlands, something like a stalemate was reached there, and continued until peace was signed.

To this war in the Netherlands England provided at first 70,000, and later 90,000 men. England had never been called upon to make such a war effort at any previous time in her history. It is not surprising that tory complaints grew that England was having to fight Dutch battles, though the complaints were unjust and mistaken. At sea, on the other hand, the complaints were not of too much effort, but of too little, and these complaints were often justified. The general equipment of the fleet was slow and inefficient. Lack of supplies and slowness in re-equipping the ships meant that the fleet often got to sea too late in the year, only to find that the French were already at sea. The situation might have been much worse but for the fact that the French repeatedly failed to take advantage of their opportunities.

James II landed in Ireland in February 1689. His success there would ultimately depend upon the French being able to retain command of the sea so as to keep him supplied. In April Admiral Herbert fought an indecisive action with the French in Bantry Bay. The French had superior numbers and were left with a tactical advantage, but they made no use of it. In fact the French made the serious mistake of turning to commerce-raiding, instead of concentrating upon securing the command of the sea. This could be a profitable undertaking, and it did inflict serious inconvenience upon the enemy, but it was not the means to win a war. The English and Dutch in 1690 had to turn to organising convoys for their Baltic and Mediterranean trade, and this for a time weakened their striking force. Thus, while Admiral Russell and thirty ships were convoying 400 merchantmen to Spain in 1690, the French were able to land another 6,000 men in Ireland. The result was that Admiral Herbert (now Lord Torrington), with only fifty ships, found himself facing the French Admiral Tourville and the Brest fleet of seventy-five ships. Torrington wished to avoid battle, rightly, since the destruction of his fleet would mean loss of command of the sea; but the government ordered him to fight. In the ensuing battle off Beachy Head he suffered the loss of fifteen ships. If Tourville had known how to make use of his victory it might have gone hard with England, but he threw away his advantage. In July, James II was defeated at the Battle of the Boyne; by August the fleet was refitted, and in command of the Channel, for the French fleet kept to Brest. Jacobite hopes faded. In 1692 Louis XIV made one final effort. He prepared an invasion of England from Havre, to be convoyed across the Channel by Tourville and the Brest fleet. Russell was at once ordered to sea. This time, with ninety-nine Allied ships, he had an enormous preponderance, for part of the French fleet was delayed, and Tourville's force numbered only forty-four. The ensuing Battle of La Hogue was a decisive victory for Britain. The French lost some fifteen ships and the rest were scattered. Winston Churchill once called this battle "the Trafalgar of the seventeenth century". This is true in that it was the end of the invasion plan, and it was the end of the hopes of the Jacobites; but unlike Trafalgar, the French fleet remained substantially in being. Their losses had been no more than those of Torrington off Beachy Head. They remained in port for most of the war, and did not risk a major battle, but so long as the fleet existed, it created a menace which England could not ignore.

This was grimly illustrated in 1693. The English government considered but rejected an attack upon Brest, and instead the main fleet was instructed to convoy a great Mediterranean fleet of merchantmen, popularly known as the Smyrna fleet, past Brest. Having safely passed Brest the main convoy turned back, and the merchantmen continued under the escort of Rooke and some twenty ships. But, unknown to it, the Brest fleet was at sea, and it came upon the convoy off St Vincent. Some eighty merchantmen and four Dutch men of war were destroyed. A great national outcry followed in England. The government were anxious to avoid an enquiry, for the real fault was theirs in not ascertaining the whereabouts of the Brest fleet, and in sending their fleet to sea so late in the spring. Two admirals were dismissed, and Nottingham resigned from the government. But again Tourville made no use of his great success. He might have seized control of the Channel, but for some reason preferred to sail into the Mediterranean, where a major battle was unlikely. But so long as his fleet existed, England was not safe. In June 1694, therefore, an attack was launched directly on Brest. But the French were prepared; the expedition was repulsed with heavy losses.

One of the interests of the wars of this period is the way in which England felt her way towards the correct strategical use of her fleet. It is sometimes said that William III was a land animal who had little understanding of the importance of sea-power. But this is to ignore his important contribution in 1694. He seems to have understood the importance which a Mediterranean fleet might have in a war against France. The Mediterranean was of first importance to England as a trade route to the Near East. But in addition, a Mediterranean fleet could blockade Toulon, and seriously hamper French military operations in either Spain or Italy. But so long as England had no naval base there, her activities must be limited to the few summer months; for the fleet could hardly reach the Mediterranean before May, and must be home again before the autumn gales in the Bay of Biscay. In 1694, however, Admiral Russell was instructed to winter at Cadiz. The idea was so revolutionary that the Admiralty refused to take responsibility for it, and the order was sent direct from the King himself. Russell could thus keep a permanent watch on the Toulon fleet. William III's sense of strategy was quite correct, as was shown in 1696. Under threat of a French invasion, the English government summoned Rooke home from the Mediterranean. The Toulon fleet of forty-seven ships of the line at once seized the opportunity to sail to join the Brest fleet, thus creating a formidable invasion fleet. It is true that the French did not make use of it, but the moral of the incident was not lost upon such students of strategy as Marlborough.

The war, which ended with the Treaty of Ryswick in 1697, was inconclusive in its nature. William had fought so doggedly in the Netherlands that it was said he did not know when he was beaten. Louis was anxious to end the war, for France was showing signs of strain, and he wished to dissolve the League of Augsburg before the question of the Spanish inheritance should be precipitated by the death of Charles the Sufferer in Spain. But to these reasons must be added the fact that the allied sea-power had gained the upper hand. Neither side could claim to have had a clear naval strategy; both sides had made many mistakes, but the advantage rested with the English and Dutch. Louis accepted a peace of surprising moderation. He gave up all his conquests since 1679 except Landau, Strasburg and Alsace, and he recognised William as King of England.

By far the greatest allied losses at sea had been at the hands of French privateers, who infested the ports from Dunkirk to St Malo, and preyed on colonial, Channel and Baltic trade. Jean Bart, the leader of the French privateers, became something of a national hero. Even when the English and Dutch arranged convoys they often sent only two or three escorting ships, and these were too weak to deter the privateers. Other privateers created havoc among the West Indian Islands. But it is doubtful whether all this effort had more than nuisance value; it could not force a decision. The French might have been better advised to have concentrated their sea-power with the single object of winning naval battles.

The Partition Treaties

In England, as sometimes happens after a great war, there was a strong reaction against continental affairs. Parliament assumed that all danger was over, and that in view of the great debt which the war had incurred, immediate economies and military disbandment should ensue. William, with a much clearer grasp of the continental situation, knew how mistaken this policy was. He was exasperated at Parliament's attitude. He wrote the Dutch Pensionary, Heinsius in January 1698:

> You cannot form an idea of the indifference with which all foreign affairs are now considered. People here only busy themselves about a fanciful liberty, while they are forced to acknowledge that they never were so free, and have nothing to apprehend from me.

Two months later, when news arrived of another illness of the King of Spain, he wrote:

> I shudder when I think of the unprepared state of the allies to begin a war, and the present dilapidated state of Spain. It is certain that France is in a condition to take possession of that monarchy, before we shall be able to concert the slightest measures to oppose it.

He had sent his favourite, the Earl of Portland, as ambassador to Versailles to sound Louis XIV. Foreign policy was conducted entirely by King William. Sometimes he showed despatches to the cabinet council, sometimes to Somers alone, and often to no English minister at all. Portland was instructed to send two letters on occasion, one of which could be shown to ministers, and the other for the King alone.

King Louis, who well knew that William III was the only monarch he had really to fear in Europe, sent Count Tallard as ambassador to England to sound William on the Spanish question. He was prepared at once to agree that the crowns of France and Spain should never be united, and to concede the point which William had most at heart, namely that the Netherlands, as Louis put it, "should be independent of any crown". In the long negotiations with Louis XIV which followed, William III was constantly suspected by English politicians of surrendering English interests to those of Holland, but an examination of his letters and despatches shows that there was little justification for the suspicion. The two essential principles he set before himself were, first, that the Spanish Netherlands should not fall into French hands, and second, that English and Dutch trade routes should be secure. His mind ran on the desirability of England receiving some guarantee of her Mediterranean trade, by annexing Ceuta, or Oran, or Port Mahon; he desired a treaty of commerce with Spain, and for all this he was prepared to see a French prince on the Spanish throne. The Emperor could be compensated by receiving the Spanish possessions in Italy; the Electoral

Prince of Bavaria might receive the Spanish Netherlands. Such was William's plan, and it seems in many respects to have been the best plan of the period. Moreover, it was remarkably similar to that which at last came about in the Peace of 1713, after eleven years of war.

William's handling of the negotiations was most statesmanlike, and was all the more difficult because, as the French well knew, both English and Dutch public opinion was set on the maintenance of peace; the English Parliament was busy insulting its King, and cutting the military force to 7,000 men, and William could speak only for two war-weary and resentful nations. In October 1698 the First Partition Treaty was concluded between William and Louis. The Electoral Prince of Bavaria was to have the Spanish throne, the Dauphin was to have the kingdoms of Naples and Sicily and the Tuscan ports, and the duchy of Milan was to go to the Archduke Charles of Austria. The treaty was concluded by William on his own authority, and without the consent of the English cabinet. The Lord Chancellor, Lord Somers, had sent the King a blank commission under the Great Seal for its conclusion. The terms were disliked in England for two reasons. First, as one writer put it:

> If the government was to be carried on by the sovereign's personal exercise of the prerogative, what had been gained by the revolution?

And second, the promised French annexation of the kingdom of Naples and Sicily would make France master of the Levant trade, and of the Mediterranean.

However, in February 1699 the Electoral Prince of Bavaria died, and negotiations had to begin all over again. The Second Partition Treaty, signed in March 1700, was less satisfactory than the first. The Spanish throne was this time to go to the Archduke Charles of Habsburg. The Dauphin was to have the kingdom of Naples and Sicily and the Tuscan ports, and also the duchy of Lorraine. The Duke of Lorraine was to receive the duchy of Milan. It is easy to see why Louis XIV (to the great surprise of William III) had so readily surrendered to the Habsburg his son's claims on the Spanish crown. The treaty would make France master of Italy, and would greatly strengthen the eastern frontier by the addition of Lorraine. William wrote gloomily about the havoc Parliament would make of these terms in their surrender of the Mediter-

ranean to the French. But on November 1st Charles the Suf-
ferer died, leaving a will assigning his entire empire to the
French prince, Philip of Anjou, and a few days later Louis
XIV decided to accept the will, instead of honouring the
Partition Treaty.

Many writers have felt that, on balance, Louis XIV was
justified in accepting the will. The Partition Treaty offered
more solid gain to France, and it is most unlikely that the
Habsburgs in challenging it could alone have defeated France.
But Louis thought much of the honour of his family, and he
certainly bargained on the war-weariness of the English and
Dutch. It is impossible, however, to believe that, in accepting
the will, he was not making a bid for European mastery.
His military and naval preparations were at once begun, and
French troops occupied key positions in the Spanish Nether-
lands in the name of Philip V of Spain. In July 1701
William III and Marlborough went to Holland to negotiate the
Grand Alliance. It was signed between England, the Dutch and
the Emperor on September 7th, 1701. The war aims of the
alliance at this time should be noted, for they were to be
changed in the course of the war. The allies agreed that
Philip V might have Spain and the Indies, but reserved
Milan, Naples, Sicily, the Low Countries, Luxembourg and
the Spanish Mediterranean islands for the Emperor. This
was close to William III's original idea, though without mention of any naval base for England in the Mediterranean.
It is not entirely clear why William and Marlborough did
not insist on the inclusion of this latter point. They certainly
wished to avoid appearing to be seeking their own aggrandise-
ment, and they had no fear of Habsburg power in the Mediterranean. Prussia, Sweden and Denmark and several of the
lesser German states were also brought into the alliance.

The War of the Spanish Succession

William had for a second time committed England to a war,
although he well knew the reluctance of the tories to endorse
the policy. But Louis XIV played directly into his hands. On
September 16th, 1701, James II died, and Louis XIV at once
recognised the Old Pretender as James III of England. There
was a general condemnation of the act in England, and it
did much to ensure that England entered the war a united
nation. Once again England was at war in defence of the

Protestant Succession. But that was not the only motive. Defoe, as so often, best summed up the attitude of the mercantile classes:

> What is England without its trade? Without its Plantation trade, Turkey and Spanish trade, and where will that be when a French garrison is planted at Cadiz and the French fleet brings home the plate from Havana? What will the Virginia colony be worth when the French have a free commerce from Quebec to Mexico behind them; what will our own northern trade be worth in time of war when the ports of Ostend and Nieuport are as full of pirates as Dunkirk and St Malo?

In short, with so many resources the French could win command of the sea, and if that were to happen, England would be doomed.

Since sea-power was at stake, it was natural that the tory argument should revive that England should act in an auxiliary capacity on the Continent, and should concentrate upon a naval and colonial war. Both William and Marlborough knew that this argument was strategically unsound. France could never be defeated by sea-power alone, while the allies, without full English support, could easily be overwhelmed. Marlborough who, after the death of William in March 1702, was mainly responsible for English strategy, wrote that England must make an even greater military effort than in the previous war. But the fleet had a vital part to play. Its main offensive function was to gain command of the western Mediterranean, blockade Toulon and hamper French military activities in both Spain and Italy.

Throughout the war command of the sea rested with the English and the Dutch. England had over a hundred ships with more than fifty guns, and the Dutch provided three ships to every five English. The French had never much more than half the Anglo-Dutch strength, and never seriously threatened the allied command of the Channel. They did, however, try to control the Mediterranean. In one respect England was in a less favourable position than in the previous war. For then Spain had been an ally, and the English fleet had been able to use Cadiz harbour. Now England had no southern European harbour at all, and without it the fleet was severely hampered. A ship could keep at sea for five or six months, but without fresh food and land relaxation, the mortality of crews was high, and without a dockyard for the careening and repairing of ships, the fleet could remain in the Mediterranean only during the summer months. The first objective, therefore, of the fleet in 1702 was the seizure of Cadiz. A great expedition sailed in July under Admiral Rooke. Rooke, however, lacked spirit. He was opposed to the whole Mediterranean strategy of Marlborough. He thought the fleet should confine itself to the protection of commerce and the like. He refused a frontal attack on Cadiz harbour, landed troops far from Cadiz, and in September abandoned the attack altogether. It was an ignominious affair, relieved only by the capture of part of the Spanish treasure fleet in Vigo harbour in October on the way home. Accordingly, in the following year the allies turned their attention to Portugal. The King of Portugal was impressed with the Anglo-Dutch command of the sea, and was ready to enter the alliance on condition he was secure from the vengeance of France. He stipulated, therefore, that the allies should agree to exclude Philip V from the throne of Spain, and that the Archduke Charles should himself come to fight in Spain. This would be greatly to extend and complicate the war aims of the allies, and in the end was to have most unfortunate results. The Dutch were rightly chary of accepting, but the tory ministers in England, especially Nottingham, the Secretary of State, insisted, and even granted Portugal the advantageous Methuen Treaty. The allies were thus committed to the conquest of Spain in return for a Portuguese alliance which served little purpose except as a base for the attack upon Spain. The tories, lacking the grasp of strategy of William III or Marlborough, continued to regard the Spanish theatre as of the first importance, whereas in fact it proved soon to be a liability.

But the strategic importance of the Mediterranean remained, and indeed increased, for in 1704 the French sent their Brest fleet into the Mediterranean to join up with the Toulon fleet. Rooke, who had been sent to the Mediterranean, was not strong enough to prevent the operation, but when he was reinforced by Sir Cloudesley Shovell and the fleet which had been watching Brest, they saw that Gibraltar was weakly defended. They sailed in, and after some tough fighting, captured it. Louis XIV at once realised its importance, and he ordered the Comte de Toulouse and some fifty ships to retake it. A sharp but indecisive battle followed off Malaga, but Toulouse retired, leaving Rooke in possession of Gibraltar. Until new moles were built Gibraltar could not form a permanent base for the fleet, but it should have formed the stepping-stone to the conquest of Minorca, and the fine harbour of Port Mahon. By a serious error of judgment, this next step was not taken until 1708.

In the continental war the French started with an enormous advantage. They seized the Spanish fortress in the Netherlands, part of the archbishopric of Cologne and the bishopric of Liège, almost before the war had begun, and thus controlled the Scheldt, the Meuse (except for Maestricht) and much of the Rhine. There were at first three main theatres of war, in the Netherlands, where Marlborough was in command, on the Rhine, where the Margrave of Baden had built the famous Stollhofen Lines, and in Italy, where in 1701 Prince Eugene of Savoy had a triumphant campaign. The Netherlands were the most difficult area for military operations, for it in effect consisted of some thirty major fortresses and some fifty other fortified places. Marlborough's strategy was always to outmanoeuvre the enemy and force them to battle, but in this he was constantly hampered by his Dutch masters, who usually wished to avoid battles, which tended to destroy armies, and required him to rely on tactical manoeuvres alone. This could certainly achieve results. In this way Marlborough in 1702 captured Venloo and Liège, and forced the French to give up the whole line of the Meuse without fighting a battle. Similarly in 1703 he took Bonn, which opened up the navigation of the Rhine. But the method was exasperating to a soldier who was a master of offensive warfare.

In September 1702 the situation of the allies suddenly worsened when the Elector of Bavaria threw off the mask of negotiation, and declared his alliance with France. The Habsburg power was enfeebled by a serious Hungarian revolt urged on by French gold. The main Habsburg military effort in Italy was held by the French armies under Vendome. It was the French plan for one army under Tallard to hold the Margrave of Baden behind his defensive lines, while another under Villars pushed into Germany to join up with the Elector of Bavaria. This was achieved during 1703. Marlborough saw clearly that unless a supreme effort was made in 1704, the Empire must fall. His intention was himself to march to the Danube if necessary. But so daring a plan had to be concealed from the Dutch. To them he said he was putting his army on the Moselle. Thus followed one of the most masterly military manoeuvres of history. The French plan was that in 1704 Tallard should attack down the Rhine, Marsin and the Elector of Bavaria down the Danube, and Vendome should launch an offensive in Italy. In May Marlborough moved rapidly down the Rhine, joined up with Prince Eugene and Prince Louis of Baden. His first objective was to knock Bavaria out of the war, and thus he devastated Bavaria for a month. The French hastened to the aid of the Elector, and the Battle of Blenheim was the result (August 13th). There were about 50,000 men on each side. Marlborough completely routed the French; casualties on both sides were heavy, but in addition the French lost some 12,000 prisoners. Winston Churchill once wrote that the Battle of Blenheim "changed the political axis of the world". It had been a moment of grave crisis. If France had crushed Habsburg power in 1704, Louis XIV might well have dominated Europe. As it was, Marlborough by his brilliant move had saved the allied cause. In one day he had raised England to the rank of a first-rate military power. Not until the days of the French Revolution would French armies again terrorise Europe. Blenheim also gave the death-blow to Jacobite hopes.

Perhaps it was inevitable that the war in the following years should seem a severe anticlimax, but it was much more an anticlimax than it need have been. Marlborough saw that the true strategic move in 1705 was to attempt a major invasion of France down the Moselle. But for this he would need some 300,000 men, and these he did not have. The Habsburgs gave him little support, they seemed content to rest heavily on their allies. The Margrave of Baden failed to join him, partly through illness, but perhaps more through jealousy of Marlborough. Finally the Dutch were as reluctant as ever to engage in major operations far from home. So the invasion plan was abandoned, and Marlborough returned reluctantly to the fortress-warfare of the Netherlands. Here in 1706 he won one of the greatest battles in history, when in four hours he shattered the French army at Ramillies, and captured their baggage, cannon and some 6,000 prisoners. Out of a fine French army of 63,000 men barely 15,000 remained. Few battles have had greater results. Villeroy, the French commander, had to abandon the whole of Spanish Flanders; Antwerp surrendered without firing a shot. Louis XIV had to denude all other fronts to raise new armies for the Netherlands. This had the most startling consequences in Italy, where Vendome had appeared to be within an ace of final victory over the Imperialists. Vendome was transferred to the Netherlands, and under the spirited attacks of Prince Eugene, the French front in Italy collapsed by the end of the year.

The terms of the alliance with Portugal, and the English seizure of Gibraltar, had necessitated the opening of a war front in Spain. An English force in Portugal was commanded by one of William III's generals, a Huguenot refugee and a fine soldier, now Earl of Galway. He was joined by the Earl of Peterborough, a restless quarrelsome character, with little experience of war, but who was appointed commander-in-chief in Spain. They were joined also, somewhat reluctantly, by the Habsburg Archduke, now styled "Charles III" of Spain. With the help of the English fleet under Sir Cloudesley Shovell, they decided to attack Barcelona, for it was thought that the Habsburg cause would be popular in Catalonia. After a fortnight's siege Barcelona surrendered, and Peterborough went off to occupy Valencia. In 1706 a threefold move was made on Madrid, Charles from Barcelona, Peterborough from Valencia and Galway from Portugal. They reached Madrid, and Charles III was proclaimed King. But dissensions broke out among the leaders; Peterborough, for reasons of his own, went off to Savoy. The French, although they had retired from Madrid, easily outnumbered the allies. As the French prepared to attack, the allies could only fall back towards the coast. In 1707 Galway was heavily defeated by Berwick at the Battle of Almanza (in which an English refugee commanding a French army defeated a French refugee commanding an English army), and by 1708 Charles III found himself pinned to Barcelona, with one single remaining fortress in Valencia, Alicante, which fell in 1709. All this was the greatest disappointment to the tories in England, for they had always regarded Spain as the most important theatre of war. In 1710, therefore, when they returned to office, they sent General Stanhope to Spain to reverse the situation. He began well, defeated Philip V at Saragossa, and advanced on Madrid, but with the arrival of French reinforcements, he was forced to retreat again. The fact was that the French were easily superior in Spain, and the Spanish people readily accepted Philip V as their king. The Spanish war had been an unfortunate legacy of tory policy, and did little to strengthen the allied cause at any time during the war.

What successes the allies had in Spain were largely the result of their command of the sea. In fact a curious reversal of priorities had taken place. It was the allied need for naval bases which originally led them into Spain, but now too much of the activities of the fleet was spent in preserving the allied cause there. The real objective should have been Minorca, and the ultimate goal Toulon. An attack was launched on Toulon in 1707, but Prince Eugene, who was in command, lacked his usual fire and determination, and the attack failed. It did, however, succeed in destroying the Toulon fleet in harbour. It was a misfortune for England that her finest admiral, Shovell, was drowned in a storm on the return voyage.

1708 saw the failure of a Jacobite raid on Scotland, but this did not upset the powerful naval dispositions destined for the Mediterranean, and at long last an attack was made on Minorca by General Stanhope and Admiral Leake. It fell easily in September. Stanhope wrote:

> England ought never to part with this island, which will give the law to the Mediterranean in time of war and peace.

Unfortunately it was too late for its capture to have a decisive influence on the outcome of this war.

Since 1704 it had been clear to all Europe that the brunt of the war was being carried by the maritime Powers. Except when Eugene was directly in command, Habsburg military power was weak and even irresponsible. As one contemporary wrote, they

> undertake sieges without cannon, ammunition or engineers, with as much assurance as they did a war without money, credit or troops.

In negotiations the Habsburgs were as haughty and unrealistic as they were inadequate in war. When the Italian theatre of war ended, the Imperialists were even more content to lean heavily on the Dutch and the English. The Dutch began to sigh for peace, and they thought it might be possible after

Ramillies. Marlborough thought otherwise. He wrote to a Dutch general:

> You must give me leave to tell you that I am one of those who believe that France is not yet reduced to her just bounds, and that nothing can be more hurtful to us on this occasion than seeming overforward to clap up a hasty peace.

So the fortress-warfare of the Netherlands continued. In 1708 the French opened the season with the capture of Ghent and Bruges. Marlborough counter-attacked, and defeated the French at Oudenarde. He then besieged and captured Lille, one of the greatest fortresses in Europe, and later re-took Ghent and Bruges. Marlborough then mooted his most daring strategic design, to by-pass the remaining fortresses, land an allied army at Abbeville, and make a direct attempt upon Paris. But neither the Dutch nor Prince Eugene, who was now fighting with him, would agree, and thus the hopes of speedily gaining a decisive victory were again frustrated.

Still, by 1709 France was in great distress. Famine and discontent were rife, and Louis was prepared to grant all that the allies could reasonably demand; to recognise the Protestant Succession in England; to give up his conquests; and even to abandon Philip V's claims in Spain. The English whig ministers had on the whole conducted the war well, but they were not the men to make the peace. They were bent on humiliating Louis; they thought his defeat so complete that he must accept any terms they demanded.[1] To all the other demands they added, not merely that Philip should be required to surrender the Spanish throne, but that Louis XIV should guarantee his deposition, even to the extent of military action. This was an absurd demand. It had formed no part of the original war aims of the allies. It was a tory addition, the result of their alliance with Portugal. What had at first seemed to be dictated by the needs of sea-power and trade, had now become regarded as part of the national interest. The Dutch rightly feared that the demand

[1] Prince Eugène thought so too. He wrote to the Emperor in May 1709: "All the facts go to show that France is quite unable to prolong the war, and we can, therefore, if we wish, obtain everything we ask for. We have only to hold together and preserve a good understanding among ourselves." This last condition proved to be too much to ask.

pushed Louis too far, and relations between them and English ministers became cool. Marlborough must bear some responsibility since he did not raise his voice clearly for peace. But he knew his favour with the Queen was waning, and perhaps he still hoped to complete an invasion of France.[2]

Negotiations broke down on whig intransigence, and by 1710 the French had recovered their strength; never again were they so weak as in 1709. The whigs had outstayed their welcome in a war-weary England. Harley, St John and the tories came into power in 1710, and peace talks began again. The tories were convinced that peace must be made. There was no further talk of deposing Philip V, but merely the requirement that the crowns of France and Spain should never be united. Great emphasis was laid on Britain's naval and commercial interests. Gibraltar, Minorca, the Hudson's Bay area, Newfoundland and St Kitts were to be annexed, and there was to be an Asiento Treaty with Spain. There was hope also of a Commercial Treaty with France. These were the terms of men who considered that balance of power was in the interests of European peace, and that Britain's interests lay overseas rather than in continental entanglements. Marlborough had meanwhile been prosecuting the war in the Netherlands with vigour. In September 1709 he fought the murderous battle of Malplaquet, in which the allies lost some 24,000 men, in the greatest carnage Europe was to see before Borodino. The French were defeated and had to fall back behind the River Rhonelle, and Marlborough captured Mons. Peace, however, seemed as far off as ever. In 1711 Villars constructed his "Ne Plus Ultra" lines of defence, which Marlborough proceeded to break through. It was Marlborough's last campaign. Now completely out of favor with the tory ministers, he was dismissed from his command at the end of the year. The best comment on the tory action is perhaps that supplied by Louis XIV:

> The affair of displacing the Duke of Marlborough will do all for us we desire.

Peace talks with the French were conducted by St John. His

2 Even Marlborough subscribed to the slogan "No peace without Spain".

task was not easy, for public opinion was set upon a "Spanish" peace. This was well illustrated by a conversation Godolphin had with Sir Gilbert Heathcote, Governor of the Bank of England, in 1709:

> Heathcote: "Pray, my Lord, don't let us have a rotten peace."
> Godolphin: "Pray tell me what you call a rotten peace."
> Heathcote: "I call anything a rotten peace unless we have Spain, for without it we can have no safety."

Such men as Heathcote had been behind the financial success of Godolphin's administration, and when the tories came in they had sent a deputation to the Queen to declare that the change of ministers would threaten the whole system of credit.[3] Nottingham and the high tories carried against the government in the Lords in November 1711 a motion:

> that no peace could be safe or honourable to Great Britain, or Europe, if Spain and the West Indies were allotted to any branch of the house of Bourbon.

and Orford had to hasten to obtain the Queen's consent to the creation of twelve additional peers to ensure a majority in the Lords. At the Congress of Utrecht, therefore, it took some courage for Bolingbroke to abandon the Spanish claims. He also refused to support the extreme claims of the Emperor. But he supported the Dutch claims to the Barrier Fortresses, and he was particularly strong in the support of the strengthening of the House of Savoy as important to the balance of power in Italy (which was now heavily tilted in favour of the Emperor). Criticism at home that the Levant trade might be endangered was forestalled by Bolingbroke's insistence that Savoy receive the island of Sicily, the friendly harbours of which he hoped would now be in addition to our possessions of Gibraltar and Minorca. Britain's territorial gains were Gibraltar, Minorca, Newfoundland, Hudson's Bay, Nova Scotia and St Kitts, and also an Asiento Treaty with Spain.

The Treaty of Utrecht, which was signed in April 1713, was a much better peace than the whigs had attempted to make. British interests were safeguarded, France was not

[3] The Queen regarded the act as an impertinence; the threat was certainly disproved by events.

humiliated, and the balance of power was preserved. But Bolingbroke had too ostentatiously thrown over his allies. Worst of all, he had seriously offended the Elector of Hanover, the heir to the throne. For these errors he was to pay dearly.

5

Party Politics in the Reign of
Queen Anne

RARELY WAS a king so little mourned as William III;
only Defoe's voice was raised to accuse the English of
ingratitude to the dead King. The accession of Queen Anne
was the signal for rejoicing, especially by the tories. They
had already triumphed during William's last years, and now,
they argued, they had a monarch after their own hearts, a
high churchwoman and devoted tory.

Anne had had a sad life. In 1683 she married Prince
George of Denmark, a good-natured, ineffective prince, much
given to eating and drinking. She had had some seventeen
children, but only one had reached childhood, and he had
died in 1700. Her life had thus been that of a semi-invalid,
in which she found consolation in a few simple things, her
religion, her husband, and her deep attachment to Sarah
Jennings. She had played with the latter as a child, was fascinated by her brilliance, and devoted to her friendship.
She had had to make the painful choice between her religion
and her father, and was never in doubt which she would
choose. In the difficult years after 1685 she was sustained
throughout by Sarah and her husband, John Churchill, and
when she came to the throne she leaned heavily upon them.
Her understanding was limited, her mind slow-moving, but
on the few fundamentals upon which she had reached certainty, she was immovable. She was no weak-willed woman.
The greatest men in the land could break on her stubborn

will. At her accession she was certain of three things: that the Anglican church must be protected at all costs, that the whigs were the hateful enemies to monarchy, and that the war against France must be won.

In 1702, therefore, a tory ministry was appointed. Its leading members among the high tories were Rochester, Nottingham and Sir Edward Seymour. Laurence Hyde, Earl of Rochester, was the son of the great Clarendon, and thus the Queen's uncle. He had been one of the principal instruments of the royal despotism during the last years of Charles II, the Hushai of Dryden's famous poem. He was made Lord Treasurer by James II, but as a sincere Anglican, he was embarrassed by James' policy. He and his brother Clarendon hung on to office without power until 1687, when they were dismissed. Now Rochester felt that he had come into his own, for Anne trusted him, and he hoped to rule through her with the help of the high church party. Seymour was a man of similar views. He had been a leader of the bitter tory opposition in William's last years, and Burnet regarded him as the ablest man in the party.

However, against these high tories stood Marlborough and Godolphin. John Churchill's career had so far been a chequered one. He had first come to Court as a page to the Duke of York in the reign of Charles II. For a time he served as a soldier under Turenne, the greatest French soldier of his day. His marriage to the penniless beauty, Sarah Jennings, in 1678 brought him into the circle of the Princess Anne. He was the victor of Sedgmoor, but in 1688 he deserted James just in time to ensure that the Revolution was a bloodless one. He served William well in Ireland in 1690, but William suspected him soon of intrigues, which may well have been a fact, and of Jacobitism, which is much less likely, and William for years made little further use of him. Yet William's crowning service to his country was to employ Marlborough to negotiate the Grand Alliance of 1701, and, before he died, to appoint him to the supreme command. Henceforth his supreme interest was to win the war. Secure in the confidence of the Queen, and in the knowledge of his own military genius, he yet needed one thing more, namely the support of a sound ministry. For this it was essential that Godolphin should be at the Treasury.

We have already seen that Godolphin was essentially a man of business and an excellent financier. As he had served Charles II, James II and William, so now he was devoted to Queen Anne, to Marlborough and the prosecution of the war against France. Certainly no one understood the business of government so well as he did. It followed, therefore, that Anne's first government was, from the start, divided. The high tories of the Rochester–Nottingham–Seymour camp looked for tory and Anglican victories; they wanted an Occasional Conformity Bill, and a Place Bill, and were convinced that if there must be war, it must be mainly a naval war. Marlborough and Godolphin, on the other hand, wanted an end to religious dissension, and a vigorous prosecution of the war by land and sea.

To understand the politics of Queen Anne's reign we should note that there were two points of view which may roughly be described as whig and tory. The whigs, well organized under the junto, stood for the "principles of 1688", toleration for dissenters, the Protestant Succession and the defeat of France. The high tories believed passionately in the old order in which the Crown and the Anglican church were in close alliance; they resented the political power of dissent, and they were cool on the land war. Between the two, so to speak, was the moderate tory view of Harley, which was less interested in religious controversy, feared the "republicanism" of the whigs and the growing power of the executive, and, at least until 1708, accepted the necessity of the war against France. But the politics of the period cannot be understood only in terms of ideas. To begin with, the government in 1701 controlled some thirty-eight seats, and could count upon a further hundred votes of men, both whig and tory, who together might be said to make up a Court party. There were also a Country party of some 150, mainly country gentry, quite unorganised, whose attendance was not good, and whose votes were often unpredictable, but a majority of whom might be expected to support the government. In addition there were over 200 Members of Parliament representing family connections; about eighty in 1701 belonged to the junto and their friends; roughly the same number were high tory; Harley had some twenty followers and Marlborough and Godolphin twelve. Although there were usually whig and tory points of view on any important subject, men accounted whig or tory did not always vote according to their labels.

The Queen's active intervention in the elections of 1702

on behalf of the Anglican party was said materially to
have increased the whig defeat, but she soon found it necessary to choose between the high tories and Marlborough and
Godolphin. In 1702 the triumphant high tories carried an
Occasional Conformity Bill through the Commons, though
it was defeated in the Lords. They found a new champion
in Henry St John, a brilliant though dissolute young man,
who earned a reputation as a parliamentarian by his part in
the victory in the Commons. When Rochester persisted with
his Bill in 1703, the Queen resented his factiousness and independence, and, to his immense surprise, suddenly dismissed him. He at once became the leader of the high tory
opposition. In 1704 Nottingham and Seymour were also dismissed. In indignation the high tories attempted to "tack"
the Occasional Conformity Bill to the Land Tax Bill and
thus ensure its passage through the Lords. But in this they
failed, for the moderate tories in the Commons led by Harley refused to support the move; and they were no more
successful in the following year with a Place Bill.

In these parliamentary conflicts Godolphin entered increasingly into alliance with Harley. Harley was fundamentally a man of the middle way, with a real political instinct
for what was possible, and an uncanny knack of estimating
public and parliamentary opinion. He was certainly trusted
by many moderate members of the Commons, yet he was,
when the test came, deficient in the art of leadership. He
preferred backstairs and subtle methods, and often his
manoeuvres led nowhere. Even when his energy was lacking
his instincts were often right, and, in the first half of Anne's
reign, he proved a valuable ally to Godolphin. In 1704 he
became Secretary of State, and St John, hungry for the glam-
our of power, became Secretary at War.

The fact was plain that whereas the high tories were bent
on factious opposition, the whigs were anxious to support
the war. The high tories lost heavily in the 1705 elections,
and the question arose how long the whigs, well disciplined
and led by the junto, would continue to support a government from which they were excluded. At first the Queen was
adamant against their being offered any office. Her point of
view was simple. The whig junto were "republicans" (which
meant not literally republicans, but "intent upon dominating
government in their own interests") and enemies of the

Anglican church. We have seen how little the events of the reign of William III had supported this estimate of the whigs, but in her few simple convictions Anne was all but immovable. As she wrote simply to Godolphin in 1705:

> I dread falling into the hands of either party . . . Do all you can to keep me out of the power of the merciless men of both parties.

Yet necessity forced her to give way gradually. One by one the junto had to be satisfied. Sunderland and Walpole were given minor appointments in 1705, and Lord Cowper became Lord Keeper.

It was a beginning, and Godolphin was thus able to withstand the tory attempt to embarrass him in 1705–6. They proposed that the Electress Sophia, as the heir to the throne, should be invited to live in England. They argued that if the government supported it they would alienate the Queen, who hated the idea of a rival Court in England; but if they opposed it, they would alienate the Electress. But the attempt failed miserably. The government, with whig support, instead brought forward the Regency Bill, which carefully defined the machinery which should come into operation on the death of the Queen, in order to ensure the Hanoverian succession. The Act was passed in 1707 and it was this machinery which worked so well in 1714 in defeating possible Jacobite plans.[1]

Union with Scotland

Whig support was essential, not only for the continuance of the war effort, but also to carry Godolphin's great Act of Union with Scotland in 1707. Union with Scotland came about, not as a result of a growing warmth between the two nations, but because of a realisation on both sides of the Border that the only alternative to union was war. The reign of William III was a time of economic disaster, as well as political strife, for Scotland. It was a desperately poor country, until recently torn by religious strife. The Scots felt that they had all the disadvantages of a union with

---

[1] The Act also repealed two of the anachronistic clauses of the Act of Settlement, one relating to the privy council, and the other to the exclusion of Placemen from the House.

England, with none of the advantages. They never saw their king; their government too often appeared to be directed from London; yet they were excluded from all the great commercial advantages of empire and foreign trade which a real union with England would entail. In 1695 the Scots attempted to form a Company on the model of the English East India Company; but Scotland was miserably poor and devoid of capital, and English merchants saw to it that the Company raised capital neither in London nor from the Dutch. Then between 1698 and 1700 the Company made three attempts to establish a settlement in Darien (Panama). All three attempts failed, and the Company lost £200,000. Scots' bitterness against England was increased, for their difficulties were blamed on English hostility. The Scots hated the English as overbearing neighbours, while the English looked on the Scots as little better than barbarians. Yet it was clear to statesmen that unless this problem was solved, Scotland might once again drift into the French camp against England. William III's dying words urged a union with Scotland. Accordingly in 1702 Commissioners were appointed by both sides to negotiate. But the tory ministers in England were not happy about a union with a Presbyterian state, and whig merchants were not anxious to incur Scottish competition in trade; and negotiations broke down.

Then the Scottish Parliament took a hand. By the Act of Security (1703) it provided for the ending of the single monarchy with England after the death of Queen Anne, unless the problem of union had meanwhile been settled. The Act caused annoyance in London, and the whigs retaliated by passing the Alien Act (1705), which threatened the Scots with the exclusion of their exports to England unless they repealed the Act of Security, or agreed to a union. In spite of the popular hostility on both sides, wise men saw the obvious solution. In 1706 negotiations began again. In nine weeks agreement was reached. Scotland gave up her Parliament, but received full safeguards for her religion and for her legal system. Scotland in future was to be represented in the English parliament by forty-five M.P.s and sixteen peers, the latter to be elected by the nobility. As part of the financial settlement, England paid compensation to those who had lost in the Darien scheme. The Treaty was signed in July 1706, and passed through both Parliaments in 1707. There was much opposition and some rioting in Scotland, but

in England there was profound relief that the menace
from Scotland was removed. Few measures have been
productive of so much good as the Act of Union with Scotland. The benefits to Scotland were great. From being a poor
country Scotland made great strides towards industrialism
and trade. Glasgow grew from a fishing village into a prosperous port; the Clyde became one of the great industrial
areas of Britain. In the eighteenth century Scotland became
one of the great intellectual centres of Europe, the Uni-
versities of Edinburgh and Glasgow being famous for their
teaching of medicine, philosophy and economics. So far from
Scotland becoming some mere appendage of England, it enjoyed a great intellectual and cultural renaissance during the
late eighteenth century, with the names of Adam Smith,
David Hume, Robertson, Dugald Stewart, Sir Walter Scott
and Robert Burns. The union with Scotland must be accounted one of the great achievements of the eighteenth century,
and the greatest act of statesmanship of Sidney Godolphin.

Godolphin and the Whigs

The Act of Union was passed with the full support of the
whigs. Yet their rewards of office continued to be small.
All through 1706 Marlborough and Godolphin kept up their
pressure on the reluctant Queen, for the whigs were insist-
ing that at least one of their number be admitted into high
office, and it was hoped that Sunderland, being Marlborough's son-in-law, might be the least unacceptable to the
Queen. Finally, after months of resistance, she gave way,
and Sunderland became Secretary of State. She regarded it,
however, as a defeat which had been forced upon her by
Godolphin, and she never forgave him. Harley was opposed
to this "surrender" to the whigs. He was fundamentally
opposed to party government, and while he did not doubt
that some concession was needed to whigs at that point, he
thought that it should not go too far, and that the Queen's
resistance to it should be well known. Increasingly in 1707 he
gained the ear of the Queen, through his kinswoman (and
Sarah Churchill's) Abigail Hill. By 1707 it was known that
Anne was taking other counsels than those of her ministers,
and she had virtually broken with Sarah Churchill. In 1708
Harley felt himself strong enough to oust Godolphin. In
February 1708 Marlborough and Godolphin resigned. There

followed a famous scene in Council when the Duke of
Somerset said that he could not sit without Godolphin and
Marlborough, and the meeting broke up in confusion. The
whole city was in alarm, and finally Harley had to beg the
Queen to accept his resignation. Marlborough and Godolphin
returned to office, and with them the whigs in full cry: Boyle,
Somers, Wharton, Pembroke, Walpole, all found high office.

The whigs governed well. They loyally supported Godolphin and Marlborough; they provided parliamentary majorities; they had the support of the financial interests of the
City; they zealously prosecuted the war. They passed an
Amnesty Act (1709) for the relief of former Jacobites. But
they never won the confidence of the Queen, who merely
bided her time. Moreover, they made the fundamental mistake of failing to make peace. The nation was war-weary,
and Harley took full advantage of the fact to spread the
charge that it was "Marlborough's war", fought for Marlborough's personal power and profit. The high tories delight-
edly took up the cry, and revived the old charge of "the
church in danger", on the grounds that the Queen was a
prisoner of the whigs. Their most effective mouthpiece was
Dr Sacheverell. In November 1709 Sacheverell preached in
St Paul's before the Lord Mayor on "the perils of false
brethren in church and state". It was an attack, not only on
Godolphin and the whigs, but on the Revolution settlement
itself. The sermon was printed and widely circulated. The
government made the mistake of deciding to impeach
Sacheverell. The famous case came on in 1710. It was ably
argued on both sides, but the previous harvests had been
bad, discontent was rife, the war was unpopular, and the
tories turned the event into something of a triumph. Public
opinion was with them, and although Sacheverell was found
guilty, he was merely suspended from preaching for three
years. His subsequent tour of England took on something
of a triumphal procession. The whigs looked on glumly and
awaited their own downfall. Their failure to make peace had
alienated many moderate men, such as the Dukes of Argyll
and Somerset, who were sometimes known as the Juntilla,
and who in these years were inclined to throw their weight
first on one side, and then on the other, as each government
seemed to exceed the bounds of moderation. They were now
ready to back Harley. His time had come.

The Triumph of the Tories

In August 1710 Godolphin was suddenly dismissed. He had served the Queen nobly since 1702, and his union with Scotland was an act of high statesmanship, but he left office without the royal gratitude; and the promise of a pension of £4,000 a year was never honoured. Harley, now in control of the Treasury, hastily installed tory lord lieutenants and sheriffs in preparation for the coming election. The remaining whigs were driven out of office. St John became Secretary of State. In the elections of October 1710, bitterly contested, the whigs were routed. Some 270 Members of Parliament lost their seats; the whigs numbered less than one-third of the new House. Many of the tories were returned for the first time; they lacked both experience and moderation. The extremists were nicknamed the October Club, from their zeal in drinking the October ales; their enemies said they were tories when sober, and Jacobites when drunk. There thus began one of the most dramatic and eventful periods, in which the old tory party enjoyed a final period of political power, and in four years were led to political suicide and disintegration.

Both parties were well aware of the new importance of public opinion. Addison stated the whig view-point in the *Whig Examiner*; Harley employed Swift to write in the rival tory paper *The Examiner,* and he made good use of his opportunity to blacken the character of Marlborough. Harley also employed Defoe to write *The Review*, and St John had his own organ in *The Post Boy*. There soon developed between Harley and St John a bitter struggle for power. St John frankly admitted many years later that he and his friends regarded politics in those days as no more than an exciting game for political power. Having once obtained power, the next step was to secure its continuance by the destruction of one's enemies. The whigs derived much strength from the support they had received from the monied interests centred in the Bank of England and the East India Company. Harley replied by establishing the South Sea Company in the tory interest. It was a clever move, designed to interest the City in the prospects of peace and a lucrative trade with Spain. In January 1711 Harley made the first move to open peace negotiations with France, but in March he was stabbed by a French spy, and he never really recovered from the blow. The Queen was full of sympathy, and promptly made him Earl of Oxford and Lord High Treasurer (vacant since Godolphin's dismissal). He was thus now First Minister in name, but in fact power passed increasingly into the hands of St John, who now became Viscount Bolingbroke.

During the next three years Bolingbroke was chiefly concerned with three things. With the first, the making of peace, we have dealt already.[2] In the event, he made a good Treaty, but at the heavy price for the tories of the accusation of having deserted their allies, and above all at the price of the fatal alienation of the House of Hanover. George of Hanover protested strongly against the peace talks in November 1711; the ministers were alarmed, and even so good a tory as Nottingham began to turn against them. But it was too late to turn back. The ministers burnt their boats in January 1712 by dismissing Marlborough, who had rather ignominiously clung on to an appointment for long devoid of power. After a special creation of peers, the terms of a separate peace were carried through the Lords, and thus was completed the one act of statesmanship to which Bolingbroke can lay claim.

The second of the high tory interests was the destruction of their enemies. Nottingham was as keen as ever on an Occasional Conformity Bill. In 1711 he entered into an informal agreement with the whigs by which, in return for his opposition to the peace terms, they would not oppose his Bill. It accordingly became law with little opposition. The next measure aimed against the dissenters was more directly the work of Bolingbroke. The Schism Act of 1714 was an act of bitter partisanship. The most successful schools of the period were the dissenting academies. The Act required these academies to obtain a permit from the bishop of the diocese. It was hoped that thus these fertile breeding-grounds of whiggish thought would be eliminated. But happily few bishops chose to exert their powers, and in the first years of the Hanoverians the whigs repealed both this and the Occasional Conformity Act. The Schism Act, however, is an indication of the determination of Bolingbroke to keep alive the old dissensions, and shows the barrenness of his statesmanship in domestic affairs.

2 See Ch. 4.

The Schism Act was part of Bolingbroke's plan to embarrass, and ultimately destroy, Harley, now Earl of Oxford. For Harley had a dissenting background, and he was opposed to intolerance. Behind the scenes a bitter struggle for power was waged between the two. Harley's health and energies were unequal to the task. His attempt to convict Bolingbroke of gross corruption failed, and on July 27th, 1714, the Queen reluctantly dismissed him from office. Then followed four of the most dramatic and significant days in our history. Bolingbroke's dream of unrivalled power lasted only three days. On July 30th the Queen became very ill. At this point the juntilla asserted itself. Somerset and Argyll suddenly appeared at the Cabinet Council in their capacity as privy councillors. They sensed that the end was near; the Regency Act of 1707 had provided that on the death of the Queen, Parliament and Privy Council should remain in being, and seven Lords Justices should exercise the royal power. Of these the key man would be the Lord High Treasurer; but the office was vacant since the dismissal of Oxford. They persuaded the Queen, with her dying hand, to give the white staff to Shrewsbury. Bolingbroke's power was at an end. On August 1st Queen Anne died.

Well might Bolingbroke write that fortune bantered him. For the third subject with which his mind had been concerned had been the Succession. He knew that the extremism of tory policy since 1710 had alienated many. Above all, he knew that the Elector George of Hanover detested the tories; his accession to the British throne would spell the destruction of Bolingbroke's power. Yet he knew also that a Jacobite restoration was possible only at the price of civil war. Before his plans matured farther, the Queen died. On August 16th a message from Hanover ordered him to hand over the seals of office. His papers were seized. He hurried to Marlborough for advice. Perhaps with his tongue in his cheek, Marlborough solemnly told him that his life was in danger. Bolingbroke waited no longer; he fled to France.

Thus ended the last four years of power of the old tory party. They had stood for much that was good; peace with France, recognition of the Bourbons in Spain, concern for commercial and naval interests. Yet these things were overshadowed by the breach in the Grand Alliance, the alienation of the House of Hanover, and the bitter party and religious conflicts which they promoted at home. They failed to recognise the growth in England of a great body of moderate opinion, of whom Defoe was the most splendid mouthpiece, who looked for other and more fruitful things than the old controversies. Bolingbroke, with all his brilliance, himself failed to recognise it, and he must bear the chief blame for the tory catastrophe.

6

The Triumph of the Whigs and the
Age of Walpole

George I

GEORGE I HAD never thought highly of his chances of becoming King of England; he had never troubled even to learn English. But Baron von Bothmer had been sent as Hanoverian minister in London, and he soon established close relations with the whigs. When Queen Anne died, the Lords Justices, headed by Shrewsbury, at once assumed office, and to their number the new King nominated a further eighteen, of whom all but two were whigs. There was no disturbance. Few people could be enthusiastic about the accession to the throne of a middle-aged German, yet George I came with a powerful claim upon their loyalty, for he had been called to the throne by Act of Parliament, and his peaceful accession would put an end to many fears of renewed civil war. He was now aged fifty-four, with a wide knowledge of European affairs, and with a reputation as an active soldier. Beyond this there was little to endear him to his subjects. He was a heavy, dour, loveless man. Since 1694 he had kept his wife imprisoned in Hanover, and he contented himself with two hideous and grasping mistresses, who lost no opportunity to feather their nests in England. He never attempted really to understand, still less to love, England. He well understood that his dual position made him one of the most powerful monarchs in Europe, and he sought to exploit the situation to the full. But he had little of William

III's industry, and he was content to leave much of the business of government to his ministers. Cold, stiff, shy and parsimonious, he rarely appeared in public. He was surrounded by Germans, and at first entirely dependent upon the advice of Bothmer. But that advice was on the whole sound. It was that he should appoint the right ministers, and trust them.

George I was really interested only in foreign affairs. It is doubtful how far he understood English institutions, or how far he really cared about them. He could not discuss them in English. He talked with his ministers in French, but some, such as Somers, Cowper and Walpole, knew no French, and the latter had to make do with bad Latin. In Cabinet Council he was silent, and he soon gave up attending. It is probable that he signed many a document without real understanding of its contents. Yet it would be quite wrong to suggest that George I was a nonentity. He had both British and Hanoverian ministers; and what he could not learn from one he could learn from the other. In the eyes of Europe he appeared a powerful monarch bestriding the narrow world like a colossus. Perhaps, above all, he was fortunate in his British ministers. For the first half of his reign was the period of the great Lord Stanhope, and in the second half he had the services of Sir Robert Walpole.

Among the politicians of the time there was a rapid change of personnel. Of the whig junto, Wharton died in 1715 and Somers and Halifax in 1716. Marlborough was re-appointed Captain-General of the forces, but he had a stroke in 1716 and took no further part in affairs. Sunderland continued in office, but the two ministers upon whom George I appeared at first most to rely were Lord Townshend and Earl Stanhope. Townshend was well known to the King even before his accession, and Bothmer regarded him as a foremost champion of the Hanoverian succession. He was an honest and industrious, but turbulent and erratic, minister. He had the misfortune in politics to be overshadowed first by Stanhope, and then by Walpole, and in the end he won immortality only in the turnip-field. Earl Stanhope, on the other hand, his fellow Secretary of State, was a statesman of the first order, and gifted also as a soldier, diplomat, orator and man of culture. The Prussian Minister in London not unjustly described him as: "the only Englishman I know possessed of a universal spirit." In foreign affairs he returned, as we shall see, to the great European tradition of William III and the whigs, and his policy was so completely acceptable to the King that the two worked in perfect harmony.

The reaction against the tories was complete. The whigs were triumphant in the elections of 1715. Many a moderate tory found it easy to drift into the whig camp. Even Nottingham himself, that pillar of the old tory cause, was so zealous for the Hanoverians that he sat in the government with the whigs for the first eighteen months of the new reign. A secret committee of the Commons reported on the tory maladministration of the previous four years. The impeachments of Bolingbroke, Ormonde and Oxford were voted. The first two had fled, but Oxford stood his ground and was sent to the Tower.

The '15 Rebellion and Whig Consolidation

The atmosphere of crisis was heightened by the Jacobite rising of 1715. The ease with which the whigs dealt with it should not lead us to underestimate the danger as it appeared in 1715. The sense of dissatisfaction with the German dynasty was widespread; the country gentry and clergy were tory, and the tories were disgruntled at their wholesale eviction from office. On the other hand, King, Parliament, the whigs and the monied interests proved to be a powerful combination. The French menace was still fresh in people's minds. The Jacobites had little to offer beyond a vague appeal to the nostalgia of the past. To the new Britain of Protestant toleration and commercial expansion the Jacobite cause was strangely anachronistic. In the Highlands they raised 10,000 supporters, but in England their strength was negligible. The whigs acted with great vigour. Possible leading Jacobites, Sir William Wyndham and Lord Lansdowne, were arrested. A small rising in Northumberland collapsed when faced, at Preston in Lancashire, with government troops half their number. Neither Bolingbroke nor the Old Pretender had much faith in the chances of success. By the time the latter arrived in Scotland in January 1716 his supporters had shrunk to a mere 4,000. On the approach of Argyll and a superior army, they retired into the Highlands and disintegrated. Some thirty or forty executions were the extent of the government's proscription. The extent of the rising had been the result of the continuance of the feudal conditions in the Highlands, and Northumberland, in which a few clan or feudal chiefs could call out their followers to rebellion.

The most important result of the '15 Rebellion was the Septennial Act of 1716. The whigs defended the measure on the grounds that it would be dangerous to have an election as early as 1718 in view of the Jacobite menace, and that frequent elections encouraged turbulence and increased corruption. The tory William Shippen put up a strong argument against the Bill. He argued that the measure was merely the means by which the whigs sought to entrench themselves in power and guard themselves against the will of the people. He called it, "perhaps our last struggle for the liberties of those we represent". But the Bill passed into law by large majorities. Various estimates have been made of the importance of the Act. Speaker Onslow said it began the emancipation of the Commons from the control of both the Crown and the Lords. It certainly gave the Members of Parliament a longer period in which to achieve experience and assurance. But, above all, the Act may be said to have consolidated the Revolution Settlement. It greatly increased the prestige of the whigs; it enabled them to establish themselves in power, and without the Act they could hardly have ruled Britain during the next forty years.

In the final test, however, the whigs prolonged their period of office, not by manipulating the constitution, but by the policy they pursued. Under Stanhope, their foreign policy was brilliantly successful; in contrast, their domestic policy appears often halting and narrow. But in general the whigs were aware of, and respected, the growing spirit of moderation of the time which was so well expressed by Defoe, when he wrote:

> I have had frequent opportunity of conversing with people of the first condition; no one worthy to be thought a statesman has really been either whig or tory, or governed in the least by the principles of such, according to the common acception of them.

The same idea is to be found in the important estimate of parties in England, written by the Huguenot Paul de Rapin-Thoyras in 1717. He argued that no party could be trusted to rule, for the high tories would bring back despotism, the moderate tories would be too tolerant of the prerogative; the extreme whigs would be republicans, and the moderate whigs would reduce the Crown to the condition of a doge of Venice; the extreme dissenters would destroy the established church, and the Anglicans would destroy the dissenters. He concluded:

> It is certain the true good and advantage of the kingdom is not to be found in any of the views which the heads of the two parties seem to have an eye to. The only method that can in time restore peace and tranquillity is to let the government remain upon its ancient foundations, and the church in the condition wherein the Reformation placed it.

On the whole the whigs agreed, and the fundamental reason for their continuance in power during the reigns of George I and George II is that on the whole they avoided faction, and gave Britain moderate, peaceful and tolerant government. In spite of the external wars of the period, the years 1714–60 are years of good government and peaceful development.

The party conflicts of Queen Anne's reign had often appeared as matters of life and death. In contrast, with the virtual disintegration of the tory party, political conflicts now assumed the dimensions of personal squabbles. The first friction among the whig leaders soon appeared, between Townshend and Stanhope. Townshend resented the confidence which the King placed in Stanhope and he was opposed to Stanhope's "Hanoverian" policy. In 1717 Townshend was dismissed. Walpole, whom Townshend was pleased to regard as his protégé, at once resigned the Chancellorship of the Exchequer. The government could ill-afford the loss of his financial experience, and the growing divisions among the whigs gave rise to a new kind of Opposition, one entirely free from all taint of Jacobitism. Moreover the whig dissensions received a new importance from the quarrel which developed between George I and the Prince of Wales. It dated from 1716, when the King left the Prince as Regent while he returned to Hanover. It flared up in 1717, and at one stage the Prince was under arrest for four days, and was then ordered to leave the Palace. In January 1718 the Prince bought a house in Leicester Square, which henceforth became the social centre of the Opposition to George I's ministers. Townshend, Walpole and the tory leaders met there freely.

Walpole and William Pulteney, in particular, revealed

their parliamentary skill in attacking the government. They opposed the standing army, they attacked financial administration and the "Hanoverian" policy of Stanhope. But the greatest chance came in 1719 with the Peerage Bill. This was in fact a continuation of the policy of entrenching the whigs in power. The tory creation of twelve peers in 1711 in order to secure the passage of the Peace terms through the Lords had been widely resented. The government now proposed to limit the King's power to create peers to six above the number then existing. Such a law would make the House of Lords virtually impregnable, and equally so the control there of the Sunderland–Stanhope faction. The Bill aroused the opposition of both Oxford and Nottingham, but above all it provoked the bitter attack of Walpole, who rallied the dissentients with a famous speech in which he called on Members of Parliament not to deprive themselves and their descendants of the chance of sitting in the Lords. The Bill was defeated by a majority of ninety-two, the government's biggest defeat. The Townshend–Walpole group had had their revenge. Sunderland and Stanhope could no longer leave such dangerous men in opposition. In 1720 Townshend returned as President of the Council, with Walpole as Paymaster of the Forces. In the following year the bursting of the South Sea Bubble deeply implicated the government and led to its break-up. Aislabie, the Chancellor of the Exchequer, was sent to the Tower. Stanhope dropped dead in the effort to defend himself from charges of corruption. James Cragg committed suicide, and his son, the Secretary of State, died of smallpox. Walpole became First Lord of the Treasury and Chancellor of the Exchequer, and, on the death of Sunderland in the following year, he became the unchallenged head of a new government. For the next twenty years Walpole was to govern Britain in so unrivalled a fashion that he has rightly given his name to the age.

Sir Robert Walpole

Sir Robert Walpole was born in 1676, the son of a well-to-do but simple Norfolk farmer. In 1701 he became Member of Parliament for King's Lynn, and at once threw himself into the whig cause. At first his only friend was Lord Townshend, who had once been his father's ward, and it was Townshend who introduced him to the leaders of the whig junto and into the Kit-Cat club, where he first met the great

whigs of the day, Somers, Wharton, Halifax, Addison and
Steele. With neither birth nor riches, Walpole had to rely
upon his talents. His first appointment was at the Admiralty
Board in 1705, where he could show his administrative skill.
In 1708 he became Secretary at War, when he was responsible
for the equipment and recruitment of Marlborough's armies.
His talents were such that he was one of the last whigs to
be dismissed when the tories came in in 1710. He at once
threw himself into Opposition, and two of his pamphlets on
tory finance proved extremely embarrassing to the government, so that in 1712 they attempted to silence him by
charges of corruption. The charges were trifling, but he was
found guilty and sent to the Tower for a short time. When
he returned to the Commons in 1713 he was recognised as
one of the most effective of the whig leaders.

In George I's first government he became Paymaster. Walpole was hard up, and this was a lucrative office in which,
as it was said, a man "might get some flesh on his bones".
His brother-in-law, Townshend, was Secretary of State. Walpole certainly feathered his nest according to the normal
practice of the day, and soon began to live in great magnificence. In 1715 he was Chancellor of the Exchequer. In 1717,
as we have seen, he followed Townshend into Opposition,
kept up a steady pressure on the government, dealt them a
severe blow with the defeat of the Peerage Bill, and returned to office in 1720. Dr Plumb has shown that Walpole's
part in the affair of the South Sea Bubble was not as remarkable as was formerly supposed. There is no evidence that
from the first he saw through the fallacies of the scheme, and
his own successful speculation was not in South Sea stock.
Nor did the situation require great financial skill in clearing
up the mess once the Bubble had burst. As Dr Plumb writes:

Generations of historians have praised him for repairing his
country's ruined finances, yet for this there is no foundation
in fact. The finances repaired themselves.

What he did do was to provide conditions of stability in
which confidence was quickly restored, and he was content to draw a veil as quickly as possible over the past. He
aimed quite steadily at his own political power, and the
death of Sunderland in 1722 left the field clear for him. He
proceeded to give the country greater peace and stability than

it had known since the days of the Tudors. It should be noted that he came into power, not on some imagined wave of popular support, but by the choice of the King, who indeed had little alternative, since apart from Townshend and Walpole, all the great whigs of the past were dead.

George I indeed accepted Walpole only grudgingly; it was not until he had shown that he could give sound government that the King was won over. Dr Plumb has shown that in his early years of office Walpole was ceaselessly concerned with the fight for political power. In May 1722 he unearthed a Jacobite plot in which the violent and restless Bishop Atterbury of Rochester was implicated. Walpole made much of it. Habeas Corpus was suspended, troops were drafted into Hyde Park and a fine of £100,000 levied on the unfortunate Roman Catholics to pay for them. Atterbury was banished, and a petty lawyer was hanged and two other small fry imprisoned. All the evidence goes to show that Walpole dreaded Jacobitism, and he was always vigilant in watching for possible outbreaks. His spies were always active among the Jacobite exiles. But he saw how the fear of Jacobitism could be used to buttress his own power, and he always made much of the dangers.

Walpole had little experience of foreign affairs, and in his early years of office he leaned heavily upon Townshend. Townshend had been critical of Stanhope's extreme continental policy, and he was suspicious of the French alliance. But he did not advocate a fundamental change of policy. Walpole, however, was frankly suspicious of European entanglements. He wrote to Townshend in 1723:

> In a word, my politics are to keep free from all engagements as long as we possibly can. . . . I am mightily inclined to caution.

In these circumstances conflict between Walpole and Lord Carteret, Townshend's fellow-Secretary of State, was inevitable. Carteret longed for a spectacular foreign policy. Then in 1724 came the affair of "Wood's Ha'pence", and Swift's *Drapier's Letters*. Wood had received a contract to provide Ireland with a new coinage, and from the deal the King's mistress made £10,000 profit. Wood's contract was entirely legitimate and reasonable, but Swift stirred up a host of ill-informed opposition in Ireland, and Carteret was known to have supported it. Walpole acted characteristically. Carteret was dismissed from his office, and appointed Viceroy of Ireland, in which office he must deal with the disturbance he had helped to create. He was succeeded as Secretary of State by the Duke of Newcastle. Newcastle and his brother Henry Pelham had been devoted followers of Sunderland. They now became equally devoted to Walpole. They were delighted with the favours Walpole showed them, and Walpole sensed that they would be better allies than Carteret could ever be. Henceforth the government virtually consisted of Walpole, Townshend, Newcastle and Pelham, and in the end the Pelhams became Walpole's heirs and successors. The most disappointed politician of the time was not Carteret, but William Pulteney, a brilliant orator and politician, and a man of great personal magnetism, who had resigned with Townshend and Walpole in 1717, but now received no reward. Walpole chose his friends carefully, and always sought to exclude those who might rival his own supreme power. When Pulteney began to attack Walpole in 1725, he was at once dismissed from his lucrative but powerless office of Cofferer of the Household. Henceforth he became the centre of a growing opposition against Walpole.

For the next two years Walpole's government ran smoothly, but it received an uncomfortable jolt in June 1727. On June 11th George I died on the road to Hanover, and what ensued is brilliantly described in the *Memoirs* of Lord Hervey. Walpole heard of the death on the 14th and at once rode to Richmond to inform the new King, George II. The quarrel between George I and his son had never really healed, and all men assumed that any minister of the late King could not survive under his successor. George II had his own minister ready, Sir Spencer Compton, the Speaker of the Commons. Walpole was instructed to take his orders from the latter. He certainly thought his power at an end, for he told Compton he desired only some sinecure as a mark of royal favour. But he had a trump card to play. On June 15th he had a private audience of the King, and offered him a Civil List £200,000 greater than George I had had, with an additional £100,000 for the Queen, just double what any Queen-Consort had had before. Only Walpole could carry such sums in the Commons. The King was won over. Walpole continued in office, and Sir Spencer Compton was placated with a peerage and the lucrative office of Paymaster of the Forces. The whole incident is important as illustrating both the way in which Walpole considered his office to be entirely dependent upon the will of the King, and also the way in which he had in fact made himself all but indispensable to him.

Walpole was never for long free from anxiety about his continuance in office, and his security after 1727 was never quite as great as before. Yet in fact George II became utterly dependent upon him. George II had learnt to like England little more than his father had done, and, as with George I, his chief delight was to slip away to the unruffled despotism of Hanover. He resented the constitutional checks which existed in England; he was always conscious of the need to assert himself, and this gave him a strutting arrogance and ill-temper which all around him noted. Yet his bark was worse than his bite, and Walpole soon learnt to manage him, with the aid of Queen Caroline. George II loved soldiering, and prided himself on his grasp of foreign affairs, yet he lacked any shred of statesmanship, and was rarely concerned with more than details. Walpole thus got his way on all essentials. He summed up the situation exactly in conversation with Hervey:

> His Majesty imagines frequently he shall do many things, which, because he is not at first contradicted, he fancies he shall be let do at last. He thinks he is devilish stout, and never gives up his will or opinion; but he never acts in anything material according to either of them but when I have a mind he should. I am going to make an odd declaration for a minister. . . . Whenever our master does wrong, it is the fault of his ministers, who must either want resolution enough to oppose him, or sense enough to do it with success. Our master, like most people's masters, wishes himself absolute, and fancies he has courage enough to attempt making himself so, but if I know anything of him, he is, with all his personal bravery, as great a political coward as ever wore a crown, and as much afraid to lose it.

We may put this another way by saying that George II was the first truly constitutional monarch England had had, for he always knew when to give way to his ministers.

Sources of his Power

We should now ask upon what the power of Walpole rested for so long. In the first place, as we have seen, it rested upon the support of the Crown. Neither George I in 1721, nor

George II at the outset of his reign was well disposed towards him, but in each case Walpole soon made himself the favourite minister. This could only have been done by giving good and secure government. It is customary for kings to give their confidence to ministers of proved ability, and having once given their confidence, to be reluctant to contemplate further changes. Walpole's policy aimed at achieving peace and stability, at securing the Hanoverian succession, and at defeating Jacobitism. His period of office may therefore be regarded as one of consolidation of the Revolution settlement. To maintain internal tranquillity it was necessary to avoid controversial and disturbing issues. In his hands the financial stability, and therefore the credit of the government, were sound. Commerce flourished. In 1725 the land tax was down to two shillings in the pound, the lowest for a generation. The old life-and-death issues of the reign of Queen Anne, such as Jacobitism and religious persecution, died away as the nation turned to commercial and industrial expansion.

Walpole was a superb administrator. No matters of detail were too small for his attention. He studied the statistics of trade and finances with meticulous care. He was at heart a Mercantilist, and as such he sought to increase both trade and revenues. In 1724 he relieved most manufactures of export duties. He also turned his attention to smuggling, which was then almost a national industry. To beat the smuggler, he transferred tea, chocolate and cocoa from the customs to excise. The result was a steady rise in revenue. He was convinced the experiment should be extended.

But then he ran into difficulties, admittedly partly of his own making. In 1732 he proposed a further excise on wine and tobacco, and also the re-imposition of the salt-tax (which he had abolished two years before) to enable him to reduce the land tax to one shilling. The Opposition at once attacked the plan, Wyndham, a high-minded tory, pointed out that the salt-tax would fall heavily on the poor in the interests of the landed gentry. Walpole replied that the gentry had carried an unfair burden of taxation since 1688 while "great towns and moneyed men pay little or nothing". Walpole always disliked the mercantile interests which so constantly opposed him. The Opposition seized their chance; Walpole's majority fell to twenty-nine. But he persisted. In 1733 the campaign against his excise reached a new fury. It was argued that British liberties would be at an end if excise officers were let loose on the country. Public opinion was whipped up with the cry "Excise—Wooden Shoes". The town was plastered with placards and ballads. The pent-up fury of twelve years' hostility to the domination of Walpole was let loose. It was in vain that Walpole gave a splendidly reasoned defence of the tobacco excise in view of the extent of smuggling; in April his majority fell to sixteen. He at once decided to drop his scheme.

The defeat was not as serious as it appeared. The solid core of Walpole's supporters had not deserted him; the Opposition had not ousted him, nor were they united on much else than a common hatred of the great man. Yet the crisis had shown how much the Opposition had grown, not only in numbers, but also in great names. They now numbered Lord Carteret, the Earl of Chesterfield, Lord Cobham, William Pulteney, Sir William Wyndham; enough to offer the possibility of an alternative government. But those who had opposed Walpole and yet were in receipt of favours felt the crack of the whip. Chesterfield was dismissed from his Court appointment, the Duke of Bolton and Lord Cobham lost their commands, and similar retribution fell on a number of small fry. Walpole showed that a man could not expect to hold office from a government he did not support.

This leads us to consider the second source of Walpole's power. He was a great parliamentarian, an accomplished orator, sensitive to the feeling of the House, in command of the facts, always ready to intervene in a debate and give the cool, common-sense point of view. His mastery of the House of Commons we can catch from the fragments of debates which have survived. No amount of organisation would help an incompetent or lazy minister to retain office for long. When Walpole prevailed in debate it was often because of the intrinsic superiority of his arguments over those of his opponents. But there was careful organisation as well. In this respect Newcastle and Henry Pelham were invaluable assistance. "Organisation" certainly did not begin with Walpole. Lord Cowper had written to George I at the beginning of his reign that it was always possible for the King to obtain the majorities he wanted in the Commons, and Rapin-Thoyras wrote in 1717:

A tory ministry may almost constantly depend upon getting

a tory Parliament, and a whig ministry a whig Parliament.

In the eighteenth century the practice was for the Crown to appoint the ministry, and the ministry to organise victory in the ensuing elections. Walpole developed the practice into a system. In most counties he had his organisers without whom victory would have been impossible, for example, Sir Thomas Wentworth in Yorkshire, and Richard Edgcumbe in the West country. Government influence, when well administered, would always beat the Opposition in a general election. This was why the Opposition increasingly raised the cry of corruption against him. Walpole did indeed extend his power by the most careful exercise of patronage. The trouble was that there were not enough good things to go round; it must therefore be carefully husbanded. No man could expect favours if he did not give political loyalty in return. Dr Plumb writes:

> From 1722 to 1727 Walpole seized whatever chance came his way to draw patronage under his control; no place was too small for his attention, no person too humble to be considered; a flattering word, a half-made promise, even the hint of future benevolence could serve a purpose.

Church patronage was carefully organised in his interest by the efficient Edmund Gibson, Bishop of London. Army patronage, on the other hand, caused Walpole much more annoyance, for this George II insisted on reserving for himself. Walpole once bitterly complained of the practice to Hervey:

> How many people there are I could bind to me by getting things done in the army you may imagine. . . . I never ask for the smallest commission by which a member of Parliament may be obliged, that the King's answer is not "I won't do that; you want always to have me disoblige all my old soldiers; you understand nothing of troops; I will order my army as I think fit; for your scoundrels of the House of Commons you may do as you please; you know I never interfere, nor pretend to know anything of them, but this province I will keep to myself".

These words give a good indication of the relationship between the King and his minister, of the extent of Walpole's power, and its limitation.

The Opposition to Walpole

Without such organisation Walpole could hardly have survived, for he was surrounded by enemies, and in spite of all his efforts, opposition grew. To understand Walpole's position, we should at this point ask two questions; who were the Opposition to Walpole, and what were their objectives? We have already seen that Walpole was a masterful man who resented independence in his colleagues, and was almost morbidly suspicious about possible rivals for his power. Thus Carteret was excluded from foreign affairs in 1724; he remained in obscurity in Ireland until 1730, and then was dismissed altogether. Carteret was a proud and independent spirit, and he resented his treatment. Similarly Chesterfield was one of the greatest noblemen of the time; he had a quite unjustifiable reputation as an expert on foreign affairs, and he stood high in the favour of the Court. For years he was ambassador at the Hague, but his opposition to the Excise scheme of 1733 led to his immediate dismissal. William Pulteney was another proud spirit whom Walpole drove into implacable opposition by his failure to offer him any responsible office. After Walpole himself, he was the finest orator in the Commons, and his popularity in the country made him a powerful figure. Yet for over twenty years Walpole successfully parried his attacks. Another implacable enemy was Bolingbroke. Dismissed from the Pretender's service after the failure of the '15, Bolingbroke had at once set about securing the reversal of his attainder. Walpole strongly opposed his return to England, but Bolingbroke's well-placed bribes with the King's mistress, the Duchess of Kendal, had their effect, and in 1725 Walpole was overruled. Bolingbroke at once threw himself into opposition to Walpole. On one occasion he even had a private audience of George I, in which he, quite unsuccessfully, attempted to blacken Walpole's name in the eyes of the King. He then entered into league with Pulteney to plan a campaign against Walpole. The two cultivated relations with Leicester House, and in 1726 they started *The Craftsman* (which lasted until 1750) as a bitter Opposition paper, which caused Walpole constant annoyance. But Bolingbroke could never shake off the character of a dangerous charlatan and self-seeker. It is possible that he did the cause of the Opposition more harm than good by his presence. He soon fell out with Pulteney, and finally in 1735 he gave up the struggle, and withdrew to France, where he attempted to establish a new reputation for himself as a philosopher. The final estimate of Bolingbroke must be that he was a brilliant but dangerous and unprincipled man, and Britain was well rid of him.

To these disappointed men must be added the tories, led by Shippen and Sir William Wyndham. Shippen was an acknowledged Jacobite who eschewed plots and intrigues, and enjoyed opposition for its own sake. He had no desire for office, and drew his strength from a nostalgia for the past. Sir William Wyndham always avoided Jacobitism. He was a good orator and an honest man, an effective critic of Walpole's policy, but lacking the stature and consequence of the whig Opposition leaders. His most effective attacks on Walpole were during the Excise crisis of 1732–3. The tories were not always in opposition to Walpole. They approved of much of his policy.

Outside Parliament the chief opposition to Walpole centred in the City of London. The monied interests were on the whole opposed to Walpole; they were bellicose, suspicious of France, often resentful of the Hanoverian connection, and from time to time bent on strong measures against Spain. As early as 1725 Walpole had to curb the independence of the City of London, at that time whipped up by the turbulent Duke of Wharton and his paper *The True Briton*. He forced through a Bill disfranchising some 3,000 freemen, and giving the aldermen the power of veto over the proceedings of the Common Court. Henceforth Walpole was able to secure his own candidates as Sheriff, and the City itself gave him little further trouble. But public opinion there remained hostile to him. The press and stage were a constant source of annoyance. *The Craftsman, The True Briton, The Champion, Common Sense* were all at various times Opposition papers. Walpole answered them in his own papers, *The Daily Gazette, The London Journal, The Daily Courant* and *Free Briton,* and on balance he had the better of the paper war. The stage was particularly virulent in its attacks upon him, and Henry Fielding was the most effective of the opposition dramatists. His play with the unlikely title *The Historical Register for the Year 1736* was an almost open attack upon Walpole. Walpole retaliated with the Play House Act of 1737, nominally in the interests of morals, requiring plays to be submitted to the Lord Chamberlain for approval. The Act effectively ended the stage attacks upon him, and Henry Fielding turned to win an immortality in another branch of literature, which he would never have won as a dramatist.

What were the grounds of so much opposition? Often, as we have seen, it was a matter of injured pride and thwarted ambition. Walpole was in office for a quite unprecedented length of time. It was inevitable that a number of place-hungry people should have resented his seemingly interminable enjoyment of office. Moreover Walpole exercised more power and for a longer time than any minister since 1660. The old fears of an over-mighty subject were aroused. It was inevitable that comparisons should be made with the position of Fleury, the "premier ministre" in France. The Opposition accordingly attacked the "corruption" by which Walpole seemed to keep himself in power. All the old fears of an all-powerful executive were easily touched off. Hence the passions stirred by the Excise scheme. It was an age in which the liberty of the subject was passionately defended, and in which freedom of speech often overstepped the boundaries of licence. It was natural that the great man of the age should be the chief object of attack.

Many of the attacks on Walpole were factious, and without much consistency. But there was also a genuine controversy over policy, especially foreign policy. We have seen that there were two traditions of foreign policy which might roughly be called whig and tory, the former pursuing a full engagement in continental affairs, the latter resentful of European commitments and preferring a disengagement from Europe, a reliance upon the fleet and the furtherance of British commerce. Townshend's policy had on the whole been in the whig tradition, but Walpole was anxious to avoid European commitments,[1] and disagreement between the two led to Townshend's retirement in 1730. The Opposition found it easy to attack Walpole from two somewhat contradictory angles. Townshend's policy at the time of the Treaty of Hanover (1725) was denounced as subordinating

[1] See Ch. 8.

English to Hanoverian interests. If Walpole sought to work in harmony with Fleury, he was denounced for his subserviency to France. Any attempt to increase the meagre armed forces at a moment of crisis was denounced as an attempt to maintain a standing army. Yet when Walpole attempted to pursue a policy of peace with Spain, he was denounced for his neglect of our prestige and commercial interests.

To illustrate this we should look to the most effective of Walpole's critics, the followers of Lord Cobham nicknamed the "Boy Patriots" or "Cobham's Cubs". Cobham, the wealthy owner of the great house of Stowe, gathered round him a group of brilliant young men, the Grenvilles, the Lytteltons and William Pitt. Cobham had been dismissed from his command for his part in the opposition to the Excise scheme, and henceforth he led a spirited opposition against Walpole. His followers annoyed Walpole by entering into close relations with Leicester House (for there had now begun a second generation of conflict between the King and the Prince of Wales). Pitt in 1737 ostentatiously supported the Prince against the King, he opposed the increase in the standing army. He opposed Walpole's attempts to make peace with Spain; and finally, when war with Spain began, he attacked Walpole's handling of the war. They repeatedly made attacks on the supposed subordination of England to Hanoverian interests, and Pitt had later to pay dearly for his gratuitous insults to George II.

For over twenty years Walpole had the upper hand of his critics. During his first ten years of power the Opposition could rarely muster a hundred votes in the Commons, though in the second decade the number steadily increased. The Opposition lacked unity among themselves. Lord Hervey wrote that:

> Lord Carteret and Lord Bolingbroke had no correspondence at all; Mr Pulteney and Lord Bolingbroke hated one another; Lord Carteret and Pulteney were jealous of one another; Sir William Wyndham and Pulteney the same; while Lord Chesterfield had a little correspondence with them all, but was confided in by none of them.

Walpole eventually fell because a great peace minister did not prove a successful war minister, and because his failing health made retirement necessary. His final satisfaction was to see that few of his enemies should share in the inheritance. The heirs to Walpole were not Pulteney and Carteret, but the Pelhams, and Walpole's system was virtually to remain intact for the rest of the reign of George II.

7

The Pelhams and William Pitt

IN THE ELECTIONS of 1741 Walpole's majority dropped to about twelve, and between then and 1742 his government suffered seven defeats in the Commons. Finally, in January 1742, he insisted on the King accepting his resignation, and George II, with tears in his eyes, agreed. Walpole was the first Prime Minister to be driven to resign by defeats in the House of Commons. For twenty-one years he had successfully held the balance between the two great powers of the Commons and the Crown, and his fall was a victory for the Commons. Dr Owen has commented:

> The Opposition made no claim yet to determine whom the King *should* employ; it restricted itself to asserting that under certain conditions it could insist that there were some ministers whom he should not employ.[1]

Walpole's fall showed that patronage and influence alone were not sufficient to retain even the cleverest parliamentarian in office.

The King could not save his favourite minister, but he could keep out of office the many who had brought about Walpole's fall. The new ministry was essentially Walpole's without Walpole. The Duke of Newcastle and Henry Pelham remained. They took in Carteret, whose German policy was highly acceptable to the King. They fobbed off Pulteney with a peerage as Earl of Bath and a powerless seat in the

[1] An excellent study of this period is J. B. Owen's *The Rise of the Pelhams* (Methuen).

Cabinet. It was the end of his political influence; the great orator and most effective of Walpole's critics had failed to win the favour of the Crown, and now lost his influence in the Commons. The remainder of the array of the Opposition to Walpole, Chesterfield, Bedford, Cobham and his "Cubs", Pitt, Lyttelton and George Grenville, Bubb Doddington (as well as the tories) received no office.

The effective members of the government were first Newcastle, immensely industrious and well-meaning, extremely unsure of himself, envious of everyone, a constant prey to fears, yet for ever absorbed in the details of government. Entirely devoid of statesmanship, he none the less was well acquainted with the business of government. He had learnt from Walpole the intricacies of patronage, and he delighted to attend to them. He is an excellent example of what can be achieved in politics by the infinite capacity for taking pains. Second, his brother, Henry Pelham, a timid and retiring man, but a man of integrity and moderation, and an excellent man of business, respected by all who came in contact with him. Third, Lord Hardwicke, their brother-in-law, a great lawyer with a reputation for sagacity, to whom Newcastle was often glad to turn for advice. Fourth, Lord Carteret, who, considering himself as a genius in politics, conducted himself in the grand manner; cared little for public opinion or his colleagues, but relied on the well-known support of the Crown.

The Pelhams, the first three, worked in close harmony together, and they were able to count upon a majority of about a hundred in the Commons. But they were always jealous of the influence of Carteret with the King. So long as Carteret's foreign policy brought success the Pelhams curbed their fears, and the Battle of Dettingen (June 1743) may be taken as the high-watermark of his power and prestige. But thereafter the foreign situation deteriorated; [2] difficulties increased abroad and the Opposition at home, led by Pitt, attacked the whole Hanoverian policy of Carteret, and even the person of the King. Finally, in November 1744 the Pelhams presented the King with an ultimatum: he must choose between Carteret and them. George II failed to find alternative ministers, and on November 23rd accepted the inevitable: Carteret resigned. The Pelhams then

2 See Ch. 8.

constructed the Broad-Bottom Administration by bringing in a sufficient number of the Opposition to make life peaceful. Thus places were found for Chesterfield, Gower, George Lyttelton, Bedford, Sandwich, George Grenville and Anson. Henry Pelham was extremely skilful at these negotiations. He won over the City of London, and even brought some tories into his government. There was one significant omission. There was no office for Pitt. He had gravely offended the King, and now had to pay the price.

There was one thing the new Administration lacked: the confidence of the King. The power of the latter is in fact well illustrated at this point. George II made no attempt to conceal his contempt for his ministers. He resented the enforced resignation of Carteret (now Earl Granville, from whom he still took advice). He believed the Pelhams were seeking to reduce him to a figurehead. It rankled with him that after Dettingen his ministers would not let him command in the field. He once burst out to Hardwicke: "Ministers are the kings in this country", and he treated them with studied hostility. In 1745 came new dangers, the British troops were defeated at Fontenoy in May, and the Jacobite rebellion broke out in June, and neither event improved the ministers' relations with the King. Pelham wrote in September:

> The conduct of [the King] is worse than ever. . . . We are not permitted either to give our advice or to act in consequence of any advice that is given. . . . I do know that if successors could be found for my brother and myself, there would be no hesitation in removing us whether we would or no.[3]

Meanwhile Pitt's attacks in the Commons had redoubled after his exclusion from office, and in January 1746 they insisted that he be brought into the Ministry. The Pelhams resigned in February; George II failed completely to find an alternative ministry, and had to ask the Pelhams to return, with Pitt in office. It was this incident which gave rise to the picture of "the King in toils", namely that George had lost his power of choosing ministers. But the crisis had been of his own making; he had treated his ministers badly without giving any thought to the consequences. It was a great

3 Owen, op. cit., p. 280.

victory for the Pelhams, who in the elections of 1747 restored their majority to about 125. Henry Pelham was undisputed master of the Commons, and thereafter George II learnt to respect him and to rely on him almost as he had done on Sir Robert Walpole. When Pelham died in 1754 the King was in genuine anguish, and declared, "I shall now have no more peace."

The government of the Pelhams rested upon the skilled management of the Commons, the careful elimination of opposition, the support of the King after 1746, sound administration and especially a sound financial policy. Henry Pelham kept taxation low, gained the support of the City, and reduced Consols to three per cent.

The '45 Rebellion

One of their spectacular successes was the suppression of the '45 Rebellion. This was really an incident in the War of the Austrian Succession. Jacobitism had long been an anachronism and an irrelevance in eighteenth-century England, but it was still fostered by French hostility, and could still raise an echo among the Highland clans. It is doubtful, however, whether the French regarded it as having more than nuisance value. An expedition of 15,000 Frenchmen, headed by Marshal Saxe and Prince Charles Edward, sailed from Dunkirk in 1744, but was driven back by storms. In 1745 the French were engaged elsewhere, and Charles Edward, against their advice, landed in Scotland in July with only seven attendants, and raised his standard at Glen Finnan. The governing fact was that the Pelhams were unprepared, and Sir John Cope could muster less than 1,500 men. Thus the Prince was able to occupy Edinburgh, and on September 21st he routed Cope at Prestonpans. For a brief month Charles Edward revived the regal glories of Edinburgh, and then with 5,500 men set out for England. As Wade was at Newcastle with 12,000 men the Prince slipped across to Carlisle, and by December had pushed as far south as Derby. There was panic at the news in London, but the Jacobite success was more apparent than real. For England had failed to rise; only about 300 men had joined him, and his own Scots followers were deserting fast. By December Charles Edward was back at Stirling and thereafter it was just a matter of time before the Duke of Cumberland extinguished the final bedraggled forces of the Young Pretender on the field of Culloden in April. There followed a five-months' pursuit of Charles Edward, and his eventual embarkation for a perpetual exile in September. The rising had had a certain dash and vigour about it, but the Jacobites had too little to offer, and England remained loyal to the Hanoverians. Even in Scotland the advantages of the Union were more apparent than they had been in 1715, and the Jacobite support was correspondingly less. The revolt would never have had the success it did but for the continental war.

Cumberland's suppressions were severe enough to earn him the title of "Butcher". Some eighty people were executed. A severe Disarming Act was passed. Highland dress was forbidden, and kilts had to be converted into trousers. The old clan jurisdictions, which had been thought to be the cause of much of the trouble, were abolished. For years afterwards the government maintained a close watch upon the activities of the Young Pretender, who retired to Italy, but in fact Jacobitism was dead.

William Pitt

The fate of the Pelhams was in future to be so closely bound up with William Pitt that we should look more closely at the career of that great man. His grandfather was the famous "Diamond" Pitt, once Governor of Fort St George, the first of the nabobs to make his fortune in India. He had returned to England with his diamond which he sold for £100,000, and set up as a landed gentleman. He was always a haughty and violent man, and he undoubtedly transmitted madness to his family. William Pitt was born in 1708. He was educated at Eton, Oxford and Utrecht. Even at school he suffered severely from what was called gout, yet he seems to have set his heart on an army career. In 1731 he took a commission in the 1st Dragoon Guards, and a few years later told a friend that he had read all the military books there were. He had been at Eton with George Lyttelton, and his brother had married Lyttelton's sister. It was natural, therefore, that, without wealth or influence of his own, Pitt should enter into the political circle of Lord Cobham. For Lord Cobham was "the founder of the dynasty and palace of Stowe". A soldier who had won distinction under Marlborough, Cobham had established one of the most magnificent country houses of the century. A fiery whig, he had gathered around him the "Boy Patriots", his nephews, Richard Grenville and George Grenville, George Lyttelton and Pitt, and he led his group in persistent attacks on Walpole. Pitt entered Parliament for his brother's rotten borough of Old Sarum. In the eighteenth century a young man without political influence needed the aid of a patron, and Stowe was the centre of a great political circle of influence. The connection meant that Pitt would be in opposition to Walpole. Walpole had his revenge, and in 1736 he was dismissed from his commission.

The centre of the opposition to Walpole was Leicester House, and Cobham and his friends were welcomed there by the Prince of Wales. In 1737 Pitt became a groom of the bedchamber to the Prince. Whenever possible he defended the Prince's interests to the annoyance of the King, who detested his son. Much of his opposition was merely factious, as when in 1738 he proposed the reduction of the standing army at the very time when his friends were calling for war against Spain. Any stick was good enough with which to beat Walpole at this time, and when war began they had even greater opportunity to attack Walpole's conduct of affairs. Yet the fall of Walpole in 1742 brought no office for Pitt and his friends. Pitt renewed his attacks, this time on the foreign policy of Carteret. Pitt's argument was that British foreign policy was subordinated to the needs of Hanover, and that Carteret was the mere servant of the King. He called him "an execrable or sole minister, who had renounced the British nation". He never lost an opportunity of being insulting to George II. He opposed the employment of German mercenaries; he opposed the continuance of the Hanoverian subsidy, and even the war itself. All this was much in the nature of opposition in any age, and in part it was self-advertisement, and the recognised way to bludgeon one's way into office. But Pitt went too far. His attacks on the King passed the bounds of decency, and he could hardly have been surprised at finding himself excluded from the Broad-Bottom Administration. After a period of waiting, therefore, Pitt in 1745 returned to open opposition. The result was the Constitutional Crisis of 1746 which, as we have seen already, the Pelhams won. Pitt gained a place, at first Vice-Treasurer of Ireland, and then, two months later, Paymaster-General. Lord Rosebery wrote:

The King shed tears as Pitt knelt before him. A constitutional Sovereign had these bitter moments.

By now Pitt had shaken off his connection with Cobham,
and his appointment to office meant a breach with Leicester
House. Pitt stood alone, with only his ability to rely upon.
Without political influence of his own, he instinctively felt
the importance of public opinion, and he went out of his
way to court it. His record of opposition had given him
some standing, especially in London, but a politician who
took office usually quickly lost the popularity he had had
in opposition. Pitt did something to offset this by ostentatiously refusing to take the valuable perquisites which were
attached to his office of Paymaster-General. He was a poor
man, and could ill-afford the loss, but both he and his son
maintained throughout their lives a reputation for probity
which few other politicians of the century could equal.

From 1746 until 1754 Pitt remained curiously quiet. His
office was a lucrative one, but entirely devoid of power.
Much of his time was spent eating his earlier words, and admitting that many of the things he had said as a young man
were faulty. He was at pains to show the King that he was
no *frondeur,* and Pelham soon gained a high opinion of him;
he wrote in 1750:

I think him the most able and useful man we have among
us.

But for all these good words, Pitt received no promotion. He
therefore ceased to give the ministry much support in the
Commons. He was often ill; he settled in Bath from time to
time, and absented himself from Parliament for long periods.

His hopes rose again when Pelham died in 1754. Pelham
had been so much the key man of the government that Pitt
felt that it could hardly go on without being strengthened.
He thought little of the ability of Newcastle; his hopes were
placed upon Hardwicke. He wrote to Hardwicke in March
a letter which, with much circumlocution, hinted that Pitt's
support could not be indefinitely continued without a share
in effective power. The ministry was reconstructed, Newcastle
took the Treasury, but there was still no promotion for Pitt.
Most galling of all was the fact that a complete nonentity
named Sir Thomas Robinson was given the office of Secretary

of State which Pitt felt was surely his due. Pitt then wrote two of the most splendid letters of his life, one to Newcastle and one to Hardwicke. He had, he said, given the government loyal support since 1746, yet he had seen nonentity after nonentity promoted over him. He could not go on; he must retire from politics:

> The weight of irremovable royal displeasure is a load too great to move under; it must crush any man; it has sunk and broken me. I succumb, and wish for nothing but a decent and innocent retreat.

So Pitt brooded until November 1754, and then suddenly he came out in open attack on the ministers. Newcastle had just won an election, and was busy gathering all power into his own hands. On the 25th the debate was on a disputed election which at first merely amused the House. Then Pitt rose with that majesty which henceforth he always displayed in debate. His oratory could be a terror to ministers: the House was trifling with the liberties of the nation; they must rally to their responsibilities:

> unless you will degenerate into a little assembly serving no other purpose than to register the arbitrary edicts of *one too-powerful subject.*

Ministers sat pale and cowed; everyone knew that this was a personal attack upon Newcastle.

Newcastle was alarmed. He knew that war was within sight; he feared Pitt's attacks upon the subsidy treaty he had just negotiated with Hesse-Cassel. And Pitt had renewed his connection with Leicester House. Frederick, Prince of Wales, had died in 1751, but the Princess of Wales was continuing the political game on behalf of her son. Nor were Pitt and Leicester House Newcastle's only worry. There was also the Duke of Cumberland, who might be Regent for the young prince if George II died, and who had his own political protégé. Henry Fox was a man of great common sense, a great House of Commons man, fond of the bottle, and primarily concerned to win for himself a fortune and a peerage. In 1755, rather than have Pitt, Newcastle brought in Fox as Secretary of State. Thus in November Pitt redoubled his attacks. He opposed the Russian Treaty, and the pre-occupation of the ministers with the defence of Hanover, and he attacked the neglect of the fleet. He was accordingly dismissed from his office.

Yet Pitt made no impact upon Newcastle's parliamentary majorities until military disaster shook the nation. In 1755 Braddock had been slain in America. In 1756 the French captured Minorca; in America Fort Oswego fell; in India Calcutta was captured. In October 1756 Henry Fox resigned: Newcastle had been bent on excluding him from effective power, and he saw no reason why he should have to share the ignominy of defeats which were none of his making. The King asked Granville if he should take Pitt. Granville replied: "Well, Sir! You must take somebody!" Then the King revealed his real objection to Pitt:

Ah! but I am sure Pitt will not do my [German] business.

However, he agreed to negotiations. There followed a confused period, for Pitt absolutely refused to serve with Newcastle. The reason was his conviction that Newcastle could not share power with anyone. The only real alternative to Newcastle was Henry Fox. Pitt would serve with Fox, but not under him. Eventually a makeshift government was formed under the Duke of Devonshire, with Pitt as Secretary of State. It was doomed to failure. For Pitt had virtually no personal followers; as Newcastle said: "he flung himself upon the people and the tories". It was not enough. No ministry could survive without Newcastle's carefully prepared majorities. In April 1757 the ministry collapsed. For twelve weeks England remained without a government at a crucial moment in a great war. Then public opinion took a hand. Pitt's stock was rising in the country. First the City of London, and then other cities, made him a freeman, and in Horace Walpole's words: "for some weeks it rained gold boxes". Finally, in great secrecy, there began the negotiations for a Pitt–Newcastle coalition. Pitt agreed on condition he had the appointment of the "efficient" offices of state, that is those especially concerned with the conduct of the war, the Admiralty, the Secretaryship at War and the Exchequer. So the coalition was formed; the King readily accepted it, and the country rejoiced. It was only just in time, for Prussia had just been routed at the battle of Kolin. In July Cumberland was defeated by the French at Hastenbeck, and in September signed the ignominious Klosterseven, by which he laid down his arms.

The Pitt–Newcastle Coalition

The coalition was always an uneasy one. Pitt insisted on having the last word on the conduct of the war, subject to the occasional interference of the King; yet Newcastle was never content to leave things to him. Apart from Newcastle's constitutional incapacity to share power with anyone, there was a deep division between them on policy. For Newcastle, although he well understood the colonial struggle, regarded Europe as the main theatre of the war. Pitt, on the other hand, placed the colonial and naval theatres first. In Newcastle's mind there was always the idea that the House of Commons was his; Pitt's followers were a mere handful; he might have to put up with Pitt for the duration of the war, but he would dispense with him as soon as the war was over. In fairness to Newcastle it must be admitted that Pitt was an exasperating, almost an impossible, colleague. He despised most of the members of the government, Mansfield, Hardwicke, Holdernesse, Legge, but above all, he despised Newcastle, and he made no attempt to conceal it:

> Fewer words, if you please, my Lord, for your words have long lost all weight with me.

Pitt knew that, apart from Earl Temple, William Beckford and a few tories, he was politically friendless, and he had neither the health and stamina nor the influence to build up a connection. He sought to rely, therefore, upon his genius as a minister, and upon his popularity outside Parliament. It was an insecure foundation for power in the eighteenth century.

They differed also over the cost of the war. The Seven Years' War was much more expensive, in terms of annual expenditure, than any previous war. By 1759 it was costing some £20,000,000 a year, at a time when the revenue was about £7,000,000. Newcastle, who had learnt principles of financial probity from his brother, was horrified at the growing debt. But Pitt, who knew little about such matters, seemed unrelenting in his demands for yet greater efforts and yet more expenditure.

THE PITT–NEWCASTLE COALITION

Yet with all these difficulties, Pitt stands forth as one of the greatest war leaders of history. His effect upon the nation was electric. During 1756–7 there was the deepest foreboding at the outcome of the war. On the day that Pitt came into power the Earl of Chesterfield reflected the prevailing pessimism:

Whoever is in, or whoever is out, I am sure we are undone, both at home and abroad: at home by our increasing debt and expenses; abroad by our ill-luck and incapacity. . . . We are no longer a nation. I never yet saw so dreadful a prospect.

During the following two years Pitt's victories turned the nation from gloom to exhilaration, and Horace Walpole was fearing to miss a morning's papers lest he should miss another victory. The House of Commons passed Pitt's measures with hardly a dissenting vote. It is a very different Chesterfield who writes in January 1759:

The estimates for the year are made up; and what do you think they amount to? No less than twelve millions; a most incredible sum, and yet already all subscribed, and even more offered! The unanimity in the House of Commons, in voting such a sum, and such forces, is not less astonishing. This is Mr Pitt's doing, and it is marvellous in our eyes.

Pitt's ascendancy over the Commons was not only a matter of his victories. He was the greatest orator of the century. Unfortunately mere fragments of his speeches before 1760 have survived. We should perhaps today regard them as too figurative and pompous. He was a great actor, and all his life studied carefully the right gesture, the exact moment of entry, the most effective flourish. It has been said that Pitt "lived in blank verse, and conducted himself in the heroic metre". Yet we know that his speeches held the House spellbound. Chesterfield said that they had "the strength of thunder and the splendour of lightning"; and when that thunder roared around the head of some unfortunate minister it was indeed a terrible experience. Several experienced witnesses believed that his speeches were unprepared, and that he allowed the subject to unfold as he went along; they therefore seemed to lack precise order and material. Horace Walpole wrote:

Though no man knew so well how to say what he pleased, no man ever knew so little what he was going to say.

He thought that Pitt was simply borne along by his feelings once he had begun to speak. But when Walpole came himself to retire from the Commons, he said he did not regret it, because there could never be a greater orator than Lord Chatham. The listener was left above all with the sense of the grandeur of both the subject and the man. Henry Grattan said, many years later:

Perhaps he was not so good a debater as his son, but he was a much better orator, a better scholar, and a far greater mind. Great subjects, great empires, great characters, effulgent ideas and classical illustrations formed the material of his speeches.

On October 25th, 1760, in, as Horace Walpole wrote: "the greatest period of the glory of this country and of his reign", old George II died. We have seen that he has some claim to being regarded as the first genuinely constitutional monarch in our history. The power and independence of ministers had made substantial advances in his reign, and on the whole their policies prevailed. Yet the ill-will of George II was sufficient to keep Pitt out of effective power for fifteen years after the fall of Walpole. Carteret came in in 1742 as the special favourite of the King, though this was not sufficient to save him from a fall two years later. Newcastle lived in perpetual agitation at the prospect of disagreement with the King, or at some rumour that he was bestowing his favour elsewhere. The King took the greatest interest in appointments, and regarded military affairs as peculiarly his own province. He was resentful of ministerial attempts to decide who should receive army commands, and in this Pitt had sometimes to give way to him. His influence in foreign policy is seen most clearly at the time of the negotiation of the Russian Treaty in 1755–6.[4] His first concern was always with Hanover; he loved his Electorate, and was always longing to escape there, where he would be free from the constitutional restrictions he so resented in England. With all the political difficulties of his reign, it was soon to be looked back to by many politicians as a golden age of political quietude and stability.

4 See Ch. 8.

8

Britain in Europe
(1714-92)

Britain and the Baltic

THE REIGNS OF William III and Anne saw an enormous extension of Britain's diplomatic and military activity in Europe. Britain was intimately concerned in the fate of the Low Countries, in the fate of Spain, in the part played by Savoy in the balance of power in Italy, in the balance between Bourbon and Habsburg, and in her own emergence as a Mediterranean power. Another area in which Britain had vital interests, strategic and commercial, was the Baltic. In 1688 the two major powers in the Baltic were Sweden and Denmark. Sweden was a great, though over-extended empire, controlling the coasts of Finland, Ingria, Estonia, Livonia, Pomerania and the mouths of the Elbe, Weser and Oder. To Britain the trade of the Baltic was of the first importance in vital materials, iron, copper, timber, pitch, tar, hemp and flax, in short the "naval stores" without which the fleet could not put to sea. Before the eighteenth century they could hardly be obtained from elsewhere, so it was natural that England should have had a long tradition of friendship with Sweden. William III tried to bring Sweden into the war, and for a short time in 1690 Swedish troops fought in the Netherlands against France. In 1697 Charles XI of Sweden died, leaving as successor his fifteen-year-old son, and Sweden was at once attacked by Denmark, Poland and Russia. In 1700 Sweden signed a defensive alliance with England and the Dutch, and an Anglo-Dutch fleet helped Charles XII to attack Copenhagen. The Danish fleet found itself heavily outnumbered, and could only make peace. Thus Charles XII achieved a bloodless victory, depending upon the command of the sea. The English and Dutch tried hard to induce Charles to make a general Baltic peace, but instead he plunged into a great war of Polish conquest which was finally shattered when Peter the Great of Russia crushed Swedish military power on the field of Poltava in 1709.

Charles XII repeatedly demanded further aid from England and the Dutch, but after the outbreak of the war in the west in 1702 they had no sea-power to spare. Moreover, relations became strained because Charles XII used his fleet to try to prevent Anglo-Dutch trade with the Baltic provinces which Russia had occupied. Such an attempt to cut off vital naval stores during a great war must be resented. Yet, on the other hand, by 1710 English ministers were becoming alarmed at the possibility of the total collapse of the Swedish power, and the domination of the Baltic by Russia. Britain was indeed in a quandary, unwilling to fall out with either Sweden or Russia, wanting only a balance of power in the Baltic and the opportunity for uninterrupted trade, but without sufficient sea-power to influence events so long as the war against France continued. In 1714 four men-of-war were appointed to convoy British trade in the Baltic, but they were informed by the British Minister to Denmark that they would be attacked by the Swedish fleet, and had to turn back.

With the fall of the tories and the accession of George I Britain returned to a vigorous continental policy. George I, who had for long been one of the most active politicians in Europe, but had remained neutral in the Swedish war, in 1714 suddenly joined against Sweden and seized Bremen and Verden, ports which would be of the first importance to Hanover, all the more so now that the Elector was also King of England. In 1715 Sir John Norris and an Anglo-Dutch fleet of thirty-two ships were sent to the Baltic to convoy the trading ships of the two nations, some 300 in all. He was not otherwise to interfere in the Russo-Swedish war, for there was no desire to complete the destruction of Swedish naval power. In 1716, however, when Charles XII was ill-advised enough to threaten support of the Jacobites against George I, Norris was instructed to join with the Danes in preventing a Swedish invasion of Norway. On the other hand, George I wished to do nothing to aid Russia, for there were now 40,000 Russians in Mecklenburg, and he feared them more than the Swedes. Moreover, public opinion in England was resentful of being involved in fighting George I's battles against Sweden for Bremen and Verden. So, apart from preventing the invasion of Norway, the fleet confined itself to convoy duties.

Then, in 1718, Charles XII was killed, and Sweden was forced to seek a hasty peace. George I's plan was to persuade the Swedes to surrender Bremen and Verden in return for help against the Russians, and in 1719 Lord Carteret was sent to Stockholm to conduct the negotiations. The Swedes, in their exhausted state, could only agree. Bremen and Verden were ceded to Hanover in return for a million crowns, and the British fleet was to be sent to the Baltic to protect Sweden from Russia. George I, however, could do nothing to moderate the demands of Peter the Great, and Sweden was deprived of all her Baltic provinces by the Treaty of Nystad (1721).

It is evident that George I used British power to the full to further his Hanoverian interests, but it will be seen that British interests rather than Hanoverian largely dictated policy throughout. Britain had vital trading concerns in the Baltic upon which her very naval power depended. Good relations with Sweden were thought to be a prime British interest for many years both before and after 1714. If relations were strained in the period 1710–19, it was because of the activity of the Swedish fleet and Charles XII's support of the Jacobites, as well as the seizure of Bremen and Verden. But the same cannot be said of Anglo-Russian relations. Peter the Great never obstructed British trade; his detestation of George I was because of the refusal of the latter to meet the claims of the Duke of Holstein in Schleswig. This question was of no concern at all to Britain, but it had the effect of turning Russia, a potential ally of Britain, into an enemy. This, rather than the Swedish policy, was the real misfortune of the Hanoverian connection.

Stanhope and the Quadruple Alliance

It was thought most convenient to deal with the complicated Swedish question as a whole, but it must now be set in the wider context of European relations following the Treaty of Utrecht. We have seen that Bolingbroke negotiated a sound peace, which in fact secured for Britain all her essential interests, the command of the sea, increased colonies and new facilities for trade. But to many a whig he had surrendered nearly all that England had been fighting for, in surrendering Spain to the Bourbons. Moreover, in largely deserting the Dutch, the Emperor and even the Elector of Hanover during the negotiations, he had committed a serious tactical error, which sealed the fate of the tories when George I came to the throne. But once the treaty was signed both the King and his new whig ministers had the strongest motives for maintaining it, for it contained the European recognition of the Protestant Succession in England. It is true that Louis XIV at once turned his thoughts to aid for the Jacobites, but he died in 1715 before his plans were effected. The Regent Orleans, who ruled for the infant Louis XV, was also regarded with the greatest suspicion by the whigs, but his position in France was weak, and his claim to the French throne, should Louis XV die, was challenged by Philip V of Spain. He needed, therefore, the goodwill of George I. George I equally needed to be sure that France would not aid the Jacobites. Moreover, he needed an understanding with France in Baltic affairs, for France had a tradition of friendship with Sweden. To George I this Swedish question was no mere side issue, but one of the first importance.

In May 1716 Britain signed a new defensive alliance with the Emperor. News of it greatly encouraged the able Foreign Minister of France, Dubois, to attempt to cut through the ice of suspicion between Britain and France by journeying to The Hague and to Hanover to meet Stanhope, and to work out an agreement. The outcome was the Triple Alliance, signed between Britain, France and the Dutch (January 1717), a defensive alliance for the maintenance of the Treaty of Utrecht. The whigs were insistent that the test of French goodwill should be the expulsion of the Pretender from France and the demolition of the defences at Mardyke. At the same time George I accepted the Regent as mediator with the King of Sweden in the affair of the Jacobite conspiracy which the latter was said to be supporting.

The Anglo-French entente was almost at once put to the test. Elizabeth Farnese, the Queen of Spain, who, far more than Philip V ruled the country, was bent on upsetting the Utrecht settlement. Her minister, Alberoni, seized on a technical breach of the settlement when the Emperor and Savoy exchanged the islands of Sardinia and Sicily, to send a powerful fleet to occupy both islands. It was by no means certain that the Regent Orleans would wish to risk a conflict over such a question, but Stanhope hurried to Paris, and in July 1718 scored a great personal triumph when the so-called Quadruple Alliance was signed (though the participation of the Dutch was never a reality). The three Powers agreed to uphold the terms of the Treaty of Utrecht; Spain was invited to join the alliance within three months, the alternative being war. Sir George Byng was sent to the Mediterranean, and at the appointed time sought out the Spanish fleet off Cape Passaro and captured fifteen of the twenty-nine ships. Thus the Spanish invaders were cut off. In 1719 French troops invaded Spain, and a British squadron captured Vigo. Meanwhile Byng enabled the Austrian army to occupy Sicily. Spain had no alternative but to abandon Alberoni and his policy.

The management of the whole affair was to the greatest credit of Stanhope. France had been reluctant to go to the lengths of war; the whole English policy of the Regent was unpopular in France. But George I's government took the view that the maintenance of the Utrecht settlement depended upon Anglo-French accord, and that with it, the defeat of Spain was inevitable. The whole policy marked a complete return to the continental policy of the whigs of the 1689–1710 period, and the Anglo-French entente proved itself the most powerful instrument for peace in Europe. In England the policy had general support, for it was in accord with both whig and tory principles, for, as Defoe wrote, it was feared that the Spanish possession of Sicily would be ruinous to Levant trade, and if Spanish naval power grew, the West Indies would not be safe.

The entente was much less popular in France, for many argued that France was being diverted from her true interests, which lay in an alliance with Spain. Dubois tried to combine this policy with his own by proposing a triple alliance of France, Spain and Britain. The whigs strongly approved of this: Carteret put their point of view very clearly:

> The union between France and Spain is inevitable. I would not be left alone with the Imperialists, who will never hear reason when it tends to moderate their pretensions. . . .

Nothing can be so fatal to us as France and Spain coming to a good agreement exclusive of us.

This new Triple Alliance was concluded in June 1721, and in February 1722 a Congress opened at Cambray at which Britain and France attempted to bring about a settlement of Austro-Spanish differences. It would be pointless to enter into its discussions, for they dragged on for years, and were no nearer solution at the end than at the beginning. Meanwhile, between 1721 and 1723 there was a rapid change of personnel. Stanhope died, and British foreign policy passed into the hands of Townshend and Walpole, and Newcastle soon replaced Carteret as the other Secretary of State. The Regent Orleans died, and after the short period of the Duc de Bourbon, policy was controlled by Cardinal Fleury.

Walpole and Townshend

The two great conflicts in Europe at this time were that between George I and Peter the Great, and that between Spain and the Emperor. Fleury tried genuinely to heal both conflicts. Both changed dramatically in 1725, the first by the death of Peter the Great, the second by a sudden reversal of Spanish policy and the signature of the Treaty of Vienna between Spain and the Emperor (April 1725). Europe was much alarmed at this latter move; a conspiracy against the Utrecht settlement was at once suspected. Lord Townshend, who was in Hanover with the King, at once created the League of Hanover between Britain, France and Prussia for the mutual guarantee of territories. This had the advantage of securing the French guarantee, not only to Bremen and Verden, but also to Gibraltar and Minorca.

With the threat of war in sight, British naval power came into play. Admiral Hosier was sent to the West Indies to prevent the sailing of the Spanish treasure fleet, without which Spain was powerless to make war. Sir John Jennings was also sent with a squadron to Naples to bring pressure upon the Emperor (1727). Spain replied by a feeble and unsuccessful attack on Gibraltar, but she soon found the Imperial alliance useless, for George II's diplomacy was active against the Emperor among the German princes, and the British fleet watched Naples. Moreover, the Emperor proved himself no more ready to satisfy the ambitions of Elizabeth Farnese in

Italy than he had been before the alliance. Accordingly in
1729 she changed sides again, and by the Treaty of Seville
Britain and France agreed to recognise the succession of Don
Carlos to Parma, and Spain virtually dropped claims to the
return of Gibraltar. This Treaty left the Emperor isolated,
but hostile to the Spanish succession in Parma.

British foreign policy had continued to look in two different directions at once. Townshend was chiefly concerned
with the threat from the Emperor; Walpole was chiefly concerned with maintaining peace with Spain. Walpole had concluded the Treaty of Seville unknown to Townshend while
the latter was in Hanover. The breach between the two
rapidly widened, and in May 1730 Townshend retired from
the government. Henceforth foreign policy was Walpole's
own. He turned at once to placate the Emperor, for unless
the latter could be persuaded to accept the Treaty of Seville,
war in Europe was inevitable. The negotiations were not
easy, but in 1731 they were concluded by the Treaty of
Vienna. The Emperor agreed to suppress the Ostend Company, which had annoyed English merchants since 1722;
and he recognised the Spanish succession to Parma. In return for these great concessions, England recognised the
Pragmatic Sanction, which guaranteed the succession rights
of Charles VI's daughter, Maria Theresa. This agreement
was a brilliant success for Walpole's diplomacy. It was a
triumph for his policy of peace, and it marked his complete
ascendancy over George II, for Walpole's policy had ousted
the more "Hanoverian" policy of Townshend. Throughout he
had relied on the goodwill of Fleury in France. It is true that
Chauvelin, the new French Foreign Minister, was anti-British
and preferred a Spanish alliance, but for the moment harmony between the three western Powers had been achieved.

Walpole's peace policy was maintained through the War
of the Polish Succession. Neither George II, nor even Newcastle, the Secretary of State, approved of Walpole's policy.
They saw the attack on Austria to be a French attempt to
upset the balance of power. The danger was all the greater
because in 1733 France signed the Family Compact with
Spain. The defeat of the Emperor could leave Britain isolated and in danger. Walpole did not deny the danger, but
he preferred to rely on diplomacy. Fleury skilfully prolonged
negotiations with Britain during the war, but was careful to
avoid an agreement. When France signed the Treaty of

Vienna with the Emperor in 1738 she stood forth as the arbiter of Europe. Don Carlos was now King of Naples; France received the reversion of Lorraine; the Bourbon Family Compact still held. Walpole's government was now convinced of the danger from France, and he saw this as a strong reason for avoiding conflict with Spain. Public opinion, however, thought otherwise.

The Anglo-Spanish Conflict

We saw in an earlier chapter how important a part Spain had played in British foreign policy since 1688. This was because of the strategic importance of Spanish power in the Netherlands and the Mediterranean. It arose also from the fabulous wealth of the Spanish empire in America. That empire, in the weak state of Spain, was a standing temptation to a maritime power. Hundreds of miles of coastline in South and Central America were virtually undefended. Every year the Spanish treasure fleet sailed from Havana with its annual blood transfusion to the feeble Spanish state. Every year Spain became less capable of providing its colonists with slaves and manufactures. By the Asiento Treaty, signed at the time of the Treaty of Utrecht, Britain received the right to send 4,800 Negroes a year to the Spanish empire, together with a single ship of not more than 500 tons with manufactures. But it was unlikely that a whole century of buccaneering in the Caribbean would cease at the mere signature of a treaty. No doubt the South Sea Company was the biggest smuggler of all. The Spanish on their side appointed "Garda-Costas" to put down smuggling. But as they were unpaid, and lived off the ships they seized, they seized foreign ships wherever they could, whether they were smuggling or not. They certainly preyed on lawful as well as unlawful commerce, without much interfering with the actual activities of the smugglers, whose articles of trade were too valuable to the Spanish colonists to be discontinued.

Steadily an Anglo-Spanish colonial conflict grew, the Spanish protesting against British smuggling, the British protesting against the illegal seizures of the Garda-Costas. The negotiations were carried on most ineptly by Newcastle, who was anxious not to risk the Asiento Treaty, and yet was afraid of the attacks of Pitt and Boy Patriots in the Commons. At last in 1739 agreement appeared to have been

1 Woburn Abbey, Bedfordshire

2 Classical Architecture: The Marino Casino, Clontarf, Dublin. Mr. John Betjeman has called this "the most perfect classical building in these islands!"

3 "Gin Lane," William Hogarth's famous study
of the London underworld

4 KING WILLIAM III (1689–1702)
The ablest monarch to sit on the English throne
since Queen Elizabeth

5 SIR ROBERT WALPOLE (1676–1745)
A great Parliamentarian, and man of business, coarse, tough
and masterful, he dominated English politics for over twenty
years.

6 WILLIAM PITT, EARL OF CHATHAM (1709–1778)
Most contemporaries were agreed in regarding this majestic
and lonely figure as the greatest man of his age.

7 CHARLES JAMES FOX (1749–1806)
He was warm-hearted, genial, the centre of a devoted circle
of friends, yet he spent most of his political life in opposition.

8 The famous Jonathan Fairbanks home in Dedham, Massachusetts, a fine example of the homely early colonial architectural style. Its central portion was built in 1636 and it is supposed to be the oldest frame house in the U.S.A.

9 The home of Revolutionary Governor Jonathan Trumbull in Lebanon, Connecticut, was built in 1740 and illustrates the transition period between stern early colonial architecture and a more pretentious Georgian period.

10 Mount Vernon, the home of George Washington, first President of the United States. The house was built by Washington's brother, Lawrence, in 1743, but later was renovated and enlarged by George Washington.

These three pictures contain an important clue to the origins of the American Revolution. The first reflects the rough and rugged life of the early settlers. The second and third show the progressive stages towards wealth and civilisation during the eighteenth century, a development too little appreciated in England.

11 WILLIAM PITT (1759–1806)
Cold, austere, a great administrator, he was in office for
almost the whole of his political career.

reached, and by the Convention of El Pardo Spain agreed to pay £95,000 compensation. But nothing was said about the fundamental rights of trade in the area, and the Opposition attacked the agreement as quite unsatisfactory. Spain thought so too, and instead in June 1739 suspended the Asiento and cancelled the offer of £95,000. War was not inevitable. Walpole himself was unprepared to admit the Spanish claims to "right of search" on the high seas, and he could not accept the suspension of the Asiento. The war of 1739 has sometimes been represented as a mere fabrication of the Opposition in the Commons, who wished to embarrass Walpole, but this is unfair. It was inevitable that there should be conflict between an active commercial nation such as Britain and a moribund empire such as the Spanish. Certainly the war was popular among the London merchants. Captain Jenkins was their hero, even though Alderman Beckford said that in fact he had both his ears intact! This was thought of as a war in defence of trade; Professor Pares has called the war of 1739 "a sudden and noisy explosion of imperialism". It was widely thought that the Spanish colonists might rise and throw off Spanish rule, and that thereafter the whole area would be open to trade. Anson was even sent to the Pacific coast to join up with the expected rising.

Newcastle was for a vigorous war, Walpole was for an economical one. In the end the efforts were futile. Admiral Vernon captured Porto Bello and demolished its fortifications, but his attack on Cartagena failed. Next he attacked Santiago, which also failed. Finally he tried Panama, but when the town refused to surrender, Vernon sailed away. Apart from a feeble expedition to Venezuela in 1743, that was virtually the end of the Spanish war. The only great achievement of the navy was Anson's voyage round the world. He inflicted little damage on the Spaniards, though he captured a galleon of Mexican silver. The real distinction lay in the perilous voyage across the Pacific and the avoidance of the French on the return to England. Vernon's attacks had been suitably described by the Opposition as "breaking windows with guineas", but he did succeed in keeping the Spanish treasure fleets from reaching Spain, which they did only once in nine years.

Walpole was always afraid that the French would take advantage of the Spanish war to attack Britain, and in fact a

French fleet was sent to the Mediterranean in 1740 with in-
structions to seek out Vernon's fleet and destroy it. This it
never dared to do, and thus an uneasy peace was maintained between Britain and France until 1744.

The Anglo-French Conflict, 1740–63

By then a general European war had developed. In 1740
the Emperor Charles VI died, and his daughter Maria Theresa found herself attacked by Frederick of Prussia and
Bavaria, and France and Spain were ready to take advantage
of her plight. Britain came in as an auxiliary of Austria
under the Treaty of Vienna of 1731. This treaty had been
equally invoked in 1733 without success, but Walpole was
now forced to recognise the threat of France to the balance
of power. After Walpole's fall in 1742, Carteret was the real
author of Britain's foreign policy for the next two years. His
policy was a return to the whig policy of the reigns of William III and Anne. He wished to organise a Grand Alliance
against the House of Bourbon. He cared nothing for Prussia's threat to Maria Theresa. In 1742 he persuaded Maria
Theresa to win the alliance of Savoy by a promise of territorial compensation in the Milanese. The British fleet suddenly appeared in Naples harbour and gave Don Carlos
twenty-four hours to proclaim his neutrality, which he had
no alternative but to do. He persuaded Maria Theresa to
make peace with Prussia, thus surrendering Silesia (Treaty of
Breslau 1742). In this way he hoped to concentrate the war
against France and Spain.

In 1743 Carteret's policy appeared to be succeeding. In
1744 it collapsed, for Prussia again attacked Maria Theresa,
Austria foolishly attacked Naples, and the French invaded
the Netherlands and prepared to aid the Jacobites. With his
policy crumbling about him, Carteret was forced out of office
by the Pelhams.[1] In 1743 Carteret had put the "Pragmatic
Army" (a mixed force of British, Hanoverians and Hessians)
on the Rhine, and it was this army which defeated the
French at Dettingen in 1743. The French attack on the
Netherlands in 1744 was more formidable, and in 1745
Cumberland was defeated in a gallant battle at Fontenoy.
Thereafter the British force was recalled to deal with the

[1] See Ch. 7.

'45 Rebellion, and the French under Marshal de Saxe were left triumphant. Yet when the Treaty of Aix-la-Chapelle was finally signed in 1748 none of the great issues of the war, namely the Austro-Prussian rivalry, the Habsburg-Bourbon rivalry, and the colonial issues were settled.

The colonial conflicts rapidly broadened and deepened in character after 1748. The Anglo-Spanish conflict had been primarily a matter of trade; the Anglo-French conflict was concerned with territorial domination in America and India. The Anglo-Spanish conflict had been the result of exuberant commercialism; the Anglo-French conflict went deeper; in America it was a matter of life and death. To the colonists Newcastle's Treaty of 1748 revealed how little the mother-country realised the issues involved. This was hardly just to Newcastle, who watched with apprehension the development of the French plan to build a chain of forts on the Ohio, "so as to reduce us", he wrote in 1754, "to a bare narrow possession on the sea-coast, and for this they think *we* will not venture a rupture". Newcastle determined to act. General Braddock was sent to evict the French from the Ohio, and Admiral Boscawen virtually precipitated war in May 1755 by attacking a French convoy bound for the St Lawrence.

Newcastle still clung to the necessity for alliance with Maria Theresa, but she was no longer interested. She was determined to make another bid for the recovery of Silesia, and this made another European war inevitable. In these circumstances her Foreign Minister Kaunitz preferred a French alliance to a British. With war in the offing, George II was greatly disturbed at the danger of Hanover's exposed position. To the annoyance of the Opposition in the Commons, in September 1755 he signed a treaty with the Tsarina Elizabeth by which 55,000 Russian troops would be employed to defend Hanover if attacked, and paid for by Britain. This alarmed Frederick of Prussia, who feared a Russian attack on both flanks, and he offered George II Prussian troops for the defence of Hanover. This was more acceptable to George than the Russian treaty, and the Convention of Westminster was signed in January 1756. Thus by devious means a diplomatic revolution had been effected. The alliance with Austria was at an end. In May Maria Theresa completed an alliance with France, and thus the Habsburgs, Russia and

France stood forth as a mighty combination for the destruction of Prussia.

Newcastle knew that a war was coming, yet his preparations were feeble. He knew that the French might attempt an invasion, yet Pitt's plan for the creation of a militia of fifty thousand was thrown out of the Lords on the government's advice. Instead he urged the King to bring over Hessian and Hanoverian troops. Newcastle, with all his industry, entirely lacked a broad strategic conception of the coming war. Pitt jeered at his fears of a French invasion, and declared that the amount of money spent on Hessian troops "would have conquered America". All Pitt's speeches were infused with ardent patriotism. He said that he wanted "to call this country out of that enervate state that 20,000 men from France could shake it . . .". He wished "to see that breed restored which under our old principles had carried our glory so high". In January 1756 the French, instead of invading England, determined on an attack on Minorca. Admiral Byng was despatched with ten old and leaky ships in April; he was fifty-two and had never held a command during an action; After an indecisive action with the French on May 20, he retired to Gibraltar. As a result Minorca fell. Byng was at once superseded and recalled and placed under close arrest. He had certainly shown a lack of spirit, but the real fault lay with the government, who had first allowed the fleet to fall some seventy ships below strength, and had denuded the Mediterranean of a naval force. But this did not save Byng, who was court-martialled and shot. News of other disasters followed quickly. Fort Oswego on Lake Ontario, and Calcutta both fell to the French. In June 1757 Prussia was routed at Kolin. In July Cumberland was routed by the French at Hastenbeck, and in September he signed the Convention of Klosterseven, disbanding his army and leaving Hanover to the French.

Pitt came into power in 1757, like Winston Churchill in 1940, to put new heart into the nation and to find a new strategy for the war. Like Marlborough before him, Pitt saw the war as a single strategic whole. The object of the war was the conquest of America; the secret of success lay in sea-power, but command of the sea required the French to be tied down in Europe, and hence the importance of military operations in Europe. First, France must be blockaded; French overseas trade would thus be eliminated and supplies

prevented from reaching the colonies. To tie down troops
in France, commando raids must be attempted on the French
coast. Troops not needed in the colonies must be sent to
Germany, and finally Frederick must be aided by subsidies.
For Britain could find money more easily than men, while
Frederick could find men more easily than money.

So Pitt persuaded the King to repudiate the Convention
of Klosterseven, and supersede Cumberland by Ligonier as
Commander in Germany. He was aided by Prussia's recovery
and Frederick's great victory at Rossbach in November 1757.
Pitt paid him a subsidy of £670,000 but refused Newcastle's pressure to send him troops. He did, however, send
some troops in 1758 to aid Ferdinand of Brunswick seize
the line of the Elbe river. Pitt's commando attacks were not
in themselves successful—against Rochefort in September
1757 and against St Malo and Cherbourg in 1758—for losses
in manpower were inclined to be heavy, and the old joke
of "breaking windows with guineas" was revived against him.
But they did serve to pin down troops in France which might
otherwise have been used in Germany. The command of the
sea in European and American waters was maintained
throughout the war, and thus the French colonies were
starved of defence and supplies. When in 1759 the French
did attempt to bring their main fleet out of Brest for an attempted invasion of England, Admiral Hawke pursued it
into Quiberon Bay and inflicted a great defeat. So complete
was the British command of the sea that in 1761 Belleisle itself was captured. Pitt's main military effort was in the
colonies, and that we shall deal with in the next two chapters.

Command of the sea placed Britain in the position of
being able to capture French West Indian islands. In previous
wars this had not been an objective because British sugar
planters resisted the acquisition of further sugar islands,
which would bring down the price of sugar. In the Seven
Years' War another consideration arose. Some "counter"
would be needed at the peace talks which could be exchanged
for Minorca. Thus Guadeloupe was captured in 1759, and
the French sugar planters found themselves much more
prosperous than when under French rule. The so-called "neutral islands" (St Vincent, Dominica, St Lucia and Tobago)
were easily occupied. Thus when the peace talks came, argument raged in England whether it was better to use Guadeloupe or Canada as "counter": the trade of Guadeloupe was

certainly more valuable than that of Canada. In 1762 the last great French island fell when Martinique was captured, and the prospect was opened up of the complete domination of the French West Indies. It is often said that when the Earl of Bute returned Martinique and Guadeloupe to the French as part of the peace terms, he did so in deference to the sugar planters. This is unlikely, for the planters were too afraid of French attacks to want them back. Bute returned them to make a harsh peace more palatable to the French.

The Anglo-Spanish conflict had officially ended in 1750, when Britain surrendered the Asiento. But complaints of smuggling went on, and the British continued to cut logwood in Honduras. However, Spain was determined to avoid further war, and when the Seven Years' War began Ferdinand IV and his minister, General Wall (an Irishman), observed strict neutrality. But in 1759 Ferdinand was succeeded by Charles III (formerly Don Carlos). He greatly feared the growth of British power, and hoped to regain Gibraltar and Minorca, and in 1761 he signed an alliance with Choiseul, the French Foreign Minister. Pitt's secret service was excellent, and he was soon in possession of the whole correspondence.[2] He informed the Cabinet in 1761 and demanded immediate war with Spain; speed was necessary as Pitt hoped to seize the Spanish treasure fleet then on its way to Cadiz. Newcastle was against the extension of the war, and only Temple supported Pitt. In September, therefore, Pitt resigned. By November despatches from the ambassador in Madrid made war with Spain a certainty. Bute then, perhaps afraid of the consequences if he did not, rushed into war. The campaign was crowned with brilliant success. The great city of Havana, the richest jewel in the crown of Spain, was captured and one-third of the Spanish fleet destroyed. Spain then capitulated. Choiseul was also convinced of the need of a speedy peace.

By the Treaty of Paris (1763) Britain gained French Canada and in the West Indies, St Vincent, Tobago, Dominica and Grenada, though the French regained Martinique and Guadeloupe. In India the French retained factories only as trading-stations. Britain regained Minorca in return for Belleisle. Britain kept Senegal but restored Goree to France. Spain gave up Florida in return for Havana and acknowledged

---

[2] The letters are among Pitt's correspondence.

the British right to cut logwood in Honduras. France ceded Louisiana to Spain. Manilla, captured from the Spanish after the conclusion of the peace, was restored.

The Bute government was attacked for several aspects of the peace. Some attacks were no doubt actuated by the dislike of Bute, and by followers of Pitt, but some arguments are worth consideration. Those who argued that Canada was not worth the sacrifice of Guadeloupe have been disproved by history. Pitt certainly thought Canada his crowning achievement. Pitt seems to have felt that the terms fell between two stools, for they were severe enough to warrant French hostility, yet not severe enough to prevent her contemplating a war of revenge. Some like the Duke of Bedford thought that too complete a British victory must lead to a European counter-alliance against Britain. Pitt and his followers were bitterly critical of the desertion of Prussia. For Bute withdrew the subsidies to Prussia in 1762, and made peace with little reference to his old ally. There was substance in this charge, yet Russia made peace in 1762, and Prussia was no longer hard-pressed. With all the criticisms, however, the Treaty of Paris remained an enormous success, ending as it did perhaps the only really profitable war in our history.

Foreign Policy 1763-92

We have repeatedly spoken of two trends of foreign policy in the eighteenth century, the "whig", requiring full participation in European affairs, and the "tory" requiring limited participation in European affairs, and the vigorous prosecution of maritime, commercial and colonial interests. It will be realised that the terms "whig" and "tory" here refer to the origins of the policies, and do not refer to the party of any men happening to advocate them. Thus Stanhope and Carteret had pursued the "whig" policy, while Walpole leaned rather to the "tory" policy. It was the genius of Pitt to find a balance between the two policies so that he had the best of both worlds. After 1761, however, there was a sharp reaction against continental commitments. The alliance with Prussia was abruptly ended in 1762, and thereafter Britain was isolated in Europe. This was not entirely the fault of the British government. Britain needed allies only against France. But Austria was still an ally of France, and Prussia and

Russia were concerned with the fate of Poland and Turkey, not with France. Our important trade connections with Russia provided an argument for a Russian alliance, but neither Power was interested in the designs of the other, and talks which began in 1763 soon lapsed. Frederick of Prussia was loud in his denunciations of British perfidy; the only man he respected in England was Pitt. Pitt claimed to be able to restore the Prussian alliance, but he failed to do so when in office in 1766.

There was much pessimism among politicians in the years after 1763. The enemy was France, and it was commonly supposed that France would one day attempt a war of revenge, yet little effort was made to keep Britain in a state of preparedness. Both the army and the navy were neglected; Admiral Hawke resigned as First Lord of the Admiralty in disgust at the neglect. Britain failed to help the Corsican rebels, and their romantic leader Paoli, and stood by help-lessly while France conquered the island (1765–8). In 1770 the Spanish attempted to expel the British settlement from the Falkland Islands. Chatham's speeches made it clear that the fleet was in such a state of unpreparedness that if Spain forced the issue, Britain could not fight. In fact Spain gave way and the crisis passed, but the moral of the story was not lost upon France, where British naval weakness was noted. Still Lord North persisted with his policy of economy, with the result that in 1775 Britain was woefully unprepared. In 1778, at a time when France could count on sixty-five capital ships and sixty-two frigates, Britain could spare only six ships for home defence, and had virtually to abandon the Mediterranean. It is true that in June 1779 the home fleet was augmented to thirty, and an indecisive engagement was fought with the French off Ushant, but a complete naval victory at that point might have changed the course of the war. When Spain declared war in 1779 the Franco-Spanish fleet was nearly double the British in home waters, and only French incompetence saved Britain from invasion. In 1780 Britain declared war on the Dutch to prevent the smuggling from St Eustatius, and in the same year Russia organised the Armed Neutrality of the Northern Powers to protect neutral trade. Neither of these events put as great a strain upon Britain as might have been expected, but Britain lost command of the sea, and this was the prime reason for the loss of the war. But for the superiority of the British sailor and of officers such as Rodney, the results would have been much worse. The periodic visit from the British fleet enabled Gibraltar to withstand a siege from 1779 until the end of the war.

Britain's prestige suffered severely as the result of the war. Not only was she at war with France, Spain and the Dutch, and opposed by the Armed Neutrality, but the public opinion of Europe was ranged against her as well. It was the need to restore British prestige which was uppermost in the mind of the Younger Pitt when he came into power. The first step was financial stability; the next was the strengthening of the navy. In 1784 the peace establishment of the navy was raised from 15,000 to 18,000 and £2,500,000 were set aside for shipbuilding. His Commercial Treaty with France aimed at a new era of good relations with Britain's old enemy. In the United Provinces a struggle for power was going on between the Orange Party, backed by Prussia, and the Republicans, backed by France. In 1787 the Orange Party won, with Prussian aid, and Pitt hastened to use the opportunity to restore the traditional alliance with the Dutch, and his father's alliance with Prussia. In 1788 the Triple Alliance was made, and thus Pitt ended Britain's isolation. The main achievement of the Triple Alliance was to save Sweden from a Russo-Danish attack in 1790. But it must be admitted that it was for most purposes an unreliable instrument of diplomacy. In 1790 Pitt was concerned at the advance of Russia against Turkey in the Balkans, for he was sensitive to the possibility that Russia might appear as a Mediterranean power. In 1791 Pitt sent an ultimatum to Catherine of Russia protesting against the seizure of the port of Oczakov, and looked to Prussia for joint action. But Prussia refused to co-operate, and when Russia rejected the protest, Pitt could only submit, for action without an ally against Russia appeared impossible. A greater success was had against Spain in 1790, in the affair of Nootka Sound, because this did not require an ally. The Spanish evicted British settlers from Nootka Sound on Vancouver Island on the grounds that the whole coastline was Spanish. Pitt took a strong line, and obtained a vote of credit from Parliament. Spain hesitated in order to discover whether it was likely that France would aid her, and when that proved unlikely, gave way and recognised the rights of the British settlers.

In 1792 Pitt's eyes were on Europe. Not only was Poland

in its death throes, but Austria and Prussia were at war with France. Before the end of the year the French Revolution appeared to be a threat not only to the monarchical system of Europe, but also to the balance of power. As at the beginning of the period of this book, so at the end; Britain was again on the verge of a twenty-year struggle with France.

~ 9 ~

The American Colonies: from Mercantilism to Independence

Mercantilism

THE PRIME MOTIVE for colonisation in the seventeenth and eighteenth centuries was economic. This is not to deny the deep religious motives of the Pilgrim Fathers, or of the Quakers of Pennsylvania, but even with these there was a strong underlying purpose of achieving a new life of security and prosperity. But whether the motive was predominantly economic, as in the settlement of Virginia, or with strong religious overtones, as in the New England settlements, colonial activity under the first two Stuarts was almost entirely the work of individuals; there was no national or governmental policy to that end. In Virginia, the first settlement was the work of a commercial company; in New Plymouth it was the work of a stout-hearted religious sect; in Maryland it was the result of a grant to a favourite of Charles I (Lord Baltimore). Though the early Stuarts sometimes looked on tolerantly at colonial activity, they were rarely in a position to give it much active assistance.

Cromwell took a more positive view. A decisive development of his time was the growth of English sea-power until it could challenge the Dutch mastery of the seas in the same way that Queen Elizabeth had challenged Spanish supremacy in the previous century. Colonies then became an important factor in the struggle for national power. The seizure of Jamaica gave England a highly strategic position in the

West Indies; the first Dutch War revealed a new naval strength, and the first Navigation Act dealt a blow to Dutch commercial supremacy.

From the Restoration onwards something like a colonial policy began to emerge, for colonies were now seen as a mere aspect of the age of Mercantilism. The Mercantilist saw western Europe divided into several "national" units each engaged in a great struggle for national power. Power was the ultimate objective but power was seen in the first instance primarily in terms of wealth. In this the Dutch were the schoolmasters of Europe. They were a small people, having only recently achieved national independence, yet the wealth acquired by trade had made them one of the powers of Europe. It was no wonder, therefore, that Colbert in France, and men like Cary and Sir William Petty in England, studied the Dutch example carefully, to discover the secret of power.

All were agreed that the first necessity was sea-power. Sir William Petty wrote in 1677 that farmers, artisans, seamen, soldiers and merchants "are the very pillars of any Commonwealth", and he argued that seamen were in fact soldiers and merchants as well, for they protected these shores, and carried trade throughout the world. Skilled seamen, who were engaged in trade in peacetime, manned English warships in time of need.

Mercantilists thought of external trade as being much more important than internal trade. Sir William Petty explained the Mercantilist view-point quite clearly:

> The great and ultimate effect of trade is now wealth at large; but particularly abundance of silver, gold and jewels; which are not perishable, nor so mutable as other commodities, but are wealth at all times, and all places: whereas abundance of wine, corn, fowls, flesh, etc., are riches but *hic et nunc.*

It followed, therefore, in Petty's argument, that:

> the Wealth of every nation consists chiefly in the share which they have in the Foreign Trade with the whole Commercial World, rather than in the Domestic trade of ordinary meat, drink, and clothes, etc., which bring in little gold, silver, jewels, and other universal wealth.

The Mercantilists thought of world trade as of a cake of fixed size, so that it followed that the larger the slice the

English took for themselves, the less there would be for others. Petty argued exactly on these lines, when he estimated that the total number of people in the world with whom the English and Dutch would be likely to trade was 80,000,000, and that the total value of the trade was £45,000,000. He then proceeded to calculate what share of that trade the English could expect to enjoy.

Mercantilists thought of England as in some sense a fortress engaged in war with the other "fortresses" of Europe. Merchants and seamen were like raiding parties sent abroad to capture as much of the world's wealth as possible. It followed that in such warfare England needed to husband her resources and see that they were used to the best advantage. It was in this light that colonies were viewed. Colonies were not necessarily welcomed by Mercantilist writers, for in drawing off some of the best of the manpower of the mother-country, and in requiring to be defended by the mother-country, colonies might be a source of weakness. Petty, for instance, pointed out that the way in which some American colonists were scattered over the country, without much regard to the amount of land they could actually cultivate, made for weakness rather than strength.

A colony was justified in so far as it created opportunities for shipping, and in so far as it produced goods which the mother-country could not produce in sufficient quantities for herself, and would otherwise have to purchase from foreigners. By this test, for instance, Barbados was an admirable colony. It employed a large amount of shipping, both in the slave and the sugar trades, and it provided the mother-country with an essential produce which she could not grow for herself. On the other hand, the New England colonies at first seemed of little value. Petty wrote that the New England settlers were merely engaged in agriculture and cattle-rearing, and they might as well be doing it in Ireland as in America. So,

> As for the people of New England, I can but wish they were transplanted into Old England or Ireland.

There was little question of "pride in Empire" in the thought of the century after 1660. Each colony was valued according to its contribution to the Mercantilist system. It was assumed that the colony would be best employed producing raw materials which the mother-country needed, which would create work, and render her self-sufficient. Thus the West Indies would produce sugar, rum, molasses, logwood, Virginia would produce tobacco (in whose interests the mother-country suppressed tobacco-growing at home), and later the New England colonies produced naval stores which relieved us of dependence on the Baltic trade.

The basis of the Mercantilist system was laid by the Navigation Acts (1651–73). The essential principles were, first, that all British trade should be carried either in British ships, or in the ships of the country with which we traded, but not in the ships of a third (i.e. Dutch) power. "British" here included the colonies, and colonial trade was confined to "British" ships. Colonial goods could be exported only to Britain if they were "enumerated". The main "enumerated" goods before 1764 were tobacco, sugar, cotton, rice, molasses, furs, and naval stores; after 1764 the list was much longer. The first idea was that these were the colonial products in which the mother-country was most interested. It was argued that even if the producer had only a restricted market in which to sell his goods, at least he had the monopoly of an assured market. The system certainly did not prevent a very rapid colonial expansion in the eighteenth century. By 1760 it is estimated that the colonial trade gave British merchants a profit of about a million pounds a year, which was not excessive. The colonial trade was certainly of the greatest importance to Britain, and colonial customs revenue was an important part of the Crown's income.

The American Colonies

The situation in the American colonies in the period after 1688 may be summarised as follows. Some colonies, like Massachusetts, were directly under the Crown, others, like Pennsylvania, were proprietary. But whether the governor was appointed by the Crown or by a proprietor, he had a difficult task. He enjoyed responsibility without power. He and his council (nominated in London) constituted the executive, but internal taxation could be voted only by the Assembly, elected by the landowners on a property franchise. The history of the relations between governor and Assembly in most colonies is the story of one long struggle, in which the Assembly usually won; for the British government was often not interested, and gave the governors ill-support. London retained the veto over colonial legislation, and it was not anxious to assert its power farther than that. Most governors were able and honest men, driven to desperation by the selfishness of Assemblies which refused sometimes even to provide for their own defence. As the latter could even withhold the governor's salary, they usually held the whip-hand.

The New England colonists were a tough, independent people, who in the 1670s had had to fight a devastating war against the Mohawk Indians. In the following years they rapidly built up a prosperous living, growing provisions which they sold to the West Indies, selling naval stores to the mother-country, and shipbuilding. Massachusetts was the most troublesome, refusing from the first to obey the Navigation Acts on the ground that "the laws of England are bounded within the four seas, and do not reach America". They also refused to accept religious toleration, and in consequence, in 1684, their charter was cancelled. James II was preparing to form all the New England colonies into a single unit, without representative institutions. If he had succeeded here, the system would have been extended throughout the colonies, with incalculable consequences. But with his fall, colonial liberties were restored. So far the colonies had always been regarded as lying within the royal prerogative, but after 1688 Parliament increasingly asserted its control. Still, one can hardly say that there was a "system" of colonial administration. There was a Board of Trade and Plantations, set up in 1696, fulfilling some of the functions of a modern Colonial Office, but these were merely advisory, and in practice important decisions, when taken at all, were taken by the Secretary of State, the Admiralty or the Secretary at War.

Virginia was in the unfortunate position of being entirely dependent upon a single crop, and she probably suffered most from the Navigation Acts which required her to sell tobacco only to Britain. The price of tobacco fell ruinously, and in 1668 was only one farthing a pound. As a result, in 1675 Nathanial Bacon led a farmers' revolt; but he soon died and the revolt collapsed. The eighteenth century was well established before Virginia improved economically. The Carolinas also experienced great difficulties in their early days. Sir John Colleton, the Earl of Shaftesbury and others obtained a charter to found Carolina from Charles II, as a commercial venture. Attempts were made to produce naval stores, provisions, rice, indigo and furs, but progress was slow, and by

1700 there was a population of only five thousand, half of them Negroes. Profits to the proprietors were few, and in 1729 they were glad to sell out to the government.

Much more vigorous was the Quaker settlement of Pennsylvania. The Quakers were one of the great dynamic forces in the later seventeenth and eighteenth centuries, and left an indelible mark upon American history. William Penn was the son of Admiral Sir William Penn, the conqueror of Jamaica. As a friend of the Duke of York he was granted Pennsylvania in 1681 in return for a loan. The Quakers had neither a church nor a priesthood, and Penn believed in real religious and political liberty. He called his colony "the Holy Experiment", and granted it a full charter of privileges. It soon became a highly prosperous colony, selling provisions to the West Indies. Its people became some of the most industrious, cultured and civilised people in the world, and they exercised a great influence in the formation of the American way of life. Pennsylvania has been called "the first large community in modern history where different races and religions lived together under the same government on terms of equality".

In the eighteenth century two further colonies were added. Georgia was founded in the first instance as a charitable institution, but it was encouraged by the government as a bulwark against the Spanish. James Oglethorpe and a number of philanthropists founded it as a refuge for discharged debtors, and the first batch, sent out in 1733, founded Savannah, and received fifty acres each. Slavery was at first forbidden, as was rum, but when the colony could not get on without either, the ban was lifted. Even so, the colony remained poor and thinly populated for a long time, and mainly concerned with rice-growing. The proprietors were very glad to turn the colony over to the Crown in 1752. The last American colony to be founded was Nova Scotia, in 1749, and it was the only one to remain loyal during the American Revolution.

Sir William Petty estimated the population of all the colonies in his day (excluding slaves) at half a million, and although this estimate included also the West Indies, yet the fact remains that the British American colonies had a far larger population than either the French or the Spanish settlements. Even so, the actual area of settlement by 1700 did not amount to much more than a narrow coastal ribbon

from Maine to Virginia and again in Carolina. There were
vast areas of unoccupied land, but already a strategic conflict was emerging. In 1682 the great French explorer, Sieur
de la Salle, starting from Canada, sailed down the Mississippi, called the area Louisiana, and set up the French flag
at the place where New Orleans was later to be. But Louis
XIV was quite uninterested in colonisation, and La Salle's
attempt to found a settlement there failed. In the north, the
English and French were kept apart by the existence of the
powerful Iroquois peoples to the south of Lake Ontario. But
both English and French fur traders were pushing out to the
rich territories of the Ohio valley, and a conflict could not
long be postponed.

Expansion and Colonial Rivalry

When William III became King of England, he at once
committed England to war with France, and thus the English
and French colonists were also committed to war. French
colonists were encouraged to attack English frontier settlements, and privateers preyed on English fishermen and
traders. In 1697 the French began the effective occupation
of the Mississippi area. By this time English fur and pelt
traders were pushing out from the Carolinas in search of the
valuable deer and buffalo skins, and thus the conflict extended southwards. The colonists urged England to annex
the whole area up to the Mississippi, and snuff out both the
French settlements in Louisiana, and the Spanish settlements
in West Florida, but the government let the opportunity
pass. The colonial conflict during the War of the Spanish
Succession amounted to little. The Spaniards attacked
Charleston in 1706, but failed to take it, and in return the
English burnt Pensacola in 1707. In the north the Massachusetts colonists captured Port Royal in Nova Scotia, but
a British attack on Canada in 1711 failed miserably. By the
Treaty of Utrecht (1713) Britain obtained the Hudson Bay
area and Nova Scotia but as France retained Cape Breton
Isle, and built there their main naval base of Louisbourg,
the British gains must be accounted small. There was no
mention of the south at all.

There followed now in the colonies a generation of peace
and rapid expansion. In 1713 the population of the American
colonies was about 360,000; a half-century later it was

1,600,000; and if the population more than quadrupled, the area of occupation tripled. There was a steady stream of immigrants, English, Scottish, Irish, German religious refugees, French Huguenots, and the like. These were the best years of Mercantilism, and the rapid growth of these years is the best justification for the system. In England and Europe there was a steady rise in the prices of colonial produce, and in the colonies, in consequence, a general prosperity. The English colonists had perhaps the highest standard of living in the world. In addition to the trade with England, there grew up a most lucrative American trade with the West Indies, where there was a great demand for provisions, meat, vegetables, salt, fish, timber and horses. These were well supplied from New England, and also from Baltimore, which was founded in 1729, and exported grain to the West Indies, as well as tobacco to England. New England also exported to England ship timber, naval stores and fish; Virginia exported tobacco, South Carolina exported rice and indigo, New York exported pelts and furs. In return for the provisions exported to the West Indies, New England imported sugar and great quantities of molasses, from which they distilled rum. But here arose a difficulty in the operation of the Mercantilist system. For the sugar and molasses of the British West Indian islands were much more expensive than those of the French. The New Englanders therefore bought from the French instead. In 1733 the British planters persuaded the government to pass the Sugar or Molasses Act prohibiting the trade with the French islands, but the colonists simply ignored the Act, and the mother-country did not see fit to enforce it. In other respects, too, she was prepared to relax the Mercantilist system when it pinched, as in 1729, when the export of rice direct to Europe south of Cape Finisterre was permitted by Act of Parliament.

Mercantilism assumed that the colonists would be most profitably employed in producing the raw materials needed in Britain and Europe, and that manufactured goods could best be supplied by the mother-country. From time to time, therefore, Acts were passed forbidding colonial manufactures, for instance of woollens in 1699, of beaver hats in 1732, and of iron goods in 1750. These Acts have often been pointed out as indicating the restrictive and even oppressive character of the Mercantilist system, and so they might have been if they had ever been enforced. But in fact it appears that they were almost entirely disregarded. In spite of the law, the Americans spun their own woollen cloth, wore their own beaver hats, and by 1760 had a prosperous iron industry.

A more serious objection to Mercantilism was the fact that the colonists always had a serious imbalance of trade with Britain, that is to say, the colonies bought more from Britain than they sold to Britain. Now the colonies produced no precious metals, and Britain foolishly and shortsightedly refused to permit either the export of coin to the colonies, or that the colonies should mint their own coins. There was, therefore, usually a chronic shortage of coin in the colonies. Some colonies attempted to meet the difficulty by the issue of paper-money, but it often depreciated in value, and commercial transactions were constantly hampered. As a matter of fact, the illicit trade with the French and Spanish often gave the colonists enough money to continue trade with Britain.

In spite of such difficulties, the half-century after 1713 were years of great prosperity and progress for the colonies. The roughness of life of the early settlers gave way to peace and a more gracious living. Travel to England was by no means impossible; well-to-do colonists sent their sons to England to study the law. Books were imported; colonial newspapers started; English fashions in dress eagerly copied. The beautiful colonial-style houses, built of wood, well painted, with white doors with fanlights, can still be seen in towns like Boston and Annapolis. About 1733 Jonathan Edwards started a great religious revival, known as the "Great Awakening", which overran New England like a fire, and was similar to Methodism in England. (Indeed the two movements were closely connected, for George Whitefield was greatly influenced by Edwards' writings, which he read while in Georgia in 1739.) The beginnings of the American educational system are also to be found in this period, for Yale, Princeton, Dartmouth, and Brown University were all founded during the colonial period.

French expansion in America proceeded much more slowly than the British. New Orleans was founded in 1718, but twenty years later had a population of only 3,000 Europeans. For one thing, the French were hampered in their development by the fact that the Iroquois Indians in the north, and the Cherokee and others in the south, on the whole continued to be allies of the British. Spanish settlements in

West Florida continued to be thin. During the Spanish War, which began in 1739, General Oglethorpe failed in an attack on the Spanish town of St Augustine in Florida, and a Spanish attack on Georgia in 1742 was no more successful. When in 1744 the British and French colonists once again found themselves at war there were the usual skirmishes along the New York–New England border, but the only really important incident in the American colonies was the capture of Louisbourg. Governor William Shirley (1741–57) of Massachusetts was one of the most popular and successful governors of the period. He and the colonists had suffered much from the privateers operating from Louisbourg, and they were angered at the dilatoriness of the British government in dealing with them. Shirley therefore hit upon a madcap scheme by which he and a handful of colonists, aided by the fleet, would launch a frontal attack on this strongly fortified naval base. The attack so took the French by surprise that they surrendered. The French later tried twice to retake Louisbourg, each time unsuccessfully, but by the Treaty of Aix-la-Chapelle (1748) it was returned to the French in exchange for Madras. So long as it remained in French hands the New England colonies would not be safe from French attack, and the control of the sea would remain in doubt.

Equally important in the strategy of the Anglo-French struggle was the valley of the Ohio river. This was not only a rich area for fur and pelt traders, but also the highway for the French from Canada to the Mississippi, and equally for the British of Virginia if they wished to expand inland. In 1747 Thomas Lee of Virginia founded the Ohio Company to open a route from the Potomac to the Ohio for Indian trade. In 1753 the Marquis Duquesne was sent by the French to establish a chain of forts in the area. In 1754 the young George Washington, aged twenty-two, and a lieutenant colonel in the Virginia militia, was sent with a small force to forestall them. But the French had already built Fort Duquesne. Washington fired the first shots of a new colonial war, but then retired. The British colonists were anxious to try their strength with the French. They numbered 1,250,000 to the French 50,000; Massachusetts wished to capture Louisbourg and the whole of French Canada, and Virginia wanted the Ohio. France was not eager for a colonial war, but in England the Duke of Newcastle, though he was much concerned at the European implications of war, felt it necessary to give some support to the colonists. Thus General Braddock and two regiments were sent to Virginia. In 1755 he marched from Virginia to Fort Duquesne. He was an old soldier of great experience, but he was over-sanguine, and his force was cut to pieces by an enemy he hardly saw. Franklin said he always thought him over-confident, but Washington thought he was an honest man who had simply been unfortunate. He was, however, made a convenient scapegoat at the time, and has remained so ever since. In the same year Governor Shirley failed to take Fort Niagara, and the French strengthened themselves on Lake Champlain by building Fort Ticonderoga. Finally, Admiral Boscawen allowed 3,000 French troops to reach Canada. This was the position when a general war broke out in 1756.

The best comment on Lord Loudoun, who was now sent as Commander-in-Chief in America, was that of Benjamin Franklin:

> On the whole I wondered how such a man came to be entrusted with so important a business as the conduct of a great army; but having since seen more of the great world, and the means of obtaining, and motives for giving place and employment, my wonder is diminished.

He lacked spirit. He failed to attack Louisbourg because he was not sure of the command of the sea, and he allowed the French to take Fort Oswego and Fort William Henry. When Pitt took charge of the war in 1757 he was at once superseded.

Pitt brought an entirely new vigour and spirit to the colonial war. With a genius for strategy, organisation and leadership, he brought a new vision to the war. In 1756 few people in England gave much thought to French Canada; at best it was an entirely secondary objective in the war. Pitt made its conquest a principal object of his strategy. He blockaded Louisbourg; he tied down as many Frenchmen as possible in France; he saw to it that wherever offensive operations were planned the British strength substantially outstripped the French. In 1758 Brigadier John Forbes was sent to capture Fort Duquesne; Lord Howe and General Abercromby were sent against Lake Champlain, and Admiral Boscawen was sent to take Louisbourg. Lord Howe was killed, and Abercromby failed to take the forts on Lake

Champlain, but Boscawen took Louisbourg, and Forbes took Fort Duquesne, which he renamed Pittsburg. Bradstreet also took Fort Frontenac on Lake Ontario, a key position in severing French communications between Canada and the Ohio valley.

1759 was the *Annus Mirabilis* for Britain. The Battle of Quiberon Bay cut off French reinforcements for Canada. Fort Niagara fell to Sir William Johnson and General Prixeaux. Amherst captured Crown Point and Ticonderoga. Finally Wolfe, a master of strategy and tactics if ever there was one, at the age of thirty-two, with only 5,000 men, completed the capture of Quebec. Montreal remained to be taken by Amherst in 1760, and the conquest of French Canada was complete. Never in her history did Britain fight so profitable a war, and, for a short time at least, she experienced an enormous sense of achievement, such as was reflected in David Garrick's:

> *Come, cheer up my lads! 'tis to glory we steer,*
> *To add something more to this wonderful year;*
> *To honour we call you as free men, not slaves,*
> *For who are so free as the sons of the waves?*

By the Treaty of Paris, French Canada and Spanish Florida were ceded to Britain. France compensated Spain for her loss by ceding to her Louisiana. Luckily for England a plan to exchange Canada for the island of Guadeloupe was defeated by the hostility of the English sugar planters.

It was a glorious achievement, but the problems which remained were so great, and of so novel a character that in the end they broke the Empire which had just emerged. For during the twenty-odd years of war which preceded the Treaty of Paris there emerged a new situation which was not understood by more than a handful of men. Until 1740 it could be said that Britain possessed a number of separate colonies in the West Indies and North America mainly for the purpose of trade. These colonies existed primarily for the economic benefit of the mother-country. In return for the part they played in the Mercantilist system the mother-country protected them against foreign enemies, but in other respects very largely left them alone. By the 1750s the position was changing. What had been merely a number of commercial colonies was becoming a territorial empire. A new idea of power was emerging, and with it the question of how the whole should be organised.

The issue was dramatically presented in 1754, when the Board of Trade ordered a congress of colonial delegates to meet at Albany to discuss common colonial problems, including defence. This was in itself a recognition of the fact that the fragmentated character of the Empire was outmoded. Benjamin Franklin, one of the wisest men of his day, had already published in his newspaper, *The Gazette*, a cartoon of a snake cut into pieces, each bearing the name of a colony, and underneath, the caption "Join or Die". Franklin was intensely loyal to Britain, and proud of the new British power. He was chosen as one of the delegates of Pennsylvania at the congress of Albany, and he submitted to it a plan for the re-organisation of the Empire. He proposed that the colonies should have a single governor-general, appointed and paid by the Crown, possessing the power of veto, and presiding over a grand council chosen by the provincial assemblies. His prime duty would be defence and the expansion towards the west, where, Franklin saw, would come a struggle with the French, the colonies would retain their independence in local affairs, but the acts of the grand council would be subject to the approval of the King-in-Council. It was, in short, a plan for a federalised Empire.

Franklin's plan was accepted by the Albany Congress, but rejected both by London and the provincial assemblies. Franklin wrote:

> The assemblies did not adopt it, as they all thought there was too much *prerogative* in it, and in England it was judged to have too much of the democratic.

Statesmanship consists in large measure in the vision of what is the great need of the moment. Franklin had it in 1754, and so did Governor Shirley, but they were almost alone. The Board of Trade did produce another plan, but it excluded the colonists from a share in the choice of the council, and it explicitly reserved the right of Parliament to tax the colonies without representation. Franklin at once pounced on the defects of the plan. In his letters to Shirley he wrote that the Empire should be considered as one. All were British subjects and were entitled to the same rights:

The British colonies bordering on the French are properly frontiers of the British Empire, and the frontiers of an empire are properly defended at the joint expense of the people in such an empire. . . . I should hope that the people of Great Britain and the people of the colonies would learn to consider themselves as not belonging to a different community with different interests, but to one community with one interest, which I imagine would greatly lessen the danger of future separations.

He wrote that it would be absurd to suppose that the men who were hazarding their lives carving out new countries and increasing the commerce of the mother-country, had thereby forfeited their rights as Britons. It was:

an undoubted right of Englishmen not to be taxed but by their own consent given through representation. . . Compelling the colonies to pay money without their consent would be rather like raising money in an enemy's country than taxing Englishmen for their own public benefit.

The whole incident of the Albany Congress and the subsequent correspondence is worth careful study because it contains so clearly the issues of the later struggle. The organisation of the Empire could not remain as it was. There were three possible developments. Either a new discipline and control would be imposed on the colonies from London; or some sort of imperial federation would be worked out in full co-operation with the colonists, or there would be separation. Because the third possibility was the course which history took, it does not follow that it was the inevitable one, but it must be admitted that the odds were heavily weighted against the other two.

The conquest of French Canada greatly strengthened the spirit of independence of the American colonists. In the course of the struggle they found a new sense of nationhood. They had begun inadvertently to refer to themselves as Americans instead of British. They no longer needed British help to defend them from the French and Spanish. Yet this was just the moment chosen by the British government to inflict new controls and indignities on the colonists. Once, when Franklin was talking to Pratt, the great lawyer, later Lord Camden and a friend of Chatham, Pratt prophesied that with the conquest of Canada the Americans would set up for independence. Franklin replied that no such idea had ever entered their heads, nor, he said, would it, "unless you grossly abuse them". "Very true," said Pratt, "that is one of the main causes I see will happen, and it will produce the event."

The American Revolution

The Seven Years' War was hardly over when the colonists felt the new strength of the mother-country. New territories had been acquired and had to be organised. The attempt at organisation gave rise to alarm in the colonies that there was a conspiracy against their liberties. There was, in fact, no conspiracy; quite the reverse. What was so alarming about the successive British governments in the 1760s was the absence of a coherent plan, and the entire lack of continuity from one government to the next. The ignorance of colonial affairs among British politicians was almost incredible. Shelburne was perhaps the best-informed, but he was in power for only a short period of time. The Grenville government did make a real study of the colonial problem, and came to a logical, if mistaken, policy, but it was in office for only two years (1763–5). Chatham, with the instincts of a statesman, was always ready to seek information at the source, and so was Burke, but apart from these men, British politicians made a sorry picture of incompetence and ignorance in the period. No one ever thought of sending out to the colonies an investigating commission under a Burke or a Shelburne, to discover the true facts.

The encroachments of the colonists had led to the fearful Indian rising led by Pontiac in 1763. It was soon suppressed, but the British government was genuinely concerned as to the fate of the Red Indians, and, until a policy could be worked out, a Royal Proclamation of October 1763 forbade any colonists to settle or purchase land between the Alleghany mountains and the Mississippi. To the British government the land really belonged to the Indians, and their rights were to be respected. To the colonists the Indians had no more right to the land than the animals they hunted. The Virginians in particular were enraged at British controls, and they crossed the Alleghanies all the same; one of them was George Washington. Whatever the moral rights of the Indians, the colonists refused to be treated as children. The

British government had meant the prohibition to be merely temporary, pending the working-out of a policy, but the misunderstanding is typical of the lack of contact between the colonists and the government in the 1760s.

Then George Grenville turned to the control of trade, and the question of the cost of colonial defence. He took the reasonable view that if the Mercantilist system was to continue, it ought to be enforced. The Sugar Act of 1764 reduced the duty on foreign molasses, but increased the duties on sugar, wines, coffee, silks and linens. Moreover the trade laws were now to be enforced, and Vice-Admiralty courts were given increased powers. As we have seen already, the Mercantilist system had been evaded for many years; in the New England states there was almost universal smuggling. These colonists simply could not afford to give up their trade with the French and Spanish West Indies. Moreover, the preamble to the Act stated that the purpose of the new taxes and regulations was increased revenue. At once men like James Otis and Samuel Adams seized upon this as "taxation without representation". Yet it was difficult publicly to take issue with the government on the subject without appearing to be defending smuggling. The Stamp Act provided a better issue.

Historians have usually been at pains to do justice to the reasonableness of George Grenville's Stamp Act, by emphasising the size of the National Debt, the need for the colonists to make some contribution to their own defence, and the fact that the colonists were given a year to make an alternative suggestion. But following hard upon the Sugar Act it could not but give the impression in the colonies that the British government had a plan to discipline them and subordinate them. The issue is also seen in better perspective when it is remembered that the tax would yield only £60,000 a year, yet the cost of defence was £350,000. It was not worth stirring up a hornet's nest for £60,000 a year, especially as American trade was worth £2,000,000 a year. But Grenville did not expect trouble, and neither did Benjamin Franklin, who was in London at the time.

The outburst of colonial opposition against the Stamp Act was the expression of a new attitude of mind among the colonists. For years they had been left largely to their own devices; they were used to self-government; they resented interference. The merchants of New England had no intention of giving up smuggling. The landowners of Virginia had no intention of being hindered in their westward expansion. The frontiersmen had no respect for either the Indians, the British government, or even the big colonial landowners who sat securely in the colonial assemblies of Boston or Philadelphia and cared nothing for the poor. And merchants and landowners alike resented the currency restrictions. The real significance of the Stamp Act was that it gave the colonists a common cause against the British government.

Thus, urged on by the merchants, the mob rose in Boston and burnt the fine house of Governor Hutchinson. Nowhere could the Stamp Act be enforced. In Virginia the fiery oratory of Patrick Henry denounced taxation without representation. The Massachusetts Assembly invited a colonial congress to meet in New York. It met in October 1765 to decide upon a common colonial policy. Thus the colonists in their own way were obeying Franklin's earlier injunction to "Join or Die". They soon hit upon the most effective way of coercing the mother-country: the trade boycott of British goods. It was at once effective. In March 1766 the Stamp Act was repealed by Rockingham's government. It is true that the Declaratory Act was passed, asserting the right of the mother-country to tax the colonies, but at the time little notice was taken of it in the colonies in the general rejoicing at the repeal.

No class was more directly affected by the Stamp Act than the lawyers, and they were well fitted to argue the case against taxation. As early as 1761 James Otis, one of the leading lawyers of Massachusetts, argued the case against "writs of assistance" (which granted authority to search for and seize smuggled goods). He called them:

> the worst instrument of arbitrary power, the most destructive of English liberty and the fundamental principles of law, that ever was found in an English law-book.

In 1764 he published a carefully argued attack on the policy of the British Government, one year before the Stamp Act. His appeal was to the principles of the British constitution: a colony, being an integral part of the mother-country, was:

> by the law of God and nature, by the common law, and by the act of Parliament . . . entitled to all the natural, essential, inherent and inseparable rights of our fellowsubjects in Great Britain.

Otis, therefore, was basing his argument upon the principles of the British constitution. He explicitly ruled out the possibility of active resistance; his tone was that of an entirely loyal British subject, and that was undoubtedly the attitude of the vast majority of Americans at the time.

But there was a logical difficulty. For it was pointed out that, in fact, ever since the Navigation Acts, Parliament *had* imposed controls, including taxation, on the colonies, without representation. Moreover, if rights were granted by Parliament, could they not also be taken away? Thus it seemed necessary to invent the distinction between *internal* and *external* taxation. It was argued that the mother-country had the right to organise trade in the interests of the Empire as a whole, but not to impose taxation for the purpose of raising revenue. This was the argument of Stephen Hopkins' pamphlet *The Rights of the Colonies Examined* (1765). (Hopkins was governor of Rhode Island.) It was this argument which gave Charles Townshend his opportunity.

No incident in the whole story of the dispute with the American colonies was more reckless and inexcusable than the Townshend duties of 1767. Townshend in effect argued that if the colonists wished to play a game of hair-splitting distinction between internal and external taxes, he would humour them. His duties on glass, lead, paper and tea would appear to be for the organisation of trade, whereas their real purpose would be to raise revenue to the extent of £40,000. There is a heavy price to pay in politics for such unprincipled cleverness. To begin with, he forced the colonists to change their ground. The distinction between internal and external taxation had been difficult logically to maintain. Now the colonists abandoned it. *Letters from a Farmer in Pennsylvania to the Inhabitants of the British Colonies* (1767–8) written by John Dickinson, constitutes a landmark in the dispute. He argued that since the distinction was too difficult to maintain, the colonists ought not to accept *any* form of taxation. Earlier the stand had usually been made on the rights under the British constitution; now this argument was abandoned in favour of simple appeal to natural law. He argued:

> that we cannot be happy without being free; that we cannot be free without being secure in our property; that we cannot be secure in our property if, without our consent, others

may, as by right, take it away; that taxes imposed on us by
Parliament do thus take it away.

Dickinson still did not advocate revolt, still less a breakaway
from Britain. He was a patriot and a moderate and this made
him more effective as a publicist than any other writer of his
day.

Still, the colonists were beginning to see that they no
longer really needed the British Empire, and that they need
not submit to its dictates. The outbursts after the Townshend duties were less violent than after the Stamp Act, and
the non-importation agreements were less generally observed.
But they were effective enough, and the British government
one by one removed the duties, except that on tea. In the
colonies the extremists were at work. Samuel Adams, a tax-
collector in Boston, became the leading spirit in the Boston
House of Representatives. He demanded nothing less than
complete self-government for the colonies, and in fact worked
relentlessly for independence. At the same time this real
objective had to be carefully concealed. Thus in the *Massachusetts Circular Letter* of 1768, written by him, he admitted
the legislative authority of Parliament over the whole Empire
so long as it did not extend to taxation without consent,
while at the same time he rejected as "utterly impracticable"
the proposal that the colonies should be represented in the
imperial Parliament; better to accept taxation than that!
Samuel Adams carefully kept the fire of resistance alight.
He organised committees of correspondence throughout the
colonies, and he circulated his statement of *Rights of the
Colonies*, which, as the Solicitor-General Wedderburn declared:

> told them a hundred rights of which they had never heard
> before, and a hundred grievances which they had never before
> felt.

He was aided in his work by other extremists, such as Patrick Henry in Virginia, Isaac Sears and John Lamb in New
York, and Christopher Gadsden in South Carolina.

By the time Lord North came into office in 1770 the situation might be summarised thus. The colonists had failed
to establish either that the constitution had been violated, or
that there was an intelligible distinction between external

and internal taxation. The theorists of the Revolution had
therefore shifted their ground. Franklin put it as a simple
alternative:

> that Parliament has a power to make *all laws* for us, or that
> it has a power to make *no laws* for us.

James Wilson of Pennsylvania accepted this, and preferred in
1770 to argue the issue on the simple basis of natural law:

> All men are, by nature, free and equal: no one has a right
> to any authority over another without his consent: all lawful
> government is founded in the consent of those who are sub-
> ject to it. . . . The happiness of the society is the first law of
> every government.

In short, it was not now a matter of the principles of the
constitution, but of what made for the happiness of the
American people. By such means the extremists steered a
steady course towards independence. But they were only a
small minority. Perhaps it is true that all revolutions are
really steered by a small minority, but for success they need
to be able to direct the many who are ready to follow. In the
colonies they could count on the "mob", the poor and discontented, who scented in the disturbances, not the means of
breaking with England, but the means of beginning some
social revolution at home. In large measure the controversy
appeared to die down during the five years after 1768, though
the extremists did their best to keep it alight. In 1770 a hostile crowd snowballed the troops and four were killed in the
so-called Boston Massacre. In 1772 a gang burnt the *Gaspee,* a
revenue ship which had run aground, but these appeared to
be isolated incidents. It was, however, the third of these
incidents which precipitated the final catastrophe, the Boston
Tea Party of December 1773.

In 1773 Lord North's government allowed the East India
Company to carry tea direct to America, thus saving shipping. Instead of paying a ninepenny duty it would now pay
only threepence and tea would consequently be cheaper in
America. The first cargo of tea to reach Boston was thrown
into the sea by a gang dressed as Red Indians. What the

Americans feared was the monopoly which the East India Company would acquire over the American market. All those merchants who had imported tea from England would now be undercut. It was an issue upon which merchants and extremists could unite. It was a victory for radicals. The British government at once decided upon punitive measures. By the Massachusetts Acts the port of Boston was closed, the Massachusetts charter suspended, and henceforth certain trials could be transferred to England. These measures could only mean that the British government intended to break the will of the colonies by force. Undoubtedly the government felt provoked, but it was foolish to play so directly into the hands of the extremists. Instead of isolating Massachusetts, the Acts united the colonies in resistance. In September 1774 the first Continental Congress of twelve colonies met at Philadelphia. Their declarations were carefully worded so as not to offend the moderates: the right of Parliament to regulate trade was still recognised, but the colonies required a complete surrender of Britain's right to tax the colonies, and an "Association" pledged the colonists to cease buying British goods.

Even at this late point an act of statesmanship from Britain would have cut the ground from beneath the feet of the extremists. The great bulk of American opinion was still moderate, and did not wish to break with Britain. Governor Hutchinson had said in 1773 that:

no line can be drawn between the supreme authority of Parliament and the total independence of the colonies.

But that was not strictly true. Benjamin Franklin had, twenty years before, suggested some federal solution, and John Adams, the moderate cousin of the extremist Samuel Adams, still favoured the federal idea. Yet the British government refused even to talk to the moderates, though Benjamin Franklin was in England. It is interesting to speculate what might have happened if Lord North had chosen to discuss the question with men such as Franklin, John Adams, George Washington and John Dickinson. Some such idea was not far from the minds of many wise Americans. Dr Joseph Warren, a leading citizen of Boston, wrote to an English friend in February 1775 that only the highest statesmanship could save the situation:

A Richmond, a Chatham, a Shelburne, a Camden, with their noble associates, may yet repair it; it is a work which none but the greatest of men can conduct.

The one act of statesmanship of Lord North's government was the Quebec Act of June 1774, successfully aimed at securing the loyalty of the French Canadians. It granted them religious toleration, and at the same time the Province of Quebec was extended to the Ohio river, thus effectively closing the door to westward expansion by the North American colonies. The effect was to satisfy the Canadians, but to infuriate the Americans. When Lord North offered them a feeble Conciliation Plan, they brushed it aside. In April 1775 the first blood was spilt at Lexington and Concord, at which General Gage lost 247 men. Boston was besieged, and the war had begun. Before we follow its course, we may pause to ask who really made the revolution in the colonies.

The American colonists were perhaps politically the most wide-awake people in the world. Their educated classes were nurtured in the tradition of Hampden, Milton and Locke. The leaders of the Revolution tended to be from three main classes, first, the lawyers and merchants, especially of New England, whose business made them resentful of interference, and very sensitive to threats to liberty. As Burke put it:

They augur misgovernment at a distance, and snuff the approach of tyranny in every tainted breeze.

Second, the landowners of Virginia, the class from which George Washington sprang, among whom the spirit of independence was strong, who were anxious for westward expansion, and who were always heavily in debt to Britain. Third, the "up-country" frontiersmen, tough, radically minded men who bitterly resented the many burdens, the heavy taxes, quit rents and shortage of paper money. To them the revolution meant primarily a social revolution. The tall, red-headed Patrick Henry was their ideal and leader. This third group was regarded as dangerous radicals by the landowners of the more settled eastern parts, but the two achieved some sort of alliance against Britain.

The American Revolution was, in fact, two revolutions in one. One was a revolt against Britain; the other was a democratic upsurge against the aristocratic character of most of the colonies. The more aristocratic and cultured classes tended to stand aside from the Revolution. They became the tories or loyalists of the war years. Luckily for the Revolution, most of the Virginian gentry supported it; the New England merchants were about equally divided, but in New York, New Jersey and Georgia the loyalists were in a majority. New York is said to have supplied 15,000 regulars to the British armies. Why then were the loyalists so ineffectual? The answer is that most of them quietly awaited the reconquest of the colonies by Britain; they sat back until it was too late to influence events. By then the threat of mob violence against them was a considerable deterrent to action.

Even after Concord, Lexington and the Battle of Bunker's Hill, the legislatures of New York, Pennsylvania, Maryland and North Carolina expressed their opposition to independence. But the radicals played their cards skilfully, and they received great help from the publication of Tom Paine's *Common Sense* in January 1776. He brushed aside all the legal and historical arguments which had previously been used. He set the Revolution in emotional terms as the struggle for independence and freedom. He resorted to wild exaggeration and misrepresentation for the purpose of discrediting England. He painted the picture of George III as a wicked tyrant. But he underlined a simple fact with great effect: the colonies had gone too far to turn back; reconciliation was no longer possible. He underlined the great spirit of idealism which was abroad in the colonies, and he converted many moderates to the cause of revolt. It was this spirit which found its expression in Thomas Jefferson's Declaration of Independence of July 4th, 1776. The form of Jefferson's argument is worth noting; he had significantly shifted the ground of complaint. The colonists had originally sought to protect their *British* rights against the encroachments of Parliament; Jefferson now claimed that they were protecting *natural* rights against the wicked George III. It was most unhistoric, but it served as an American rally-point for many years to come.

Yet the war was not popular either in America or in England. The Americans always had the greatest difficulty in raising troops, and it was rare for Washington to be in a position to take the offensive. Indeed, without his indomitable spirit it is difficult to see how the struggle could have continued. He seldom had more than 12,000 troops, and sometimes as few as 4,000. We hardly know how great a soldier he was, for he was rarely tried in battle. His great task was to keep an army in being until the British gave in. The British had a continent to conquer, the Americans had only to hold on to their homeland. Lord North's government also had great difficulty in raising large numbers of troops. In England there was a curious fatalism among politicians which made them argue either that the Americans were bound to give in shortly, or else that conquest was impossible from the start. Transport difficulties were enormous over 3,000 miles, but these were less important than the chronic failure of the British to hit upon any suitable strategy upon which the war could be fought. Perhaps the best plan would have been to have dominated the three or four most important seaports, and to have blockaded America. But too much time was wasted. The Americans at first showed a lack of public spirit which brought Washington near to despair. But the British made the mistake, not only of sending insufficient troops, but of giving the command to Sir William Howe, who was so sympathetic to the Americans that he was afraid of hitting them too hard. As one American officer wrote: "General Howe is either our friend or no general". In fact both were true. If Wolfe had not been killed at Quebec, and had been given the command in 1774, the course of history might have been different.

The early years of the war were marked by confusion, incompetence and negligence on the American side, though, thanks to French help, there was no shortage of arms and ammunition. Washington could do no more than pin Howe in Boston. Had Howe transferred his headquarters at once to New York, that state would probably have remained loyal, but he deferred the move until 1776, by which time Washington controlled the state. Howe spent his time putting out peace feelers, without really having any suitable terms to offer. Moreover, in taking New York he missed his greatest opportunity to capture Washington and his army, which would have ended the war. Even so, by 1777 Washington's army had dwindled to 4,000 men.

At last in 1777 the British Secretary at War, Lord George Germain, produced a plan. General Burgoyne had been sent to Canada in view of the attack upon Canada by Benedict Arnold in 1776. He was now to proceed with 8,000 men via Lake Champlain to the Hudson river. If he joined up with

Howe from New York, and if they could hold the Hudson river, the colonies would in effect be cut in two. So far this was a sound plan, but Germain, through sheer negligence, failed to inform Howe of all the facts, and instead of co-operating with Burgoyne, he was sent off to capture Philadelphia. This he did, but meanwhile Burgoyne, marching with a formidable amount of baggage, through miles of enemy territory, ran into difficulties, found himself surrounded, and was forced to surrender at Saratoga in October 1777. This was the decisive turning-point of the war, for it changed its whole character. Lord North never really recovered his spirit, or believed that it was now possible to conquer the Americans. In February 1778 he offered peace terms; a peace commission was sent out. (What could such a commission not have achieved in 1774!); Britain would renounce the right to tax the colonies, or to send troops there without the consent of the colonial assemblies, and all offending legislation would be repealed. If these terms had reached America in 1777 they might well have been accepted; but in February 1778 the Americans signed an alliance with France, and nothing less than independence would now be accepted.

The entry of France into the war, followed by that of Spain, in 1779, and the Dutch in 1780, together with the threat of the Armed Neutrality of the Baltic states, was the direct result of the Capitulation of Saratoga. So far the French, anxious to reverse the decision of the Treaty of Paris, and anxious also to win entry into the American market, had supplied the Americans with arms and volunteers, but they delayed open intervention until they saw an American victory in sight. With the intervention of Europe, the key to the war became sea-power. The new war found British naval power at its lowest point of strength, presided over by the most inefficient First Lord of the Admiralty, Lord Sandwich. The invasion of England now appeared imminent; Gibraltar was besieged in 1779. In fighting to prevent complete loss of the sea, Britain began to look at the American war as of secondary importance.

As early as 1776 the British had made an attempt to seize Charleston, in South Carolina, in order to link up with the large numbers of loyalists in the south, but the attempt had then failed. It was revived in 1778 when Savannah was captured; Charleston fell in 1780, and Lord Cornwallis marched inland. The ensuing battles, such as those at Cam-

den and Guilford in 1781, were fought quite as much between loyalists and patriots as between British and Americans. The Carolinas were virtually recaptured by the British,
and Cornwallis decided to prepare a new naval and military
base at Yorktown. It was the darkest hour for the Americans,
their resistance was low, and they were on bad terms with
the French. The latter could do little until they had won
command of the sea. In August 1781 Cornwallis was at
Yorktown, when the French Admiral De Grasse, who was
thought to be in the West Indies, appeared in the Chesapeake.
Washington at once seized the opportunity for concerted
action. Cornwallis found himself attacked by Washington and
fifteen thousand men from the land, and by De Grasse from
the sea. It was a brilliantly conceived plan on the part of the
Americans. On October 17th Cornwallis and some 7,000 men
surrendered.

This was virtually the end of the war, so far as the Americans were concerned. From one point of view this appears
strange, for the British still held New York, Charleston,
Savannah and some seven other points. Washington's army
was incapable of further offensive action, and Britain quickly
regained command of the sea. But Britain was concerned no
longer with retaining her colonies, but with saving her West
Indian possessions, which Rodney achieved at the Battle of
the Saintes in 1782; with defending Gibraltar, which held out
against all attacks, and with obtaining a reasonable peace
with France.

The United States owed its independence in a real sense
to the intervention of France, and the new state obtained
very favourable peace terms. By the Treaty of Versailles
(1783) the American boundaries were fixed at the St Lawrence, the Great Lakes and the Mississippi. Britain was genuinely anxious to do something for the loyalists, who were
often brutally treated by the Americans, but Lord Shelburne
could obtain no more than a meaningless promise that Congress would look after their interests. Florida was ceded to
Spain in compensation for Gibraltar. France received the
island of Tobago in the West Indies; she had the prospect of
trade with the Americans, but above all she was left with a
bankruptcy which six years later precipitated the French
Revolution.

It has sometimes been supposed that great revolutions grow
always out of great injustice and oppression, and therefore

that Mercantilism, or George Grenville, or Charles Townshend, or Lord North, or George III must have been the instruments of oppression. But, as we have seen, this was not
so. The American Revolution was fundamentally the result
of the failure of Britain to evolve a genuinely federal and
self-governing imperial system. It is sometimes said that
such an idea was "ahead of the time", but some wise contemporaries did in fact advocate it. In the absence of a suitable imperial system, the American radicals decided that they
could well do without the British connection. The Revolution
was the result, not of oppression, but of growth. Jefferson's
Declaration of Independence sought to make George III the
villain of the piece. This, too, was nonsense. George III was
responsible neither for the Stamp Act, the Townshend duties,
the Sugar Act, nor the Tea Act, but he did strongly approve
of the coercion of the colonies after 1774; he could think
of them in no other way than as rebellious subjects, and he
did prolong the war with America.

10

The British in India

"John Company"

DURING THE REIGN of Queen Elizabeth the English witnessed a great broadening of their world interests. Sir Francis Drake was a living challenge to Spanish sea-power. His great voyage round the world (1579–80) and, above all, the defeat of the Spanish Armada, created confidence in the success of overseas ventures. There emerged a fiercely mercantile spirit, and it was in this mood that the East India Company was founded in 1600, in an attempt to break into the rich Portuguese reserve of East Indian trade. The East Indies proved too difficult to penetrate, but in 1612 a factory was established in India, at Surat. A "factory" was simply a group of merchants, living together in somewhat monastic circumstances, under the protection of the local prince. By 1619 there were four such factories, all under the "President" of Surat, as well as one or two on the east coast of India. Thirty years later there were twenty-three such factories, but the number of Company employees was only ninety.

Even so, this was not achieved without fierce opposition, first from the Portuguese, and then from the Dutch. On the whole the policy of the Company was to ally with whichever was the weaker of these two, against the stronger. Thus at first there was an alliance with the Dutch against the Portuguese, and after 1623 with the Portuguese against the Dutch. The Anglo-Portuguese alliance was sealed with Charles II's marriage treaty in 1661, by which England guaranteed Portuguese possessions in the East against the Dutch, in return for the island of Bombay and Tangier. In 1668 Charles II transferred Bombay to the Company in return for a loan. Surat was proving to be a dangerous base, for it was sacked by the Marathas in 1664 and again in 1670. Gradually, therefore, it was superseded by Bombay, for, as the latter was an island, it was more easily defensible, and unlike Surat, its possession did not depend on the concession of any native prince.

The period of the Civil War in England was a time of tribulation for the East India Company, and its very survival had been in doubt. The expenses of Indian trade were high, losses at sea were heavy; it was difficult to raise capital, and the hostility of the Dutch, the most formidable sea-power in the world, brought the Company near to bankruptcy. The total annual trade of the Company was small, perhaps not more than £50,000. Its servants were ill-paid, and forced to supplement their income by private trading. In contrast, the Restoration opened a period of great prosperity for the Company, for the demand in Europe for eastern goods became insistent and highly profitable.

At first the Company traded principally in indigo, but this was soon surpassed by calicoes, for which there developed a great demand in England as an alternative to the more expensive linens. Calicoes came especially from southern India, and thus in 1641 the Company established itself at Fort St George, on the Malabar coast, at a point which they could easily fortify. For the Company was learning that they could never be safe until they had built settlements strong enough to resist the attacks of local marauders. The Company also turned its attention to Bengal, for here was to be had a valuable trade in saltpetre, essential for the manufacture of gunpowder. About 1640 a factory was established on the Hugli river, and in 1689 Job Charnock established a factory at Calcutta. Bengal also yielded a rich trade in silks, sugar, cotton and tea. Tea and coffee drinking rapidly became a habit in England after 1660, and in the reign of Queen Anne was all the rage. The Company imported tea not only from Bengal, but also in great quantities from China, and coffee from the Red Sea ports. There was also considerable trade in carpets, porcelain, lace, drugs and cotton yarn. Indeed so great was the demand for eastern goods that the Company had great difficulty in maintaining a balance of payments, for the East wished to buy less of the Company's exports of tin, lead, broadcloth, trinkets, coral ivory and manufactures than England wished to buy from the east. This imbalance of payments helps to explain the importance of the Chinese trade, for not only was China tea in great demand in England, but soon the Company learnt that it could pay for much of it with opium, grown in Bengal, instead of with precious bullion from England.

The great prosperity of the Company (it paid a dividend of fifty per cent. in 1682), and its charter of monopoly, was bound to arouse much jealousy in England. This was intensified after 1681 when the masterful Sir Josiah Child became virtual dictator of the Company. Ruthless with his enemies, he also played high politics, winning the favour of Charles II and James II by the most effective means of advancing them money. Thus the Company took on a tory complexion, and had to pay the price after the Revolution of 1688 when the whig merchants attempted to break its monopoly. Important issues were involved, for while on the one hand the Company had been too exclusive, yet it was doubtful whether the cost of maintaining and defending the eastern factories could be borne by any Company which did not possess a trade monopoly. There was also a constitutional issue involved. For the Company's charter, like seventeenth-century colonial charters, was granted under the royal prerogative. When, therefore, Parliament declared (1693–4) that it was forfeit, and that "all the subjects of England have equal right to trade to the East Indies, unless prohibited by Act of Parliament", it was in fact staking claims which amounted to an invasion of the royal prerogative. But after 1688 the Crown did not seriously contest this parliamentary encroachment, and here we have one of the most important ways in which Parliament extended its authority during the eighteenth century. Thus in 1698 a New East India Company was formed by Act of Parliament, but it found it impossible to oust the old, and in 1709, following the arbitration of Godolphin, the two Companies merged. There then followed a period of steady development and prosperity for the Company. In forty years its trade doubled, increasing from £ 1,-000,000 to £2,000,000. It paid rates of interest between five per cent. and ten per cent. Most of the Company's directors and servants desired only peaceful trade; but the circum-

stances in India were being rapidly transformed, and they entailed a revolution in the activities of the Company.

In the sixteenth century there had arisen in India the
great Mahommedan Empire of the Moguls, and Akbar the
Great, the contemporary of Queen Elizabeth of England,
had brought that Empire to its peak of power. But not even
he had been able to establish a firm mastery of southern
India, and under his successors decay set in. Akbar, himself
a Mahommedan, had wisely extended toleration to his
Hindu subjects, but this was not the policy of his successors.
The Emperor Aurangzib, third in succession from Akbar, ruled
disastrously for fifty years, pursued a policy of aggression
and persecution, and died in 1707, leaving his Empire
in ruins. His persecution gave rise to a great Hindu revival, and, about the time of Cromwell, there arose the power
of the Mahrattas under their great leader Siraji. Under their
hammerings the power of the Mogul crumbled. In the south
one of their number became Rajah of Tangore, another seized
Orissa; the Mogul was often at their mercy. As the emperors
ceased to wield effective power for long periods, their viziers,
or ministers, began to set themselves up as virtually independent rulers. Such was the Nizam of Hyderabad; another
was the Nawab of Oudh. Thus India drifted into chaos. It
is sometimes said that the arrival of the European powers
hastened this disintegration, but this is not to see the situation in perspective. The Europeans were unable to do more
than touch the mere fringe of Indian life until internal decay
gave them an opportunity for interference. Often that interference was reluctant, and made necessary by the political
confusion of the time. The English were eager for trade, but,
at least until the time of Clive, very reluctant to be drawn
into Indian affairs.

From time to time the Company had been drawn into
wars. Thus in the 1680s Job Charnock in Bengal was at war
with the Emperor Aurangzib over the question of the payment of customs, and he was forced to abandon the factory
at Hugli and withdraw from Bengal. Peace was made in
1690, and the English were allowed to return. This time they
built a fortified factory which became Calcutta. When the
Emperor's power was effective, therefore, the Company
could still be made to feel that it existed on sufferance. Still,
the Company was useful to the native ruler; its trade was
valuable, and in Calcutta or Madras the Company acted as

"zemindar" or magistrate of the city. It was easy therefore
for the Company to feel that they were too important to the
Nawab for him to wish to expel them. Defences therefore in
the first half of the eighteenth century were often utterly
neglected on the landward side, what precautions there were
being taken only to seawards against pirates and the rival
European companies.

Even by 1740 it would hardly be possible to argue that
the English had done more than touch the fringe of Indian
life, yet already the situation was very different from what it
had been a century earlier. Then a few traders had been
allowed to remain on sufferance. In 1740, on the other hand,
there were three great Presidencies, at Bombay, Madras and
Calcutta. The governors lived in regal state, with a military
force and perhaps a fleet, with their own judges and a mint.
Perhaps the total number of Britons involved was not more
than a couple of thousand; the official servants of the Company were certainly many fewer. They were mainly concerned with trade, but already they had much experience of
native politics, diplomacy and war. Calcutta was the largest.
The "white town" covered only about a quarter of a square
mile, but beyond, the "black town" contained perhaps 200,-
000 people. Its fortifications stretched for three miles; its
wharves were piled with the tea, rice, silks, muslins and cottons awaiting shipment; while farther inland there were the
comfortable houses and gardens of the European inhabitants.
Bombay numbered perhaps 100,000 inhabitants, and Madras
about 30,000. Some of the Company's servants made fortunes for themselves, but many did not. And the risks were
great. For sanitation was almost non-existent, water was pol-
luted, and British subjects died in great numbers in the heat,
at a time when medical knowledge did more to hinder than to
help the problem of human survival. Nature saw to it that
the men who first established British power in India were
young men.

The Anglo-French Conflict

The dividing line between the early period of dependence,
and the later period leading to European independence and
dominance in India, may well be said to be the period of the
War of the Austrian Succession. The man who saw the issues
of the future most clearly was the French Governor of

Pondicherry in 1742, Dupleix. He saw that, sooner or later, an Anglo-French struggle would end in the expulsion of one or the other from India. He saw also that the character of the East India Companies must necessarily change as they took on greater military responsibilities. Trade alone could not be expected to pay the bill, nor provide the bases and manpower necessary for war. The burden must in some way be passed to the soil, and that meant the Company's control of some large area of land. It would require also, though Dupleix perhaps did not sufficiently realise it, control of the seas. But Dupleix's plans would only frighten his masters in France, so he kept them to himself; and thus began the mis-understandings and mistrust between the French East India Company and himself, which were to be a principal cause of his failure.

War between England and France was declared in 1744. Dupleix waited until a small squadron arrived from the French base in Mauritius. At this the pusillanimous Captain Peyton, commanding an English squadron, sailed for safety to Bengal. The French then attacked Madras with a feeble land and sea force. There was little spirit in the English de-fence, and after six days the town surrendered, and was plundered by the French. Thus was established one of the most important principles of warfare in this period, the all-importance of sea-power. Madras had fallen easily to a com-bined attack by land and sea. But the subsequent French attack on Fort St David failed, because by then the French squadron had sailed away. On the other hand, sea-power alone was not sufficient, for when, in 1747, the English Admiral Boscawen made an unskilful attack on Pondicherry, the main French settlement, it was a complete failure. In the following year, by the Treaty of Aix-la-Chapelle, Madras was handed back to the English in return for Louisbourg. Dupleix was bitterly disappointed. But the war had not been futile in India. The Anglo-French issue was now clearly stated. A new situation had emerged. Before 1744, in theory at least, both the English and the French companies existed in the Carnatic under the protection of the Nawab. But the Nawab, in spite of a faint pro-English feeling, had been quite unable to prevent the French attack on Madras, or to prevent its fall. The Europeans learnt that they could now control events in the Carnatic, that they had little to fear from the native rulers. It was a short step, and one Dupleix was ready to take, to make the native princes pawns in the great struggle.

Dupleix sought for a great land base for French power. In 1748 there was a disputed succession to the throne of the Nizam of Hyderabad. Dupleix backed the successful candidate with military force, and for his services was rewarded by being appointed governor of all southern India. In the Carnatic he deposed the pro-English Nawab Anwar-ud-Din, and set his own candidate, Chanda Sahib, in his place. As the Nawab of the Carnatic was in theory merely the deputy for the Nizam of Hyderabad, he was now merely the subordinate of Dupleix. One point alone held out against the triumphant Frenchman. Anwar-ud-Din had been killed, but his son, Mahommed Ali, now the English candidate for the throne of the Nawab of the Carnatic, had taken refuge in Trichinopoly, where he was besieged by Chanda Sahib. If Trichinopoly fell it would be the turn of the British next, and they could hardly save themselves from being pushed into the sea. Only a desperate remedy could save them. This was the view of the young Robert Clive.

Clive was born in 1725, the son of a Shropshire lawyer and small landowner. He was a turbulent and passionate youth, and his family were relieved to pack him off to India, at the age of eighteen, as a writer in the East India Company. He was desperately unhappy in the work, and twice attempted to commit suicide. He was captured by the French at Madras in 1746, escaped disguised as a Moslem, and then found his true vocation by taking an ensign's commission in the Company's army. In 1751, with the rank of Captain, he produced a desperate plan which alone could save Trichinopoly. It was for a diversionary raid on the Nawab's capital at Arcot. The plan was accepted, and he was appointed to the command. Thus it was that with perhaps 500 sepoys and 300 Europeans he seized the town, the garrison of some 5,000 fleeing in panic. They returned later to besiege the town, and Clive held out for fifty-three days against them. When they withdrew, he pursued and beat them at Kaveripak. It was the turning-point in the Anglo-French struggle. In 1752 Trichinopoly was relieved, some 800 Frenchmen were captured, and Chanda Sahib was executed. The French had overreached themselves. The Marquis de Bussy was still a power at Hyderabad, but in 1752 he was busy repelling a Maratha invasion. Moreover, the French

East India Company were thoroughly alarmed at the extent of French commitments in India. They did not see Dupleix's plans as the condition for continued power in India, but only as expensive and dangerous. In 1754 Dupleix was recalled to France. Thus, when the Seven Years' War began, the greatest French visionary had already left India.

If the French East India Company had not understood what Dupleix was about, Clive did; his own later approach to Indian affairs was essentially that of Dupleix. Dupleix had sought to make the Deccan the basis of French power; Clive was to make Bengal the basis of British power. The opportunity was presented in 1756 by the vicious, irresponsible but highly intelligent Nawab of Bengal, Siraj-ud-Daula. He had observed the affairs of the Carnatic closely, and had seen how the alliance between a Nawab and a European power had ended in the dominance of the latter. He determined that it should not happen in Bengal. He was prepared to tolerate simple trade, but he watched with alarm the strengthening of the fortifications of Calcutta, though they were only on the sea-ward side, against the French. The Company did not seriously expect trouble from the Nawab, for they thought their trade and revenues were too important to him. In June 1756, therefore, when the Nawab suddenly attacked, he found feeble defences and a poor garrison. The garrison held out long enough for the women and children to escape by sea, and then surrendered. They were thrown into the military prison known as the "Black Hole", some 146 people in a room 18 feet by 14 feet 10 inches; in the morning there were twenty-three survivors; the others had succumbed to the heat, thirst and madness.

Madras was at first reluctant to weaken itself by sending a force to Bengal, but in October 1756 agreed to spare Clive 800 Europeans and 1,000 sepoys for a punitive campaign. Clive reoccupied Calcutta in January 1757. The Nawab was so alarmed that he signed a hasty peace, confirming English privileges in Calcutta, and restoring the plunder, of which indeed he had found disappointingly little. Clive and Admiral Watson, who commanded the squadron, did not abandon the idea of punishing Siraj-ud-Daula, but, for the moment, there were other things to do, and so they agreed to a deceptive peace. The French were too involved in the Deccan to interfere in strength in Bengal, and in March 1757, with the consent of the Nawab, the British captured Chandernagore, thus depriving him of his natural ally against the British. Then Clive entered into a conspiracy with Siraj-ud-Daula's enemies at Court. In June an alliance was signed with Mir Jafar; he risked little: he was to remain neutral until the Nawab was effectively defeated, and then he would declare his treachery and become the new Nawab. Thus it was that on June 23rd, 1757, Clive, with 800 Europeans and some 2,000 sepoys, attacked Siraj-ud-Daula and some 50,000 native troops at Plassey. Mir Jafar, commanding the Nawab's right wing, remained inactive. The Nawab was routed, captured and executed, and Mir Jafar reigned in his stead. The British were now the power behind the throne, and were soon to be the only effective power in Bengal.

The whole campaign was well described by Clive as a mixture of "fighting, tricks, chicanery, intrigues, politics and the Lord knows what". The matter of broken treaties and broken faith troubled Clive little; this was the way native princes treated each other, this was the language they understood. In other respects Clive had proved himself a heaven-born fighter, with the dash, decision and sureness of touch of a great leader. The new Nawab appointed the Company "zemindar", or magistrate and tax-gatherer, over some 800 square miles of territory. Clive received a personal gift of some £240,000, and in addition, two years later, the "jagir" by which the rent which the Company would ordinarily pay to the Nawab would be paid personally to Clive.[1] The Company thus virtually became the tenants of Clive in Bengal! In all perhaps £3,000,000 passed to the Company or to private persons as a result of the Battle of Plassey. Clive, starting with nothing, had, at the age of thirty-two, become one of the richest of the King's subjects. He at once wrote home to his old father asking him to secure him a seat in Parliament in the Duke of Newcastle's interest. So much wealth and so much power could not be acquired without grave risks and the making of many enemies. War had been made to pay. The idea spread among the Company's servants that India was a vast continent of unimaginable wealth, theirs for the taking. All this was to have an unfortunate result later.

But from the point of view of the Anglo-French struggle,

[1] It amounted to some £30,000 a year.

the conquest of Bengal was of the first importance. It provided the British with the base and the resources with which to complete the defeat of the French. If the French had established themselves as securely in the Deccan, they would have been in a similar position.

In fact, the French under Bussy continued in the Deccan until 1758. In that year the Comte de Lally, sent out by the French to drive the English out of India, captured Fort St David, and summoned Bussy from Hyderabad to aid in the siege of Madras. But his naval force under d'Aché was defeated by the English under Pocock. Thus, in December 1758, Lally at length attacked Madras, with greatly superior land forces, but without naval aid. The English Governor Pigot held out stoutly until February 1759, when Lally abandoned the siege. In the previous year he had been equally unsuccessful in an attack on Tanjore, and the combined failure was a shock to his prestige. In September 1759 the French fleet under d'Aché returned, and was at once attacked by Admiral Pocock. Both sides lost heavily, but the French eventually fled to Pondicherry. The British thus re-established the command of the sea they were not again to lose in this war. In the following month British reinforcements arrived under Eyre Coote, and in January 1760 Coote routed the French under Lally at the Battle of Wandiwash, and Bussy, the hero of the Deccan, was captured. It was the last pitched battle of the war. By April the French were effectively reduced to Pondicherry, which was then besieged by Coote. Lally resisted bravely, though he was on the worst of terms with the Company, and the garrison was desperate for supplies. When it surrendered in January 1761 the French had lost their last place in the Carnatic. In 1759 Clive had sent Colonel Forde to take over the Northern Circars, and thus, by the end of the war, the British were in control of the whole eastern coast of India, except for Orissa.

The reasons for the British triumph over the French in India may be summarised as follows. The British had established command of the sea, and without that the French could not hope to succeed. Lally in fact usually had more men than the British in the Carnatic, but they were often ill-equipped and supplied, and without sea-power his attack on Madras failed. The second reason was the master-stroke of the conquest of Bengal. Henceforth the British had a base supplying money and materials for the war in the Carnatic, while the French could be supplied only from overseas. Unless the French could dislodge the British from Bengal they were bound in the end to be defeated, but they could not even begin to threaten Bengal until they were masters of the Carnatic. Thus, after 1757 the French were doing no more than attacking the outer defences of the British in India. And the conquest of Bengal, begun even before the news of the outbreak of the Seven Years' War, was the result of the genius of Robert Clive. He was a ruthless and determined man, with an unerring judgment in strategy and in the field. Lally was personally a brave man, but he lacked the qualities of Clive.

A Time of Trouble

By 1761 French power in India was broken. British power was now great and unchallenged, but the problems presented by the new position in which they found themselves were enormous, and dominated the history of the next twenty years.

There was indeed utter confusion in the Company and among its servants. For a private trading company now found itself, as the result of war, a leading power in the Indian continent. But this involved responsibilities which the Company was not anxious, nor indeed fitted, to undertake. Their position was anomalous. They were no longer merely traders. They were the zemindar or diwan [2] for the Nawab over great areas of territory. The prime function was to collect taxes in the form of rents, but this also entailed police and judicial functions. Of course, these functions would still be performed by natives, but the supervisory responsibility would rest with the Company. This would be a formidable task at any time. Native customs and law were remote from British experience, and even the most zealous servant of the Company might unwittingly do great harm. Moreover they were few in number, and ill-paid. Clive had set an appalling example in the enormous wealth he had extorted from India, and there were many who wished to follow his example. For instance, the Company's trading privileges applied only to goods imported from, or to be exported to, Europe; they did not extent to "inland trade" in consumer goods in Bengal. But the Company's servants engaged in it all the same. For

---

[2] i.e. magistrate or tax-gatherer.

them life was dangerous and hard, and without the prospects of handsome profit would have been intolerable.

Once interference in native politics had begun, it was difficult to limit it, for the rulers themselves were often intolerable, alternately indolent and sadistically cruel. Nor is it surprising if Nawabs soon felt that since both the power and responsibilities of government were the Company's, there was little for them to do but to abandon themselves to a luxurious insignificance.

Clive had his own solution to the Indian problem. He stood squarely for the extension of British power. He thought that the British government should declare its sovereignty over the occupied areas, and he alarmed the Company by vowing that with 2,000 Europeans he could conquer all India. He saw India as the source of unlimited wealth. He was contemptuous of the natives, Hindu and Moslem alike; he thought them all "indolent, luxurious, ignorant and cowardly"; they could be ruled only by force. But all this was anathema to the Company. They wrote to him: "You seem so thoroughly possessed with military ideas as to forget your employers are merchants." They bitterly resented having to pay him the jagir of £30,000 a year. When Clive returned to England, he sought to use his wealth to capture the Company. A great struggle developed between him and Laurence Sulivan for control, and in the 1760s Company affairs, both in England and in India, were rent by the pro-Clive and the pro-Sulivan factions.

Clive's blatant attempts to capture the Company, and his crude use of wealth to bludgeon his way into British politics, were, more than anything else, responsible for making Indian affairs an issue in British politics in the period between 1763 and 1784. Clive stood for an extension of British power in India. Sulivan also loved power, but his real desire was for peace and reform. Clive entered Parliament for Shrewsbury in 1761, in the Newcastle interest. By 1768 he had his own parliamentary group of seven. As he supported Newcastle, Sulivan supported Bute. In 1763 Clive supported George Grenville, so Sulivan supported the Rockinghams. Thus Indian affairs became a pawn in the great game of British politics.

By 1764 the situation in India had become very serious. In Bengal Mir Jafar had been accounted a doubtful friend, and after some atrocious murders, he had been deposed in

October 1760 in favour of Mir Kasim. Those who supported
the latter received enormous gifts, and thus the deposition
of a Nawab became a profitable business. But even Mir
Kasim was unable to close his eyes entirely to the gross
abuses perpetrated by the Company's servants in indulging
in "inland trade". When he attempted to curb it he was declared deposed, and Mir Jafar was restored. At this Mir
Kasim massacred fifty British hostages, and fled to the
Emperor. War followed, in which the Emperor and the
Nawab of Oudh supported Mir Kasim. They were defeated by
Hector Munro at the Battle of Buxar (October 1764). Mir
Jafar was restored as Nawab, and forced to grant the right
of "inland trade". The Company had triumphed, but the rottenness of the system was apparent, not only to men on the
spot, such as the young Warren Hastings, who disapproved
of the treatment of Mir Kasim, but also to some of the Directors at home. In 1765 Clive was again sent to India to find
some order in the chaos; as he himself put it, "the Augean
stable there is to be cleaned".

If reform was all that was needed, he was indeed quite the
wrong man to send, for Clive was bent, above all things,
upon the extension of British power, not its reform. He made
peace with the Emperor and with Oudh. In Oudh he placed
a British puppet on the throne as Nawab, and henceforth
Oudh was a peaceful ally of the British. He ceded Allahabad
to the Emperor, and in return was granted the diwanni of
Bengal. This gave the Company the complete control of the
finances of the province. It is true that the Nawab continued
to be formally responsible, but all effective power rested with
the Company. The arrangement meant that the Company
could control all that really concerned it, in particular the
finances, while it left other matters to the Nawab's ministers.
Clive did frown on the practice of receiving "presents" on
the part of servants of the Company, a practice he had done
so much to initiate by his example. But the central problem
of "inland trading" he left untouched. Clive left India two
years later, the richer himself by some £200,000, to continue the political battle in England, and the real problem
of reform was left unsolved.

Nowhere was the rottenness and incompetence of the system seen in a worse light than in Madras, where the government was plagued by the greed of scoundrels such as Paul
Benfield and John Macpherson. In 1765, as part of his peace

settlement, Clive had freed the Nawab of the Carnatic from dependence on the Nizam. But at this time a big military power was arising in Mysore under the leadership of Hyder Ali, a soldier of fortune. In 1766 Madras was foolish enough to engage in war with him, and in 1768 Hyder Ali was raiding up to the gates of Madras. Meanwhile almost every member of the Company was engaged in lending money to the Nawab at ruinous rates of interest, and urging him on to war in which they saw profits for themselves. The great need of the time was, therefore, an internal reform of the Company, and the subordination of Bombay and Madras to an overriding authority in Bengal. In 1772 Warren Hastings was appointed Governor of Bengal, and the great work of reform was begun.

Warren Hastings and Reform

Warren Hastings, born 1732, was the son of a clergyman. The family was an old one, and had once owned Daylesford Manor, but had fallen on evil days. In 1750, at the age of seventeen, he went out to Calcutta as a writer in the East India Company. He built up an unrivalled knowledge of the native mind by much experience of inland trade. All his life he retained great respect for the Indian character, and for the gentleness of the Hindu. In 1772, as the favourite of Laurence Sulivan, he was appointed Governor of Bengal. It was an excellent choice. Warren Hastings was one of the greatest administrators in the history of British India, and he was now at the height of his powers. The conditions he found in Bengal were enough to daunt the stoutest heart. The government was in the utmost confusion. A great famine had swept the land, and a million people had died. The government of the Nawab was corrupt and inefficient; the Company servants were too often sunk in private trade and corruption; trade was bad, and the Nawab was heavily in debt to the Company.

Hastings decided to bring all aspects of government under the control of the British. The Nawab was gradually relegated to the position of a figurehead. His deputy, Mahomed Reza Khan, was dismissed, and not replaced. Then Hastings turned to the central problem of the revenue. The welfare of the state, and the very continuance of the Company in India, depended on the ability of the Company to remain solvent and to be able to pay for its ever-growing armies. Hastings took the view that it was impossible for the British to go into the districts of Bengal personally to collect the revenue. The land tenure was complicated, they would always be at the mercy of the local zemindars and assessors ("kanungoes"), while the temptation to be corrupt was too great. He determined, therefore, to leave the collection of revenues solely to the native zemindars, and to have them responsible to the Company's collectors. The latter he wished to be centralised in Calcutta, but as an interim measure he set up six Provincial Councils. The amount required from each zemindar was settled beforehand; what he collected over and above this sum was his own. As part of his centralising policy, and to emphasise the new control of the Company, the seat of government was shifted from Murchidabad to Calcutta.

Judicial organisation was always closely linked with that of the revenue, for revenue officers in India had always to exercise a measure of judicial power in deciding assessments and disputes. But the law was in the utmost confusion. The Moguls had imposed a Moslem law on a Hindu people, but with the decay of the Imperial power the Courts had tended to lose their authority. Hastings' plan was to leave criminal jurisdiction to the native courts, but to set up district courts under the revenue collectors for the settlement of civil disputes. A Civil and a Criminal Court of Appeal were established in Calcutta. Hastings was anxious that native law should remain untouched. He wished to stamp out lawlessness and profiteering, but he did not wish to break up the essential pattern of native life. He never spoke contemptuously of their character and customs, as Clive often did. He did, however, seek severer penalties for dacoity [3] than Moslem law allowed.

He knew that dacoity was the result of extreme poverty. He sought to increase prosperity by reform of the customs. He introduced a postal service, he reformed the currency. He forbade the Company's servants to engage in inland trade. By administrative economies he saved annually some fifty lakhs of rupees. Much remained to be done, but in two years Hastings brought order into extreme chaos. The eyes of the whole province were turned on Calcutta; the Company

[3] Brigandage, which was rife in Bengal.

was now the real ruler of Bengal. Hastings lived in great magnificence in a fine house at Alipur, for in addition to his salary, he made great profits from private trade, especially in opium with China. His powers of work were enormous; he radiated supreme confidence in himself. Not yet had his character been hardened by the worry and bitterness which later years were to bring.

With the government of Bengal in good hands, two great problems remained; the first was the relationship between the Company and the British government, and the second was the relationship between the Bengal government and the other presidencies in India. At no time in the history of British India were Indian affairs so constantly before British politicians as in the period between 1772 and 1784. For the problem was an intricate one. A company which had begun as a commercial venture had become the virtual ruler of an Indian Empire. There was then a sense of responsibility in England that this great power should be well used. But with this honourable motive there was a much less honourable one. India now presented a vast field for patronage, and patronage was a well-known aspect of political power. The political groups, the Grenvilles, the Rockinghams, the Chathamites, could not be indifferent to so important a political factor. This is not to say that all politicians were anxious for an extension of British power in India. Clive, Beckford, Colonel Barré and General Burgoyne thought that the Crown should take over the Indian conquests, but most politicians were reluctant to see so much additional power pass to the hands of the British government. But most agreed that some reform of the system was urgently needed. The unstable governments of the 1760s were unfitted to deal with so prickly a problem, but when Lord North established a firm government in 1770 it became practical politics.

In 1772 the Company had to apply to the government for a loan of a million pounds. Feeling against the Company ran high; Lord Chatham wrote: "India teems with iniquities so rank as to smell to earth and heaven." Burke, on the other hand, feared the extension of the government's power over the Company. Lord North's Regulating Act of 1773 was then a compromise. It appointed a Governor-General of Bengal at a salary of £ 25,000 a year. He was to govern with the aid of four councillors, with whom he held the casting vote. It set up a Supreme Court in Bengal. The taking of presents and "inland" trade were forbidden. The Treasury or a secretary of state had the right to see policy statements from India. Warren Hastings was named in the Act as the first Governor-General.

As it turned out, the new machinery was full of faults which had to be corrected by later legislation. Thus Hastings had no overriding power if he disagreed with his Council; nor did the other Presidencies submit readily to the supremacy of Bengal. The Act was thus the source of many of Hastings' later troubles. In fairness, we must remember the novelty of the situation. The authors of the Regulating Act were attempting to meet a situation entirely new in our history. Similarly Hastings was being asked to wield a power in India such as no pro-consul had ever had to wield in our history before. In India the problems were of the greatest difficulty, and at home he had to battle against a mass of ignorance, misunderstanding, faction and selfishness, such as is without precedent in the history of the Empire. For the next twelve years, amidst the confusion of Indian affairs, amidst its turmoils and dangers, there remained one clear beacon of light, the resolution and vision of Warren Hastings.

When Hastings went to Bengal in 1772 the greatest danger in India was from the Mahrattas. The power of the Mogul Emperor at Delhi had been reduced to a shadow. In 1771 the Mahrattas had taken Delhi, and ravaged up to the borders of Oudh. Afghans, Sikhs and Rohillas, as well as Mahrattas, were all engaged in tearing the Empire to pieces. If the Mahrattas attacked Oudh, the Company would have to go to the aid of its ally. Oudh was aware of the danger, and sought permission of the Company to conquer Rohilkund, lest it should fall to the Mahrattas. Hastings agreed, for if successful the war would strengthen Oudh without cost to the Company. Thus in 1774 the Nawab of Oudh, Shuja-ud-Daula, an old friend of the Company, conquered the Rohillas. This aggression was later held against Hastings, because Burke and his friends completely misunderstood the situation. They were ridiculously lyrical about the nobility of the Rohillas; in fact they were Pathan conquerors from Kandahar, who oppressed their Hindu subjects, and the latter were glad to be rid of them. As to the barbarities of the war, these were not Hastings' responsibility. He seized the opportunity of the war to renounce the annual payment of £325,000 a year to the

Mogul, due from the diwan of Bengal, on the grounds that the Mogul was now the prisoner of the Mahrattas, which was true.

In 1774 Hastings received his new Council under the Regulating Act. One, Barwell, was an old servant of the Company; the other three were political appointments. General Clavering was a King's Friend; Colonel Monson had seen active service in India; no one knows why Philip Francis was appointed. From their arrival in India conflict with Hastings began. Barwell usually supported him, but the others gave him constant trouble. Francis hated India, and thought it riddled with corruption. He approached every problem with a naïvety which sprang usually from an ignorance of the real facts. So quarrels in Council grew. Both Clavering and Barwell, and Hastings and Francis, fought duels. These dissensions were closely followed by native politicians and one of them, Nuncumar, saw fit to take a hand. In March 1775 he laid before the Council accusations of corruption against Hastings himself. Hastings refused to be present, but the three decided to hear them. They saw in them an opportunity of breaking Hastings' power. The evidence was obvious forgery, but the damage had been done. Everyone in the bazaar knew that the Governor had been accused before his own Council. Two months later Nuncumar was arrested and charged with forgery, and hanged. This was the second charge laid later against Hastings, that he had instigated a judicial murder against one who had dared accuse him. It is not worth pursuing the question far. Nuncumar's charges against Hastings were false; Nuncumar, on the other hand, was indisputably guilty of forgery. But his real fault had been to challenge the Governor-General. Every native understood that the prestige of the latter required the head of Nuncumar. Such were the circumstances of Eastern politics. Hastings indeed swore that he neither instigated nor influenced the trial, and that may well be true. He had only to allow the law to take its course.

The three did nothing to save Nuncumar, but they made full use of the incident to discredit Hastings in England, once Nuncumar was dead. They insisted on holding long investigations into the Rohilla war and relations with Oudh, before their arrival in India. Hastings wrote that: "the Board is occupied in collecting proofs of my demerit, and of the virtue of my adversaries". Francis disagreed strongly with Hastings over the revenue settlement. In the almost entire absence of statistics, the revenue assessments had to be largely guesswork, and Hastings admitted that in some instances they were too high. Francis wanted the assessment to be fixed in perpetuity, and the zemindars treated simply as landowners, on the analogy of the squires of England. To this Hastings was strongly opposed, as being entirely contrary to history or justice. Behind the dispute there was a fundamental conflict between the two men. Hastings respected Indian life and customs, and wished to preserve them; Francis despised them, and doubted even whether the British should have entered India at all. Francis hated Hastings, and enjoyed harassing him; on one occasion he wrote triumphantly that he had exasperated Hastings "to a degree of madness". He hoped one day to replace Hastings as Governor-General. Before long the whole service in India tended to be divided into pro-Hastings and pro-Francis factions. In England Francis had the best of the struggle; Hastings' friends were few and unreliable. In 1776 the directors of the Company voted for his recall, though the proprietors reversed the decision by a large majority. The onset of the American war, and the war with France, shelved the question of his replacement. By that time Hastings was engaged in the Mahratta war.

In 1775 the Bombay Presidency rashly took sides in a disputed Mahratta succession, and backed one Raghoba as Peshwa. But the Bengal government frowned on this interference, and required Bombay to desist. But in 1777 a French agent arrived in Poona, the Mahratta capital, and Hastings at once scented danger. He judged that a thousand Europeans, in alliance with the Mahrattas, could drive the British out of India. When, therefore, the Mahrattas renewed their request to Bombay, Hastings took a different view, and troops and ten lakhs of rupees were sent to Bombay. The Mahratta war was one of the charges made against Hastings later. Whether the war was justified turns, not on the issue of Mahratta politics, for the support of Raghoba proved to be ill-advised, but on whether the threat from France was real, and whether British prestige at that moment required an assertion of power to prevent a massing of Mahratta power against it. Hastings held that it did. Francis, on the other hand, was unalterably opposed to intervention in Mahratta politics, and greatly feared a general war. Hastings, with his profound knowledge of the Indian mind, may well have been right, for the best way of dealing with the Mahrattas was to keep them divided, but one must admit that there was, on the face of it, something to be said for Francis' point of view. The Company would have been in a stronger position to meet the real threat from Mysore if it had been unencumbered with the Mahratta War.

In 1778 the Bombay government attacked the Mahrattas before the arrival of the reinforcements from Bengal. They at once ran into difficulties and were forced to sign a disgraceful surrender, which Hastings immediately repudiated. In 1780 the reinforcements under Goddard overran Gujarat, but Hastings' masterpiece was a surprise attack from the east on the great fortress of Gwalior, whose ruler, Sindhia, had been fighting in the west. Sindhia developed a great admiration for Hastings, made peace, and eventually, in 1782, was instrumental in negotiating a general peace between the Company and the Mahrattas on the basis of the *status quo* (Treaty of Salbai). It was disagreement over Popham's expedition against Gwalior which led to the duel between Hastings and Francis, in which Francis was slightly wounded. In December 1780 he sailed for England, to continue his feud with Hastings among the English politicians. The capture of Gwalior decided the war.

Meanwhile, the entire situation had been transformed by the American and French wars. At once the command of the sea was threatened. The Company's ships had to run the gauntlet of Ceylon, Mauritius and the Cape (for the Dutch entered the war), and sustenance from England was extremely unlikely. Hastings had to make do with his own resources. In July 1780, in alliance with the French, Hyder Ali of Mysore and 80,000 men invaded the Carnatic, annihilated a force under Colonel Baillie, and devastated the land from end to end. The whole of India reacted rapidly to this set-back, for British strength depended on British prestige, and this had been severely shaken. The Nizam of Hyderabad became hostile, Chait Singh of Benares refused his war contribution, and so on. If the French fleet had driven home its advantage, it would have gone ill indeed with the British. But they did nothing until 1782, when Suffrein landed 3,000 French near Pondicherry, cut off food supplies from Bengal to Madras, and defeated Hughes in a series of naval engagements. Sir Eyre Coote campaigned bravely in the Carnatic until he was a broken invalid in September 1782 (he died in 1783). In 1783 the British were facing disaster, when the news arrived from Europe that peace had been signed between Britain and France. Mysore made peace in the following year. The war had been one of atrocity; British troops were hideously treated by Hyder Ali.

During the war Hastings was driven to desperation to raise the money to pay for the war. In these circumstances he demanded extra contributions from Chait Singh of Benares. The latter was zemindar for the Company, and not, as Burke later tried to make him, an independent prince. His usual contribution was twenty-two and a half lakhs of rupees; during the war Hastings asked for an additional five. There was nothing unusual in this; according to Moslem custom an overlord could ask for extra help when in need. Chait Singh paid at first reluctantly, then not at all, when he thought the Company's power was failing. When in 1781 Hastings attempted to arrest him, his troops inflicted serious losses on a British force. Hastings then brought up further forces, deposed him, and replaced him by a boy Rajah. If Hastings had shown weakness in 1781 it would have gone hard with the Company. Burke absurdly misinterpreted the incident later, as he did also with the affair of the Begums of Oudh. The mother and grandmother (the Begums) of the Nawab of Oudh had held on to the hoarded wealth of the previous Nawab, to which they were not in the least entitled, while the Nawab was heavily in debt to the Company. In 1782 Hasting demanded the surrender of the treasure, and eventually extorted from them one hundred and five lakhs of rupees, or over a million pounds, which were used to pay the Nawab's debts. The Nawab was entirely agreeable, the ladies in no way harmed, and they bore Hastings no grudge; indeed at the time of his trial they wrote him letters of gratitude, for they saw him as the protector of a weak and foolish Nawab. The whigs were to surpass themselves with exaggeration and misunderstanding of such issues as Nuncumar, the Rohilla War, Chait Singh and the Begums of Oudh. But these issues are for the most part trivial compared with the great services of Hastings in saving British power in India in the hour of greatest need. An alliance between the French, the Mahrattas and Mysore would have been disastrous for British power in India; the loss of command of the sea brought disaster within sight. The Company's troops fought with great bravery, but the burden of responsibility lay almost solely with Hastings. It was a heroic struggle, and Hastings was a man cast in a heroic mould.

After 1780, however, the opposition to Hastings in England grew louder and more insistent. It would be wrong to ascribe this merely to Francis and his bitter tongue. There was a long-standing feeling that things were seriously wrong with the Indian government. The subject had been constantly discussed, but thrust aside by the American war. But Burke was hot for a moral cause, and with the fall of Lord North's government in 1782, the issue could no longer be postponed. Dundas attempted a Bill in 1783, but it failed. Fox attempted his Bill in 1783. He sought to place the control of Indian affairs in the hands of seven commissioners. But he made grave errors of judgment. He did nothing to win over the Company, and he did nothing to allay the fears that his real purpose was to put vast new powers of patronage into his government's hands. In the debates Burke called the Company "one of the most corrupt and destructive tyrannies that probably ever existed in the world". But the Bill was defeated, not only by the intervention of George III, but by the tremendous unpopularity of the Coalition. Grenville, in opposing the Bill, said that its purpose was "no less than to erect a despotic system which might crush the free constitution of England". Pitt learnt the lesson, and his Act of 1784 established a Board of Control of six Commissioners consisting partly of members of the government and partly of privy councillors nominated by the King. In India the powers of the Governor-General was strengthened. In a masterly fashion Pitt linked the government of India with the British government, without increasing the latter's powers of patronage. Even Burke called the Act "as able and skilful a performance as ever issued from the wit of man". It laid down the pattern of government relations with India until 1858.

Pitt had referred to Hastings as "a very great and indeed a wonderful man", but he was critical of his administration. To Hastings it filled his cup of bitterness. In February 1785 he set sail for England. His great task was fulfilled. He had given Bengal the beginnings of a sound administration, he had saved the Company from bankruptcy, and placed it on a sound financial foundation, above all he had saved the whole British position in India in its hour of greatest peril. He came home, however, not to receive the nation's thanks, but to stand trial for his deeds.

11

George III and the Whigs

George III and Bute

THERE ARE FEW decisive breaks in English history, and 1760 is not one of them. Yet it must be admitted that the period which followed was in many ways very different from the years of George II. The reigns of William III and Anne had seen England for the first time play the part of a great Power in a world of momentous issues. In contrast, the age of Walpole and the Pelhams, though one of steady economic advance, seemed devoid of great issues until William Pitt gave voice to them again. Accordingly, politics became little more than the conflicts of rival personalities. With the Seven Years' War there is a return to momentous issues. Britain won a great empire; foreign trade was expanding, and with it industrial production at home; the cost of government was rising and the field of government activity increasing; great issues of liberty were posed, first by John Wilkes, and then by the American colonists. It is not surprising that for the first decade of the new reign the political confusion should be intense.

Leicester House had long awaited the accession of the new King. It had been the centre of the Opposition in the reign of George II, as in the reign of George I. Its nuisance value was considerable, yet it could never win a political battle, for as soon as its protégés gained office they tended to drift out of the orbit of Leicester House. Pitt was such a protégé during the 1750s. Prince Frederick of Wales had died in 1751, and since then all hopes had been on his son. The political affairs of the young Prince were directed by his mother, the Princess of Wales, a foolish, intriguing woman, and his tutor, the Earl of Bute. Lord Waldegrave has left a good picture of Bute:

> He has a good person, fine legs, and a theatrical air of the greatest importance. There is an extraordinary appearance of wisdom, both in his look and manner of speaking; for whether the subject be serious or trifling, he is equally pompous, slow and sententious. Not contented with being wise, he would be thought a polite scholar, but he has the misfortune never to succeed, except with those who are exceedingly ignorant. . . . Frederick, Prince of Wales, used frequently to say that Bute was a fine showy man who would make an excellent ambassador in a court where there was no business.

The future George III was brought up a timid, ignorant boy, with a terrible sense of his own deficiencies, which Bute seemed to take a delight in increasing. He was taught that his grandfather was a mere prisoner of his whig ministers, that all politicians were rogues, and that there must be a clean sweep when George came to the throne. To this extent there is some substance in the story that George's mother was always urging him to "be a King". As early as 1758 George and Bute were planning the composition of their first ministry. Bute certainly imagined himself a political genius capable of cleansing the Augean stables of English politics. The young George, painfully immature, saw it all in simple moral terms: the noble Bute riding to battle against the forces of darkness.

George III, therefore, began his reign with little real interest in the great victories which were bringing glory to his crown: such victories, he wrote, would only glorify his enemies, by which he meant Pitt and Newcastle. He had been taught to detest them both. In 1761 Bute entered the ministry as Secretary of State. The King had a right to appoint his own ministers, and this step was fully expected. Yet there were special reasons for alarm. For Bute was not one of the small circle of politicians who since 1714 had largely shared political places. He was hated as a Scotsman who could manipulate the corrupt Scottish boroughs. Newcastle noted with alarm that he interfered in the distribution of

patronage which was a necessary part of the elections of
1761. If anything could have cemented an alliance between
Pitt and Newcastle, it might have been the appearance of
Bute. But in fact the two hated each other. The one thing
they were agreed upon, said Waldegrave, was the determination never again to co-operate in politics. Newcastle was as
anxious as George III and Bute to bring the war to an end,
for he was driven to distraction at the growth of the financial
burden. Pitt, on the other hand, was convinced that France
must be utterly crushed, and that war must be declared
upon Spain before Spain could attack England in the following year. When the issue came before the Cabinet in October 1761, Pitt found himself supported only by Temple,
and he resigned. Pitt fell, not because of any intrigue of
George III or Bute, but because his war policy was opposed
by all but one of his colleagues. Pitt's political isolation was
thus suddenly revealed as a stark fact.

Newcastle's turn came next. Bute, and his new favourite
George Grenville, increasingly took over the control of
patronage. In May 1762 Newcastle resigned. After thirty
years and more of political power he did not really believe
that government could succeed without him. In fact, how-
ever, the long era of the Pelhams was over. Bute became
First Lord of the Treasury. He knew that the departure of
Newcastle left government organisation very weak in the
Commons. In October the Peace terms were completed, and
Bute was under no illusions about the difficulty of getting
them through the Commons in face of the opposition of
Pitt. He, therefore, brought in Henry Fox as leader in the
Commons. Henry Fox knew his House of Commons well,
but his reputation was bad. While Pitt had been winning
an empire, Fox had been feathering his nest in the Paymaster's office. He was now to complete his reputation as a
political jobber in return for the peerage he so much coveted.
The stories of his wholesale bribing of Members of Parliament are untrue, but his reputation was bound to suffer
for his alliance with Bute. For Bute was intensely unpopular;
his carriage was hissed and pelted in the streets by the mob.
In fact, the Peace terms were carried by an overwhelming
majority, and the followers of Newcastle who voted against
them were ruthlessly dismissed from office ("the massacre of
the Newcastle Innocents"). But Bute was thoroughly disillu-

sioned, and insisted on resigning (March 1763).[1] He was succeeded as head of the government by George Grenville.

George Grenville

All this was a great shock to George III, yet a breach with Bute was the prime condition of his own political development. Bute still hoped to be able to conduct affairs from behind the throne, but Grenville clamped down upon their correspondence, and extracted a promise from the King not to consult Bute (1765). The strain of this brought on the first signs of George III's mental illness, but he gave the promise and kept it, and thereafter began to develop a mind of his own. For years afterwards the whigs kept alive the story of secret influence behind the throne, but there was no substance in it after 1765.

George Grenville's short government (1763–5) proved to be a most significant one. Grenville was a narrow, humourless man, but with a good head for business and organisation. Once a member of Cobham's Cubs, he had with Pitt attached himself to Leicester House, became a protégé of Bute's, and was now his successor. He had learnt from Walpole and the Pelhams that a successful minister must be known to control patronage in order to control the House of Commons, and must be known to have the confidence of the King. If politicians learnt that there were two sources of patronage, one at Court, and one with the minister, there would be divided authority and weakness. This was why Grenville made George promise to cease communicating with Bute, and gathered the reins of patronage into his own hands. In the Commons he insisted upon loyal support, and therefore wanted all Bute's friends deprived of their offices. Now this placed the King in a very difficult position. These men were already known as "King's Friends", and this term has often been misunderstood. There were many men in politics who believed that the King had an unfettered right to choose his ministers, and that their own political obligation was to support the ministers of the King's choice, unless their consciences persuaded them otherwise. These men

---

[1] His unpopularity was completed by an outburst of opposition in the country to the government's proposed excise on cider. Any increase of taxation was hated in the eighteenth century, the excise especially so.

the King might naturally wish to reward by offices or appointments of some kind. When Bute was chief minister they received their appointments through Bute, and therefore were regarded as in some degree Bute's men. The successor to Bute would wish to have in his hands all the patronage he could muster, and would wish to dismiss these men and give their offices to his own followers. The King, however, would feel himself in loyalty bound to defend the "King's Friends". This became the great issue between George III and George Grenville, and it is the starting-point of the mistaken theories which used so to confuse the studies of this period.

Before, however, this issue came to a head, Grenville's government had done two important things. The first was to prosecute John Wilkes. John Wilkes was a clever rogue, the son of a Clerkenwell distiller, who had married well enough to set up as a country gentleman at Aylesbury. He soon entered into the circle of Stowe, and was taken up by Earl Temple (Lord Cobham's heir and successor). In 1757 he became Member of Parliament for Aylesbury and a strong supporter of Pitt. He had a clever pen, wrote obscene verses, and was a member of the notorious Hell-fire Club, founded by Sir Francis Dashwood. The fall of Pitt in 1761, and the growing unpopularity of Bute, gave him his chance. Bute in 1762 employed Smollett to produce a paper called the *Briton* as a government propaganda organ. Wilkes cleverly parodied it in June with a paper called the *North Briton*. The title itself was an allusion to Bute as a Scotsman. Some of its articles were scurrilous attacks upon the King and his favourites. It attacked the Peace terms with arguments which were close to Pitt's and finally in No. 45 he attacked the King's speech on the Peace treaty. The government saw Wilkes as the mouthpiece of the Pitt-Temple faction, and determined to crush him. A general warrant was issued for the arrest of "all connected with the publication of the *North Briton*".

There is little doubt that Wilkes intended provoking the government into retaliation, and that he was anxious for a fight. His arrest involved three important questions: Was a General Warrant legal? Wilkes knew the opinion of the Lord Chief Justice that it was not. Was the Secretary of State a magistrate capable of issuing a warrant? This was later answered in the affirmative. Was Wilkes covered by parliamentary privilege? The court at once ruled that he was, and therefore he was released from arrest. Finally Chief Justice Pratt, who was a close friend of Pitt, ruled that general warrants were illegal. Wilkes then sued the Secretary of State (Halifax) for damages and received a thousand pounds damages. Thus Wilkes pursued his intentions of making the government look foolish. But the government then persuaded the Commons to vote that Privilege did not extend to libel. Wilkes' friends were placed in a difficult position, for Lord Sandwich had been able to produce in the Lords the obscene poem, and Pitt was at pains to dissociate himself from such a writer. He declared his libels "illiberal, unmanly and detestable", but he argued that a vital point of whig liberty was at stake. It made no difference. By a large majority the Commons expelled Wilkes from the House (January 1764), and he escaped to France. This was not the last of Wilkes, but already he had had a strange victory. General warrants had been declared illegal; the government had been discredited in the eyes of public opinion; Wilkes was already a hero in London; the name of Bute was hated; the first sinister rumours of a plot against the constitution were broadcast; the issue of "Wilkes and Liberty" was already in the air.

The second important activity of the Grenville government was in financial economy. Most politicians were appalled at the enormous cost of the late war and the heavy ensuing national debt. Grenville proposed to deal with the problem in three ways. First, he instituted strict economy throughout the government departments; even the fleet was practically starved of ships. Second, he proposed strictly to enforce the revenue-producing customs duties in the colonies. Third, he passed the Stamp Act to cover the costs of colonial defence. In this narrow and pedantic way, therefore, Grenville set in motion the dispute with the American colonies.[2]

Political Confusion, 1765–70

It was, however, not the Stamp Act but the issue of patronage which brought about the fall of the Grenville government. George III felt that he could not submit to the bonds imposed on him. He turned to his uncle, Cumberland, to

[2] See Ch. 9.

find him an alternative government. After some months of negotiations Cumberland found one in the Rockingham group. The Marquis of Rockingham had basked for some years in the favour of George II as a Gentleman of the Bedchamber, and he never forgot the honour. His great territorial influence ensured him political importance if he cared to exert it. He had no political ability, and hardly ever spoke in the Lords, but he was a man of great integrity and charm, and this enabled him to retain the loyalty of his followers. But it is probable that his group would have had no more importance than another had it not been for the fact that he appointed Edmund Burke as his private secretary. Burke became the organiser of the party, and indeed the philosopher of party government.

The Rockingham government (1765–6) was from the first a weak one. Its first failure was to persuade Pitt to join it. Pitt would not sit in any government of which he was not the head, and although he was personally well-disposed to Rockingham, he utterly refused to sit again in a government which contained Newcastle (who was Lord Privy Seal). His refusal left the government weak in ability, in Townshend's words "a lutestring Administration, fit only for summer". By this he meant that it could last only so long as Parliament was not sitting. Its American policy was singularly foolish. The Stamp Act had caused riots in America. The Act might have been enforced, or it might have been repealed, but it was muddled thinking to repeal the Act and yet pass the Declaratory Act confirming the British government's right to tax the colonies. It was not, however, on this, but on personalities that the government foundered. In July it was too weak to continue, and the King sent for Pitt.

George III had matured since 1763, and he looked forward to a Pitt Ministry with some excitement. For he now saw Pitt as a great man, and moreover one with little political following of his own. He was not, therefore, a man of "connection", anxious to find places for his many friends. He might be persuaded to serve the King loyally and take under his protection the King's Friends who were so much George's concern. He was delighted to hear that Pitt intended to "dissolve all faction" and bring in all right-thinking men who would co-operate on the principle of "Measures, not Men". But he was to be bitterly disappointed. The Chatham government (for Pitt now became Earl of Chatham) was an unmitigated disaster. Among his followers were few men of ability. Temple, secretly annoyed that he was not himself head of the government, refused to join, and Pitt had to rely on the loyal but incompetent Duke of Grafton as First Lord of the Treasury and General Conway and the able but unpopular Shelburne as Secretaries of State. The brilliant Charles Townshend was Chancellor of the Exchequer, but he was entirely devoid of political judgment. At first the Rockinghams kept some places and gave the government support, but in November they resigned and went into Opposition: the Rockinghams were interested only in a government they could control. Chatham might have strengthened his government by winning the full support of the Bedford group. The Duke of Bedford was an old man, no longer interested in office, but his followers were ambitious and well organised by Richard Rigby. But Chatham failed to win them over, and they passed into Opposition. Not even Chatham could carry on a government single-handed. In January 1767 his health collapsed. He retired into utter seclusion. His colleagues were left to their own devices. Grafton was horrified, but he could get no word of guidance from Chatham. Charles Townshend was able to carry his disastrous scheme for taxing the colonies.[3] The government became one of drift; almost every principle of government for which Chatham stood was one by one overthrown.

The King's position was pitiable. He had set much store by Chatham's government, and he had given him every support. For months he fondly hoped for Chatham's recovery. He wrote to him to beg him to bestir himself, even to the extent of giving Grafton five minutes' talk and encouragement. But Chatham could only reply that he was too ill to attend to business. Finally by 1768 the government ceased to be Chatham's even in name. For Chatham was disgusted with the way affairs had been handled, and when his last ally, Shelburne, was dismissed from the government, Chatham insisted on resigning. For another year he remained in complete seclusion, and the government became Grafton's in name, as well as in fact.

The crowning blunder of the Grafton government was to renew the conflict with John Wilkes. Wilkes, in danger of

---

[3] See Ch. 9.

being forgotten in France, returned in 1768 and stood as a candidate in the Middlesex election. The times were extremely unsettled. The government was in confusion; there had been six ministries in eight years; trade was bad, and there was much unemployment and distress in London. Wilkes was elected amidst much excitement and violence. He then surrendered to the Courts upon the charges of 1764 and was sentenced to a fine and twenty-two months' imprisonment. A born demagogue, Wilkes had aroused a dangerous support among the radicals and discontented of London, and in those days there was no adequate police force to maintain order. Wilkes was not only a Member of Parliament, but was also elected an alderman of London. Grafton's government was alarmed, and by a large majority the Commons expelled Wilkes from the House. They feared his radicalism and his popular following, and thought it monstrous that an outlaw should sit among them. But Wilkes was promptly re-elected unopposed. Again the House expelled him, and again he was elected. This time Colonel Luttrell was declared elected, though he had gained less than a quarter of the number of votes cast for Wilkes.

A grave constitutional problem had thus arisen. For on the one hand the House of Commons had always claimed the right to be the sole judge of election disputes. Just as in the seventeenth century they had resisted royal interference, so now they were contemptuous of an attempt at mob-rule. Yet on the other side, it was clear that the electors of Middlesex had chosen Wilkes, and the Commons had denied them the right of representation. If a majority of the Commons could decide against the fitness of a candidate to sit, what was to prevent a corrupt majority from denying the people just representation? The charges of a conspiracy against the constitution, of a secret influence behind the throne, arose again. The unrepresentative character of Parliament was freely mooted, and thus from the Middlesex election Radicalism was born. The Radical Horne Tooke, a shady minister of the church, vigorously took up Wilkes' cause and helped to found the Society for the Defence of the Bill of Rights (1769). It was at this point that Chatham suddenly emerged from his seclusion, like some giant refreshed, to denounce the ministry in awful terms, and to point a warning. He said he held no brief for Wilkes, whose character he detested, but a great principle of liberty was at stake:

What then, my lords, are all the generous efforts of our an-
cestors that instead of the arbitrary power of the King we
must submit to the arbitrary power of the House of Commons? . . . It contradicts Magna Carta and the Bill of Rights,
by which it is provided that no subject shall be deprived of
his freehold, unless by the judgment of his peers or the law
of the land.

He continued that the very principle of the rule of law was
at stake; if it were surrendered the fundamental principle of
liberty would be at an end: rather than that should happen, he
declared in majestic tones, "MAY DISCORD PREVAIL FOR EVER!"
It was one of Chatham's greatest speeches. During 1770, in
alliance with Rockingham, he fought to get the decision in
the Middlesex election reversed. The City of London peti-
tioned the King in the same terms. Chatham's alliance with
the City was thus fully restored. By 1770 both were talking
of the need for parliamentary reform.

It may be convenient here to outline the remainder of the
Wilkes story. He continued to be excluded from the House
until 1774, when he was quietly allowed to take his seat.
After 1770, now that he was an alderman of London and
a magistrate, Wilkes became less and less interested in the
principles of radicalism. In 1771, however, a Middlesex newspaper published a report of parliamentary debates. The
Commons had always thought it important to keep its
debates secret, and the publication, as the radicals well knew,
were forbidden. The Commons sent a messenger to arrest
the publisher. Instead Wilkes had the messenger arrested for
common assault, thus forcing a conflict with the House. The
Commons summoned the Lord Mayor, Brass Crosby, Alderman Oliver and Alderman Wilkes to appear before it. Wilkes
refused to go; the other two attended and were committed
to the Tower for the rest of the session. Wilkes, however,
was left in peace. The Commons did not again attempt to
prosecute for the publication of debates, though they could
always exclude reporters from the House by reporting their
presence to the Speaker. Thereafter Wilkes largely lost his
importance. He did support the American cause during the
American Revolution, and had some sensible criticisms
of Lord North's administration. He introduced a reform
Bill in 1776 "for the just and equal representation of the
people of England in Parliament". In a witty speech he jeered
at Lord George Germain:

East Grinstead, I think, has only about thirty electors, yet gives a seat among us to that brave, heroic lord at the head of a great civil department now very military, who has fully determined to conquer America—but not in Germany.[4]

He took an active part in the suppression of the Gordon Riots in 1780. He died in 1797, an almost forgotten figure.

To complete the discomfiture of the unfortunate Grafton government, there appeared in January 1769 the mysterious figure of Junius. His letters appeared in the London press during the next three years. All the efforts of contemporaries and of historians have failed to identify Junius with any of the great names of the time,[5] but he was a most effective controversialist. It was the Middlesex election which brought him into print. He had an intense hostility to George III, disliked Wilkes as a person, but saw great issues of liberty at stake in his case. His attacks on Grafton were merciless. He believed passionately in the whig interpretation of the Revolution of 1688, and this meant the rule by the great whig families. He feared the influence of the Crown, and thought that it would be offset by a return to triennial parliaments. On the other hand, he thought that to sweep away rotten boroughs would make too powerful a legislature. His great aim was to create a united whig opposition against the royal influence. When by 1771 he saw that he had failed, the letters ceased, and Junius disappeared for ever.

Lord North

With so many disasters about it, the Grafton government collapsed; Grafton thankfully resigned in January 1770, and Lord North took his place. Lord North was a man of considerable experience. He had been a Lord of the Treasury under Newcastle, and had built up a reputation for solid financial competence; he served in both the Grenville and the Chatham governments, and in 1767 he succeeded Charles Townshend as Chancellor of the Exchequer. As Leader of the Commons he earnt high praise from Richard Rigby, who declared: "I have never known any of his predecessors acquit themselves so much to the satisfaction of the House". He was therefore one of the rocks in the quicksands of

---

[4] A reference to Germain's disgrace at the battle of Minden.
[5] See my book *Political Ideas*, Ch. VI (Gollancz).

Grafton's government. He was an excellent parliamentarian, a skilled debater, imperturbably affable and with an engaging sense of humour. He was, therefore, the man to whom George III naturally turned in 1770. He quickly restored order to government. Within a month or two he could count on a majority of a 120. He easily rode the war-scare of 1771 with Spain. In 1772 he carried the Royal Marriages Act, by which members of the royal family were required to obtain the King's consent before contracting a valid marriage. This Act was consequent on two imprudent marriages by Gloucester and Cumberland. The Opposition tried to make capital out of it, but the Bill passed easily. In the same year North showed his skill by allowing a Bill for the relief of dissenters to pass the Commons, relying on the Lords to kill it, which they duly did. In 1773 he tackled the most complicated and difficult problem of the affairs of the East India Company, and carried the Regulating Act.[6] There was a general reluctance in Parliament to interfere in the affairs of the Company, and there was a fear that in doing so they would increase the powers of government patronage which were already great enough. But the Opposition, as usual, were divided about the Bill, and there was a feeling that North had done the best possible in a difficult situation, so the Bill passed by comfortable majorities.

The Opposition, particularly the Rockinghams, were in despair. In 1774 the government of Lord North was more firmly entrenched than any government had been since 1760. Opposition groups could not maintain their identity indefinitely without a hope of office and without a rallying cry. It appears likely that the Rockinghams would have disintegrated but for two things. One was the stimulus of Edmund Burke, and the other was the onset of the American Revolution.

Burke and Fox

Burke was born in 1729, the son of a Dublin lawyer, and was educated at Trinity College, Dublin. As a young man he was fascinated with literature and hoped to make a name with his pen. In 1765 Lord Rockingham was looking round for a man of the world to act as his private secretary, and he selected Burke. From that point Burke became the organiser and the philosopher of the Rockingham whigs.

6 See Ch. 10.

Burke was ideally suited, for he venerated the aristocracy, not as individuals, for he was well aware of their defects as men, but as an institution. He believed passionately in the principle of aristocratic government; that to him was the great achievement of the Revolution of 1688. The aristocracy were fitted by nature to rule; they were born and brought up to rule; they did so reluctantly, much preferring the delights of country life to the labours of government. But this was an advantage, for they were free from vulgar ambition. They ruled as a duty, not as a self-gratification. They were the great oaks beneath which the nation lived in peace and prosperity. Burke saw the great virtue of the British Constitution to lie in the representation it gave to the great interests of the nation. For it gave an allotted place to the great landed interest, the established church, the mercantile interest, the yeoman freeholders. But the ultimate guardians of 1688 were the aristocracy.

Burke's correspondence is full of his attempts to inspire Rockingham, the Duke of Richmond and other members of his party with this ideal. He idealised them, but he was never subservient to them. He could lecture them for their reluctance to pay attention to business. He was the great philosopher of party government. Men could only make themselves felt in politics at all by banding together around a common principle. He strongly defended government by "connection". It seemed to him natural that Britain should be ruled by the Rockinghams, the Grenvilles, the Bedfords and the Pelhams of this world.

Burke gave his party a philosophy in one of the most powerful pamphlets ever written, *Thoughts on the Cause of the Present Discontents* (1770). So persuasive was it that it not only made a party, but it misled many later historians into misinterpreting the period. Burke argued that there was a spirit of disaffection abroad in the country because people feared the growth of a conspiracy against the Constitution, centred in the Court, and working by mysterious means behind the throne:

> The power of the Crown, almost dead and rotten as Prerogative, has grown up anew, with much more strength, and far less odium, under the name of Influence.

It was seeking to destroy "connection"; its power had been

shown in the Middlesex election. Burke hinted darkly that the power of Bute still cast a shadow over British politics.

Burke had a brilliant imagination and a persuasive pen, but we have seen already how inaccurate a picture he drew of the power and influence of George III. Yet it was substantially the view that nineteenth-century historians developed as "the whig view" of the period. But it was not the view of many of Burke's contemporaries. There was no constitutional rule binding the King to a small number of great whig families. Many people had resented the long domination of the Pelhams, and were glad that George III was released from dependence upon them. Unfortunately between 1763 and 1770 he had been unable to find a stable government. This was, however, far more the result of whig incapacity and disunity than the errors of George III. In 1770, when at last the King found a suitable minister in Lord North, politicians rallied to his support. Burke's theory must not be taken as representing either the truth, or the general opinion of his time; it was a brilliant figment of his imagination. Yet, with all Burke's skill, by 1774 the Rockingham whigs were in danger of disintegration, when the American Revolution came to their rescue by giving them a cause.

Again Burke supplied the philosophy. His approach to the American problem was most statesmanlike. He always held that the American question should not be argued in terms of a narrow legality. It was not so much whether the mother-country had a right to tax the colonies, but whether it was wise to do so. He thought that the Americans had always enjoyed great political liberty; they had been subject to commercial restriction, but when that pinched they had known how to evade the law. It was a mistake to change this time-honoured system by raising the new issue of taxation. He warned that the Americans had already found nationhood; it was dangerous to push them too far:

> An Englishman is the unfittest person on earth to argue another Englishman into slavery.

In 1774 he begged that the government should surrender the right of taxation in America. The weakness of Burke's position was that he still envisaged the mother-country retaining the commercial control of the Empire. But he urged the Administration to think imperially, to develop a sense of proportion, to rely, not on laws, but on the ties of affection and blood "which, though light as air, are as strong as links of iron".

When war began Burke seemed a voice crying in the wilderness. His opposition to the war aroused little support in 1775. Public opinion was solidly behind the government in their intention to teach the colonies a lesson. Among the Rockingham whigs there was in fact a deep pessimism; the Duke of Richmond, for instance, thought that the colonies were lost, and that England's sun was already setting. At best they were disposed to wait upon events. It was thus of the greatest importance to Burke that in 1774 he found a powerful ally.

Charles James Fox was the brilliant son of Henry Fox, who had made such fortunes out of the Pay Office and had become Lord Holland. His father gave him every luxury, and even had him coached in the art of gambling. In 1768 he entered Parliament at the age of nineteen, already with the reputation of a reckless gambler but a charming personality. In 1770 Lord North made him one of the Lords of the Admiralty. In 1772 he suddenly resigned; the motive was probably no more than that he hoped to win promotion from Lord North. The manoeuvre seemed to succeed, for Lord North appointed him a Junior Lord of the Treasury. But to the King this was going too far. He detested the young Fox for his dissolute life and what seemed to be lack of principle in politics. When in 1774 Fox saw fit to oppose the government, he was dismissed. He then passed rapidly into association with the Rockingham whigs, and, as seems probable, was a willing pupil of Burke, for almost at once Fox's speeches on America began to echo the arguments of Burke. Their style, however, was very different, for while Burke was monumental, almost ponderous, in his speeches, Fox had a lightness of touch which made him a born orator. He frankly opposed the war with America, and took the courageous line that it would be better to abandon the colonies than to conquer them, even supposing that were possible.

George III saw the American issue in very simple terms. The colonists were disobedient; they must therefore submit or be conquered. He entirely failed to understand how there could be another point of view. Both he and Lord North were agreed on the need for vigorous action. The King pored over plans, maps and lists of recruitment, yet neither could extract from the nation more than the feeblest response. Typical is the letter of Lord North to the King in August 1775:

> He is sorry to say that it is the opinion not only of Lord Barrington (Secretary at War) but of all those who are conversant in the recruiting business, that the number of recruits wanted cannot be expected by the next spring. The general notion is that we cannot, by that time, depend upon raising about five or at the most six thousand men. . . . *The cause of Great Britain is not yet sufficiently popular.* . . . The success of the War in America absolutely depends upon a considerable army being there early in the spring.

Since campaigns had to begin in the spring, it followed that real military effort would have to be postponed until 1777. George did everything possible to urge speed. In January 1776 he complained of the slow preparations in the Navy, and wrote to the First Lord of the Admiralty:

> I cannot too strongly inculcate the necessity of setting all official forms aside that in the least delay the engaging Transports. . . . Every means of obtaining many vessels ought to be sought.

Although the results were meagre enough, Lord North remained hearty and active until the beginning of December 1777. But then arrived the news of the capitulation at Saratoga; this disaster, and the danger of war with France, combined to destroy his energy and his will. From this point onwards he virtually abandoned the direction of the war to his fellow ministers. He was deeply depressed, and asked only to be allowed to resign. But George III would not hear of it. In November 1775 he had called North "my Sheet Anchor". In September 1777 he had insisted on paying some £20,000 of Lord North's debts to show his gratitude for his services. It was not that he regarded Lord North as an ideal War Minister. He continually wrote urging him to take heart, to bestir himself, to show some resolution. But he felt he could not part from North, for he was the only minister who would agree to continue the war. The fall of North would mean the triumph of the whig opposition. So

North continued, a miserable spectacle, writing to the King in March 1778:

> Capital punishment itself is, in Lord North's opinion, preferable to that constant anguish of mind which he feels from the consideration that his continuance in office is ruining his Majesty's affairs.

He begged the King to send for Lord Chatham.

Lord Chatham

No man in England followed the development of the American dispute more intensely than Lord Chatham. He was himself the architect of British power in North America, and he looked upon the colonies with pride. He was a complete Mercantilist; that is to say he saw the colonies in terms of commercial wealth and power. As early as 1766 he had utterly denied the right of the mother-country to tax the colonies, though it could regulate their trade. In practice this was a difficult distinction to draw, as Charles Townshend's duties showed, but it was one Chatham always tried to maintain. To Chatham, the Americans were claiming the same rights as Englishmen had claimed in the seventeenth century, and hence:

> I rejoice that America has resisted. . . . The gentleman asks when were the colonies emancipated? But I desire to know when they were made slaves.

He argued that it was futile to cause a revolution for the paltry sum of £100,000 a year, when American trade was worth two millions. Above all, he urged caution in view of the inevitable hostility of France. He opposed all the retaliatory measures of 1774, and the despatch of troops:

> This country has no right under Heaven to tax America.

In perhaps the most impassioned words ever uttered in Parliament he foretold that war must end in defeat, and that disaster would await them when France intervened. In 1775 he introduced a Conciliation Plan, yet it could muster only thirty-two votes in the Lords. Once war had begun, he feared above all the approaching conflict with France.

Finally, in April 1778, ill and weak, leaning upon two friends, with his legs swathed in bandages, he appeared for the last time in the Lords, looking, an eye-witness said, like a superior species, to make a final protest at the danger of losing the American colonies. Shortly afterwards he fainted and was carried from the Chamber. He died a month later. Not even at this time did the two sections of the whig Opposition agree, for the Rockingham whigs were for abandoning the colonies, and this Chatham would never accept.

Defeat and the Movement for Reform

After 1778 Lord North's government sank into increasing confusion. Time and time again he wrote to the King of his utter incompetence to continue to manage affairs, but all his objections were waved aside. From November 1778 the King tried to manage affairs himself, acting through two men of business, John Robinson, a secretary at the Treasury, and Charles Jenkinson, the Secretary at War. Both were exasperated at North's incompetence, and sent the King reports on the state of affairs.

Until 1779 the whig Opposition had been unable to arouse any echo of support in the country. Their opposition to the war seemed to most people to be unpatriotic, if not treasonable. But by 1779 the incompetence of the government was plain for all to see. How was it, men asked, that Lord North continued in office? One answer given was that the political system was so corrupt that public opinion could not make itself heard. The radical opposition of London and Middlesex, which had once supported Wilkes, again raised its head. Earl Stanhope had published a pamphlet on parliamentary reform in 1774. In 1776 Major John Cartwright published his famous *Take Your Choice,* calling for manhood suffrage and annual parliaments. But it was not until 1779 that an agitation for reform became widespread. In December a group of Yorkshire gentry, led by Christopher Wyvill, met together to approve a petition against the high taxation and waste of public money:

whence the Crown has acquired a great and unconstitutional influence, which, if not checked, may soon prove fatal to the liberties of this Country.

The Wilkesite radicals had been the humble discontented of

London; but the Yorkshire movement consisted of the country gentry. Moreover the movement spread to other counties,
and petitions poured in. But would the movement find leaders
among the whigs? Cartwright had urged Shelburne to head a
reform movement as early as 1777, but he had replied that
the time was not ripe. In 1779 the Rockingham whigs, and
especially the Duke of Richmond and his nephew Charles
James Fox, appeared eager to lead the reform movement.
If the whigs could combine with the county associations
(as they were called) and with the Middlesex and London
radicals, something like a national reform movement would
emerge. In March 1780 a central committee was established in
London with Wyvill as chairman. The demand was for strict
economy, 100 additional county members and annual
parliaments. Fox was chosen as parliamentary candidate for
Westminster, the most democratic borough in England. It
was argued that 6,000 voters in a total of 129 boroughs returned no less than 257 members to Parliament.

At this the Rockingham whigs drew back. Opposition to
the power of the Crown and to the government of Lord
North was one thing, but the radical proposal to attack the
borough influence of the landed gentry was quite another
matter. When the radicals talked of reform they often
meant manhood suffrage and annual parliaments. When the
county associations talked of reform they meant economy
and the increase of county representation. When the Rockingham whigs talked of reform they meant the limitation of the
patronage of the Crown. Upon this three-fold division the
reform movement split and broke down. The only link between them was Fox, and he had soon to choose. In March
1780 Burke carried the first step of his economical reform
plan when he carried against the government the abolition
of the Board of Trade. In April Dunning carried his celebrated motion "that the influence of the Crown has increased,
is increasing and ought to be diminished". The very fact that
the resolution was carried showed that royal influence was
not as strong as the whigs affirmed. The motion was more
an expression of exasperation at the inadequacies of Lord
North's government than of any clear desire for parliamentary reform.

In April 1780 some radicals, headed by Cartwright and
Jebb, and whigs, headed by Sheridan and Trecothick, formed
the Society for Constitutional Information. Its aristocratic

character was shown by the fact that its subscription was from one to five guineas. Its purpose was not agitation, but to distribute the constitutional facts, and to collect historical precedent, from the Middle Ages and the seventeenth century, to justify reform. Nothing could better illustrate the essential moderation of the reform movement.

By the late spring of 1780 the reform movement was already disintegrating. The final discouragement came with the terrible Gordon Riots of June 1780. Sir George Savile and the Rockingham whigs had carried in 1778 a Roman Catholic Relief Act. Religious intolerance was easily whipped up by agitators in the eighteenth century, and in 1779 a Protestant Association was formed with the half-witted Lord George Gordon as President. On June 2nd, 1780, a huge crowd of 60,000 people gathered in St George's Fields, Southwark, to present a monster petition against the Catholic Relief Act. The petition was presented to Parliament, and some of the crowd went off to burn Roman Catholic chapels. During the next few days there was more violence, the prisons were attacked and the prisoners freed. The house of the Lord Chief Justice, Lord Mansfield, was destroyed, together with his precious library. Next day, "Black Wednesday" saw the climax of the violence and destruction. An attack on the Bank of England was repulsed with heavy casualties. By the 9th the military were in full control. Four hundred and fifty people were arrested and twenty-five people were hanged. Gordon was tried for high treason, but acquitted after a brilliant defence by his counsel, Thomas Erskine.

What did it all mean? There is no evidence that it was planned by the Protestant Association, or the Opposition, or indeed by anyone. Religious feeling against Roman Catholics was strong; there was much social unrest in London, and there was an obvious absence of any adequate police force. There was widespread disillusionment at the war failures, heavy taxation and trade recession. All these factors seem sufficient to explain the Gordon Riots.

The results were far-reaching. The riots went far to destroy the reform movement. The rift between the whigs and the radicals widened. The governing classes became deeply suspicious of popular movements. Professor Butterfield comments:

The memory of these days had a great part in that fear of popular demonstrations which seized upon both the ministry and the governing classes of England at the time of the French Revolution.

One result was to give a further two years' lease of life to Lord North's government. Public opinion swung to the side of law and order. For more than a year the correspondence of the King and North became tranquil, almost complacent. But in November 1781 came the news of the surrender of Yorktown, and North once again lapsed into gloom, inaction and almost imbecility. Jenkinson wrote to the King that these fits were "really like the paroxysms of a disease". The end came in March 1782, when the country gentry in the Commons intimated that they could no longer support the government.

"At last the fatal day is come" wrote George III in despair. The Lord Chancellor Thurlow negotiated the formation of a government consisting of the Rockinghams and Chatha-mites (led by Shelburne), headed by Rockingham. It was an uneasy government, full of personal rivalry, for the Rocking-hams detested Shelburne, especially as the King gave him his confidence. The administration lasted for less than three months, and is important for two achievements.

First, Burke carried through his plan for Economical Re-form. He left the Civil List untouched, but swept away a number of sinecures at the saving of some £50,000 a year. He fixed his own salary as Paymaster General at £4,000, and swept away the perquisites which had enriched so many of his predecessors. Government contractors were excluded from the Commons, and revenue officers were disfranchised. The prime purpose was to reduce the influence of the Crown. It was a reform Pitt carried farther.

The second concerned Ireland. The Protestant ascendancy in Ireland had been virtually unchallenged in Ireland since 1691. The Catholic gentry were loyal and quiet, and the Catholic peasantry were mute. Discontent was at first confined to the Protestants of Ireland. There were two main grievances, first, that Ireland was economically subordinated to England, that Irish industries, especially woollen, were crushed in the interests of the English manufacturer, and that there were unfair restrictions on the export of agricul-tural produce, especially fat cattle. The second closely related to the first, was that the Irish Parliament was subordinated to the English, so that the latter could legislate for Ireland,

and thus impose economic restrictions at will. These grievances were touched off by the American Revolution. At a
time when Ireland was virtually undefended, and American
privateers were raiding her coast, Lord North could not
object to the Irish Protestant landowners, led by Henry
Gratten and Henry Flood, raising a force of Irish Volunteers. Henceforth they could speak with a new strength, and
in 1780 Lord North submitted to the inevitable, and abolished
the discriminatory laws against Irish trade. In 1782 Rockingham's government carried this farther by granting legislative independence for Ireland. Burke was an Irishman, and
Shelburne an Irish landowner, and both were anxious to
"do something for Ireland". However, their well-meaning
act caused more problems than it solved.

On July 1st Lord Rockingham died, and the government
broke up. When the King appointed Shelburne First Lord of
the Treasury most of the Rockingham whigs resigned; some,
however, like Richmond, remained in office, and thus the
Rockinghams began to disintegrate. On the other hand Shelburne was left dangerously weak. He was a subtle intellect,
with the instincts of statesmanship, but he was no leader of
men; in fact he was one of the most mistrusted men of his
time. He remained in office just long enough to complete the
Treaty of Versailles,[7] but in February 1783 was defeated
in the Commons and resigned. He had been defeated by an
"unnatural" alliance between Fox and North. The King was
deeply distressed. It appeared to be a triumph of his enemies.
He regarded North as a deserter, and Fox as bent on destroying the royal power. He consoled himself, however, with the
thought that so "unnatural" an alliance could not last. He
accepted, therefore, the Fox–North Coalition under the
nominal headship of the Duke of Portland; indeed he had no
alternative.

Some writers have attempted to defend the Coalition, argu-
ing that the alliance was not "unnatural", and that the old
enmity between Fox and North had ended with the war. But
this is to miss the point. The Coalition was a great blunder,
perhaps the greatest of Fox's career. He was right to feel
that a strong coalition was needed, but it should have been
with Shelburne, not with North. In the eyes of contemporaries he stood forth as an unprincipled self-seeker. The

---

[7] The terms were ratified in March 1783.

Coalition was entirely unsupported by public opinion. Fox had suddenly become quiet on the subject of parliamentary reform. Instead it appeared that he was concerned with creating a system of patronage of his own, by means of his India Bill. This was unfair, but it is easy to see how contemporaries could draw such a conclusion. To many he had become Carlo Khan, as much fouled by the dirty game of politics as Lord North himself. In December 1783 the King saw his chance. Lord Temple was the bearer of a message to the Lords that the King would regard as his enemies all who voted for the India Bill. The Lords took the hint and threw it out. George III sent for the seals of office, and the Coalition was at an end. Fox's "unnatural" alliance was short-lived, and now he began twenty-three years of exclusion from office. The fault was largely his own.

George III could dismiss the Coalition in the confident knowledge that he had an alternative government. On December 19th it was known in the Commons that William Pitt had accepted the office of First Lord of the Treasury at the age of twenty-four.

12

The Younger Pitt and National
Recovery

THE NAME OF Pitt was a programme in itself. It stood for high patriotism, national recovery, political purity. No man ever entered politics with a more honoured name, or was more fortunate in the moment of entry than William Pitt. For all other politicians of the day seemed tarnished with the failures and corruption of the past. North was discredited, Shelburne mistrusted, Fox had committed extraordinary blunders. All seemed unprincipled and sullied, except Pitt.

Born in 1759, the Year of Victories, he had been the great hope of his father. At the age of fourteen he entered Pembroke Hall, Cambridge, and was a serious student of Mathematics and the Classics. Weak in health, he had been prescribed horseback riding and port wine, and the latter became an unfortunate habit. In 1780 he took an active part in the County Association for Kent, and later in the year was returned to Parliament for Sir James Lowther's rotten borough of Appleby. He naturally attached himself to Lord Shelburne, the leader of the Chathamites. His first speech was in support of Burke's Economical Reform. In June he attacked the continuance of the war:

it was conceived in injustice; it was brought forth and nurtured in folly; its footsteps were marked with blood, persecution and devastation. It was productive of misery of every kind.

204

The Opposition were delighted with the new recruit. Men were reminded of his father's oratory. In May 1782, by agreement with the Opposition, he brought forward a motion for parliamentary reform, in which he argued that only corrupt influences had kept the war going for so long. The motion was lost by only twenty votes; parliamentary reform was not to have so good a division again until 1831. When Shelburne formed his government in 1782, Pitt became Chancellor of the Exchequer. His replies to the attacks of Burke and Fox were masterly. He skilfully suggested that he was unused to the sordid side of the political game; he had learnt a nobler patriotism at his father's knee:

> I can say with sincerity, I never had a wish which did not terminate in the dearest interests of the nation. . . . Unused as I am to the facetious and jarring clamours of this day's debate, I look up to the independent part of the house, and to the public at large. . . . My earliest impressions were in favour of the noblest and most disinterested modes of serving the public: these impressions are still dear to my heart; I will cherish them as a legacy infinitely more valuable than the greatest inheritance.

No man could fail to be impressed. When Shelburne fell George III offered Pitt his place. He refused, but when in December 1783 the Coalition fell, and the King repeated the offer, he accepted. John Robinson, Secretary at the Treasury, had been able to show him that in the ensuing election his majority was assured. George III had chosen Pitt in the same way as he had chosen North in 1770. Pitt had no more than a handful of personal adherents; he was in office because he was the King's choice. On the other hand, the King knew that the alternative to Pitt was Fox. It followed, therefore, that each sorely needed the support of the other. At first Pitt had great difficulties in the Commons; he was repeatedly defeated there, for the Fox–North majority still held against him. Fox carried fourteen motions against him, yet with decreasing majorities, and Fox knew that unless he could force Pitt out of office before the elections, the Opposition were bound to fail. Finally, in the elections of April Pitt was returned with an overwhelming majority (the first vote showed it to be 168). It is true that all the old methods of organisation were used, as John Robinson's papers clearly show, but there was also a real swing of public opinion in Pitt's favour wherever it could make itself felt.

Pitt at once turned to the business of government. His prime task must be seen in the light of the disasters of the American War. The finances were dislocated, trade disrupted, colonies lost, prestige shaken abroad, discontent and disillusionment at home, the administration regarded as corrupt and inefficient. The strength of Pitt lay in the fact that he had had nothing to do with the errors of government before 1780; that he projected himself on to the nation as the symbol of national regeneration; in short that he was Pitt the Reformer. George III well understood this and was content to accept it. George had always longed for a stable administration, yet he had had one only for the years 1770–5, and now he had one again. He not only accepted Pitt's financial reforms, but fully approved of most of them. Pitt in turn knew that so long as he trod warily in matters which deeply concerned the King, he would have considerable freedom of action in other respects.

During Pitt's period of office the practice of Cabinet government took a great step forward. The whole weight of government rested largely upon Pitt. His Cabinet colleagues were entirely in the Lords, and most of them, such as Lord Sydney and the Marquis of Carmarthen, were political nonentities. Pitt, therefore, exercised a personal supervision over policy and the administration of departments which gave real unity to government, exhausting though it was to Pitt himself. When he wanted assistance he turned, not to his Cabinet colleagues, but to the men of business in junior offices, Henry Dundas, the admirable Treasurer of the Navy, who also sat on the Board of Control for India and the Board of Trade, and was such a tower of strength to Pitt; his cousin William Grenville, the Secretary at War; Charles Jenkinson, President of the Board of Trade, and an expert on all commercial matters; and George Rose, Secretary to the Treasury, his devoted political organiser. These men behind the scenes were responsible for much of the business of government which Pitt appeared to conduct single-handed. Pitt required absolute loyalty from his colleagues, and in 1789 dropped Lord Sydney, and in 1792 Lord Thurlow, rather than put up with disloyalty. As time passed, George III's health became precarious; he could no longer pay the same attention to the day-to-day business of government which he had in Lord North's time. Policy was thus left more completely than ever in Pitt's hands. His mastery of the House of Commons was remarkable. A contemporary wrote:

> In solemn dignity and sullen state,
> This new Octavius rises to debate.

Another, looking for the secret of Pitt's extraordinary ascendancy, came to the conclusion that it was his eloquence which was "the key-stone of Pitt's ministerial greatness". All his life he was a lonely figure, with none of the geniality of Fox, yet no man since has achieved in peacetime such unchallenged eminence. This does not mean that he always carried his measures, for party organisation was rudimentary. He himself had swept away some of the props which patronage had supplied. He was forced to resort to the creation of an inordinate number of peerages to reward his followers. Yet his personal ascendancy was a wonder to contemporaries.

Nevertheless the limits of that power were revealed in 1788, when George III had his first attack of insanity. The whig Opposition demanded the appointment of a Regency; they argued that if the Prince of Wales was Regent, he would dismiss Pitt and put in his whig friends. Pitt realised the uncertainty of his position and played for time, for the King's doctor expected a speedy recovery. He, therefore, urged Parliament to set up a committee to look for precedents. Fox replied angrily that there were no precedents, and that the Prince was Regent by hereditary right. Pitt seized the opening ("I'll unwhig the gentleman for the rest of his life!") and righteously upheld the rights of Parliament. In January 1789, Pitt slowly drew up a Regency plan. By February he was able to announce the King's recovery. The crisis had passed, but the dependence of the minister upon the royal favour had again been demonstrated.

In 1783 Pitt had committed himself to a parliamentary reform measure, when he proposed the addition of one hundred County members and the disfranchisement of the worst of the rotten boroughs. It was a subject he had many times discussed with his friends as he sat at supper at his favourite Goosetree's in Pall Mall, and he felt bound to attempt a measure now that he was in office. In 1785 he proposed a moderate measure: the disfranchisement of thirty-six rotten boroughs and the compensation of their owners. The House refused leave for him even to introduce the Bill, and Pitt never attempted another parliamentary reform bill. There was nothing to be gained by endangering his political career by continuing the subject; the King was against the measure; and moreover Pitt saw that there was very much more important work to be done elsewhere.

His first great legislative success was the India Act, by which he carefully avoided the objections raised to Fox's Bill.[1] He also plunged into the great work of financial and administrative reform, which Pelham, George Grenville and Burke had initiated. He was greatly helped by having available the reports of committees instituted to consider reforms as early as 1781. The great problem was how to increase revenues, economise on administration and balance the budget. The eighteenth century lacked an elastic tax system, and efficient machinery for tax collection. The main sources of revenue were, first, indirect taxes on trade, that is to say, customs and excise; but these could not be increased without hampering trade, and, moreover, customs duties were frequently evaded by smuggling. Second, the land tax, which was badly assessed, and could be increased only at the price of discontent among the gentry. Third, the window tax, which was increased from time to time during the century, and led to much window-stopping and evasion; Pitt was able to abolish the tax in 1792 on houses of less than seven windows. Fourth, luxury taxes, on horses, carriages, men-servants, saddles and the like; these Pitt extended, and made their collection more efficient. It was not until 1798 that Pitt devised an entirely new basis for taxation by the use of the income tax, but he greatly improved financial administration and the yield of taxation. He declared war on smuggling, which had long been a national industry, said to employ 40,000 men. He cut the duty on tea to twelve and a half per cent., thus losing revenue, but making it unprofitable any longer to smuggle at the risk of one's neck. To defeat the smuggling of wine and tobacco he transferred them to the excise. He reviewed the administrative system and created machinery for the collection of taxes which was to stand the test of the Napoleonic Wars. He swept away a number of sinecures, and abolished the perquisites of nu-

[1] See Ch. 10.

merous offices. This was to continue the work which Burke had begun in his Economical reform, and in so far as it limited the royal powers of patronage, it might have been resented by George III. But the King admired good house-keeping. He had not realised the financial confusion which had existed under Lord North, and was horrified when he learnt the true facts. He, therefore, approved of Pitt's re-forms.

When Pitt came into power, there was an annual debt of £2,000,000, and Consols stood at only fifty-six. He found some £40,000,000 of public money mislaid through a chaotic system of accounting. For the first two years he had to resort to additional loans, and to cover the interest charges by increased luxury taxes. By 1786 he had turned the deficit into a surplus, but he was still left with a Na-tional Debt of £239,000,000. He, therefore, proposed his famous Sinking Fund, by which his surplus of £1,000,000 would be set aside every year under independent commis-sioners for the repayment of debt. This was a sound and statesmanlike proposal so long as there was an annual sur-plus. To make it certain that the fund should not be raided by succeeding Chancellors of the Exchequer, Pitt made the commissioners responsible only to Parliament. When war came, the fund lost its usefulness, for the surplus disap-peared, and the government had to borrow money at high rates of interest to pay off loans at low. But in 1786 the plan was a good one.

In 1786 Pitt negotiated his Commercial Treaty with France. This was more than an economic measure. He was concerned that since 1688 England and France had come to regard themselves as hereditary enemies. Pitt wished to crush the idea, and at the same time to open up new avenues of trade. Thus in return for admitting French wines and brandy on favourable terms, Britain secured a market for her manufactures. Pitt pointed out that while the French gained a market of 8,000,000 people, Britain ob-tained a market of 24,000,000.

In a great programme of simplifying the customs duties, Pitt had carried by 1787 no less than 2,537 resolutions. The old system was so complicated that merchants often did not know what they were expected to pay. A single article might pay as much as fourteen different duties. Pitt arranged that each article would pay a single duty, and in addition he increased the yield by £20,000.

In 1792, in an important speech, he reviewed the development of the nation since 1783. The annual surplus of £1,000,000 was maintained. The nation was at a new peak of prosperity, the result, he said, of inventions in production, and the growth of markets overseas. There stretched before the nation an endless vista of material improvement, growing comfort and happiness. But all depended upon the continuance of peace. Finally, he paid tribute to Adam Smith, whose teachings in the *Wealth of Nations* had pointed the way to his reforms, and, he believed, pointed the way to the solution of every problem of the age. In these terms Pitt paid tribute to his master. The speech may be taken as the high-water mark of Pitt during the years of peace, before the clouds of war closed upon him.

With Ireland Pitt was less successful. In 1780 the discriminatory restrictions on Irish production had been swept away, and in 1782 Ireland had received legislative independence. Pitt was anxious to integrate Irish trade with Britain in a fair and equitable system, if possible on the basis of complete free trade. He argued that some such system was the indispensable basis of future good relations between Britain and Ireland. The House of Commons accepted his plan (1785), but then in both England and Ireland merchants brought pressure to bear on their governments against the plan; each fearing the competition of the other. The plan was therefore shelved and never effected. Undoubtedly a great chance was lost of solving one of the many problems of Ireland.

A matter which redounds less to Pitt's credit was the treatment of Warren Hastings. Hastings returned to England in 1785 to find the subject of India a matter of furious controversy, and himself the object of attack. His implacable enemy, Philip Francis, had gained the ear of Burke, and the latter agreed to take up the case. Burke had studied the Indian question very deeply, had misinterpreted much of it, and in April 1786 he brought forward charges against Hastings in the Commons. Hastings was allowed to reply from the Bar of the House. On the first charge, concerning the Rohilla War, he was absolved, but on the treatment of Chait Singh Pitt spoke and voted against him, and Fox's motion was carried. In May 1787 Hastings was impeached.

The trial began in February 1788, and dragged on year after year until 1795, when Hastings was finally acquitted. It would never have lasted so long if Burke had not drawn out the case with his erudition and his oratory, to the boredom and even distraction of everyone concerned. Burke's motives were first the knowledge that whig fortunes were low and needed a rallying-cry, and second, genuine moral indignation at what he thought to be Hastings' wicked abuse of power. He never expected Hastings to be found guilty, but he thought that a moral principle should once and for all be asserted in the case of any colonial administrator, however far he might be from the seat of justice. He wanted it asserted that the humblest subject in the farthest parts of the Empire had as much right to protection as a citizen in this country. It was a noble idea, and Burke has left his mark on the growth of British Imperialism, but at the price of hounding Hastings through a trial lasting seven years. Pitt might well have intervened to expedite proceedings, but he was anxious that justice should not only be done, but appear to be done.

During these years Burke was a great advocate of the solution of the religious problem in Ireland. Ireland persuaded Burke of the need for religious toleration, for the Protestant ascendancy in Ireland meant the subordination of the Catholic five-sixths of the population to the will of the dominant Protestant minority. Burke saw that the constitutional changes of 1782 would in the end exacerbate the situation, for it removed the curb of the English Parliament on the activities of the Irish Protestant Parliament. The religious disabilities, he argued, simply kept alive the spirit of animosity and ascendancy. In his famous *Letter to Sir Hercules Langrishe* (1792) Burke argued that the Catholic disabilities were against the spirit of the Revolution of 1688, and would lead to grave conflict, if the disabilities were not removed. Pitt came more gradually to the same conclusions, and in 1791 he gave his support to a mild measure of Roman Catholic Relief, which was introduced and carried through by John Mitford.

At first sight it appears curious that Burke and Pitt should both be in favour of remitting Catholic disabilities, and yet against the repeal of the Test and Corporation Acts which offended the dissenters. Both felt that these Acts were part of the structure of the Constitution and linked with the maintenance of the Established church. Moreover, Burke in particular was influenced by the fact that many dissenters were radicals. Two of the leading radicals of the time were Dr Richard Price and Joseph Priestley. Both were products of dissenting academies, both believed passionately in religious liberty, both took the teaching of John Locke to its logical conclusion, and argued that all men had a right to the franchise; both gloried in the American Revolution and welcomed the French Revolution; both used their destructive logic to attack the constitutional abuses of the time.

The most potent radical of the period was Tom Paine, whose book *Rights of Man* (1791), in answer to Burke's *Reflections,* was a splendid piece of journalism, and became the bible of radicalism. Paine proclaimed quite simply the sovereignty of the people. All men had basic rights of which no constitution could deprive them. The British Constitution was no more than a mediaeval survival; Paine advocated the abolition of the monarchy and the hereditary peerage, the disbandment of the armed forces, a great programme of social insurance, and thus the birth of a new Age of Reason. Tom Paine gloried in the French Revolution and called for a similar revolution in England.

In England the French Revolution was at first regarded with a mixture of relief, that our old enemy was incapacitated, and interest that at long last the French had chosen to modernise their government. Fox loudly proclaimed it as the best and greatest event that had ever happened in the world. Poets and idealists were carried away with the news. Burke was the first to issue a solemn warning. In 1790 he declared in the Commons that:

The French have shown themselves the ablest architects of ruin that have ever existed in the world,

and in October he published his *Reflections on the Revolution in France,* one of the most powerful pieces of political philosophy in the language. He warned of the danger lying in the misuse of the word "liberty"; that "liberty" and "equality" were incompatible terms; and that the pursuit of equality could lead only to despotism. He said that he was not opposed to reform in France, but the French Revolution was actuated not by a spirit of reform, but by one of destruction. Liberty was safe only when it grew out of the past. Men should beware of an unrestrained reason; it should be tempered by prudence, justice and a sense of the past.

Burke's condemnation of the French Revolution led to a breach between him and Fox. It came into the open in April 1791, when Fox declared in the Commons that "their opinions were as wide as the poles asunder". He accused Burke of inconsistency, for if he had welcomed the American Revolution, how could he condemn the French? Burke, in a further pamphlet, denied that there was any inconsistency, for the very liberty for which the Americans had fought was in peril in France. Fox was deeply affected by the breach between them, and is said to have spoken in the Commons with tears in his eyes. To Fox the French Revolution was the birth of a new liberty for mankind; to Burke it was the birth of a new despotism.

Pitt did not take sides in the controversy. As time passed he came increasingly to value the British Constitution. He watched closely the onset of a European war in 1792, but appeared mainly interested in the problems of the balance of power. His essential humanitarianism was shown in his close friendship with Wilberforce, and his support of the Abolitionist cause. He envisaged the growth of the British Empire as extending the blessings of trade and civilisation throughout its extent. In a great speech in 1792 he looked forward to the day when the unhappy continent of Africa might enjoy the blessings of "science and philosophy" in a peaceful and fruitful civilisation of its own. His great pride was the commercial development and prosperity of Britain, which his financial policy was encouraging.

Yet his fears grew. The Society for Constitutional Information was revived in 1791. The London Corresponding Society was formed in 1792 by Thomas Hardy, a shoemaker of Piccadilly, and Horne Tooke. It was open to any working-class man, and was soon in touch with similar societies in Sheffield, Manchester, Scotland and elsewhere. Were they revolutionary? They often borrowed their language from France, and their ideas from Tom Paine, though much of their discontent arose from the economic conditions in the new industrial towns. One of the pamphlets which circulated in Birmingham in 1792 asked the people to remember that their Parliament was venal, the monarchy an anachronism, taxes oppressive, "your representation a cruel insult", and that "the peace of slavery is worse than the war of freedom". It is not surprising, therefore, that the King's Speech in December 1792 referred to the danger of revolution in the country. When Fox and Charles Grey urged Pitt to parliamentary reform, he replied that "this was not a time to make hazardous experiments". The spirit of subversion was abroad and, if it succeeded, would "destroy the best constitution that was ever formed upon the habitable globe". Three months later Britain was at war with France.

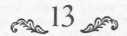

13

Law and Order

IN RAPIDLY EXPANDING societies it often happens
that traditional institutions are outgrown and break
down. There is then a period of difficulty in which various
expedients are tried out, until the right answer is found.
This was true with law and order in the century after 1688.
We have seen that it was a rapidly expanding society; life
was becoming more complex; towns were growing, and London was sprawling outwards at a prodigious rate. In spite
of the Settlement Laws labour was moving from place to
place, more rapidly than ever before. Wealth was in greater
display, and the idea that London had streets which were
paved with gold was in many a simple mind before it was
translated in to song. London seemed above all a place where
all the upper classes were on the make, and it was natural
that many of the light-fingered poor should try to be as
clever. Streets were unlit, police supervision negligible, and
the opportunities for crime, therefore, correspondingly great.

A cry went up from the governing classes in the years
after 1688 against the great increase in the wickedness of
the age. There was a general sense of insecurity. Men of
property felt that they had all too little protection against
the pickpocket, the murderer and the mob. In this they were
justified, for there was a rapid growth in the number of
thieves, robbers and highwaymen. The great majority of
the crimes were against property; there were few against
the person. John Locke had said that the prime purpose of
government was the protection of private property, yet in the

decades after 1688 it appeared that the government was conspicuously unable to fulfil this task.

The conclusion which should have been drawn was that the existing law needed more efficient enforcement. Instead it was argued that the law was not sufficiently deterrent. Accordingly law after law was passed imposing the death penalty for an increasing number of offences. The laws were introduced whenever a new wave of some crime was reported, and passed with little or no debate. In 1688 there were only some thirty offences punishable by death. By 1765 Sir William Blackstone said that the number was 160. How many it was a half-century later it is impossible to tell, because the law by then had become such a tangle that contemporaries did not themselves know, but it was certainly over 200. This was in the mistaken belief that the greater the punishment the greater the deterrent. Altogether some 190 new capital offences were created between 1688 and 1820. Thus the Waltham Black Act of 1722 imposed the death penalty for the theft of hares, rabbits, fish, cutting down trees, wounding cattle, setting fire to any house, barn, haystack or wood, and a number of other offences. An absurd situation thus arose, that the same penalty could be imposed for murdering the King and for breaking down a young tree. The penalty could be imposed equally on men, women and children over fourteen: in some circumstances it could be imposed on children over the age of seven. As late as 1833 a nine-year-old boy was sentenced to death for stealing two pennyworth of printers' colours, though the sentence was not carried out. Certainly public opinion was behind this increase in the severity of the law before 1760.

The law, therefore, greatly increased in savagery, to meet an admitted social problem of bewildering difficulty. But there were two important mitigating circumstances. First, many offences passed unpunished; and second, the criminal law might be excessively severe, but criminal procedure was most liberal and humane. The Englishman prided himself upon the rule of law. The jury system has always been one of the greatest pillars of liberty in this country, and both judges and juries were on the whole generous and humane in their interpretation of the law. In fact its operation in the eighteenth century is a good illustration of the fact that a law, to be effective for long, must be supported by public opinion. When the law outstrips public opinion, people tend to find a way around it. Thus on one occasion a certain Martha Walmesley was convicted of the theft of goods to the value of seventy shillings; but as the death penalty was imposed for the theft of goods to the value of forty shillings, prosecutor and jury agreed to value the stolen goods at eight shillings! In fact juries had a habit of valuing stolen goods at thirty-nine shillings in order to avoid the death penalty. When this situation occurs, the indication is that public opinion is ceasing to support the law.

Even when the death penalty was pronounced, there still remained the recommendation of judges to mercy, and the royal pardon. Thus between 1761 and 1765 a total of 838 death sentences were commuted to transportation or imprisonment, either on the recommendation of the judges, or by royal intervention. Statistics are not available for the enforcement of capital punishment over the whole country in the eighteenth century, but in London and Middlesex alone between 1749 and 1799, 3,680 were sentenced to death, and 1,696 actually executed. The great majority of the offences were some form of theft or fraud. However, it is to be noted that as the century drew to its close a far higher proportion of capital sentences were commuted, and by 1810, although there were 3,158 capital sentences in the whole country, only sixty-seven were actually carried out, clear evidence of the change in public opinion.

It was intended as part of the deterrent effect of capital punishment that executions should be public. In fact, however, the effect in the eighteenth century was rather the reverse. "Hanging days" were turned into public holidays. The last journey to Tyburn was usually made by cart through hilarious crowds. If the victim was brave or nonchalant he was cheered. Hucksters and pickpockets did a roaring business. So far from increasing the deterrent, the whole spectacle brutalised and familiarised. Henry Fielding, the author and magistrate, was always against public executions.

Indeed it was Fielding and his half-brother John who first pointed to the real cause of the trouble, namely the weakness of the system for keeping the peace. In the metropolis there were no less than seventy different police authorities. Only the City of London itself had a reasonable police system. There a general police system was maintained under the supervision of the mayor and aldermen, who were magistrates, and in addition the City was divided into twenty-six wards, each with its own constables, beadle and watch-men. Constables were unpaid, and held office for a year. As the duties were many and hard, the task was generally hated. Outside the City of London proper there was a maze of parishes (some 152 in all), each a law unto itself. The worst defect of all was that no constable from one parish could act officially outside the bounds of the parish. The only semblance of central authority was provided by the Police Office at Bow Street, to which were attached the best police, and also a Foot and Horse Patrol which, how-ever, could operate only on certain highways. The famous Bow Street Runners were eight officers who became legendary for their efficiency, could act throughout the country, and served as the Scotland Yard of the day. But in most parishes there was little enough supervision. Sometimes, for instance, though there was a day watch and a night watch there was no evening watch, and for three or four most dangerous hours citizens were left undefended. Even when criminals were well known, parish officials were often bribed or frightened into inactivity.

The first important change came with the Act of 1792, when seven Police Offices were established in London. Each was administered by three magistrates appointed on the recommendation of the Home Secretary. They were to be paid, and had power to appoint paid constables. Thus began the close association between the police and the Home Office, and the first step was taken towards the establishment of an efficient police system. Sir Robert Peel carried this farther in 1829.

In the eighteenth century European philosophers were much concerned with enquiring into the nature of law, and in 1764 the Italian philosopher Beccaria, in his book *On Crimes and Punishments,* emphasised several simple propo-sitions:

(*a*) that the purpose of punishment was the protection of so-ciety;

(*b*) that punishments ought not to be savage, and that cruel punishments merely hardened society to cruelty;

(*c*) that the certainty of punishment was much more im-portant than its severity;

(*d*) that excessive punishments very uncertainly carried out were bad;

(*e*) that there ought to be a reasonable scale between the crime and the punishment.

Beccaria preferred moderate penalties strictly enforced to extreme penalties ill-enforced.

These ideas were taken up in England by Samuel Romilly and Jeremy Bentham. Romilly's first pamphlet on the subject was in 1785. He was struck by the fact that (as he said in 1810):

there is probably no other country in the world in which so many and so great a variety of human actions are punishable with loss of life as in England.

He urged that the death penalty ought not to be inflicted "for a mere invasion of property", that excessive punishments frequently remitted turned crime into a gamble. Jeremy Bentham, in his *Introduction to the Principles of Morals and Legislation* (1789), argued that since punishment involved the infliction of pain it was bad, and could be justified only in so far as it was necessary for the protection of society; it ought never to be greater than was necessary to promote the general happiness of the community. All this was in accord with a growing public opinion, but it was difficult to persuade Parliament that it was safe to relax the barriers erected to defend private property. A committee of the Commons had reported in favour of reform as early as 1771, but the Commons rejected the proposal. Romilly did not open his parliamentary campaign until 1810, and it was not for another nine years that any substantial reform was achieved.

The reform of the law had not therefore really begun by 1792, but a great change in public opinion was already coming about. Men were learning that the best way to achieve a law-abiding society was not to increase the severity of the punishments, but to keep punishments in accord with public opinion, and ensure their enforcement.

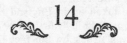

14

The Church, Methodism and the Evangelicals

IN 1688 THE Anglican clergy were placed in a dilemma; they had to choose between their church and their loyalty to the monarchy. The great majority chose the former, though many had misgivings. Some 400 of the most saintly men and best scholars among them could not bring themselves to take the oath of allegiance to William III, and became Non-Jurors, among them Archbishop Sancroft, Bishop Ken of Bath and Wells, and Bishop Frampton of Gloucester. They were in no sense disloyal; they simply retired, often into poverty, for the sake of their beliefs. The church could ill-afford to lose such men, but the way was thus open for the advancement of men more in accord with the spirit of the times.

A great opportunity was lost in 1689 to end the Protestant divisions in England by bringing the sects together on the principle of Comprehension.[1] After the great religious struggles of the seventeenth century a new spirit was abroad. The old religious controversies seemed less important. Men talked less of theology and more of a reasonable morality. We have seen that the England after 1689 was one of rapidly expanding trade and wealth. It was also the age of Isaac Newton and the new physics, Locke and the new psychology of happiness, Shaftesbury and *les douceurs de la vie*. In religion there emerged a number of men of latitude, led by the

[1] See Ch. 3.

Cambridge Platonists (Benjamin Whichcote and Cudworth, the Master of Clare College, Cambridge), who argued that there was no conflict between reason and religion. John Locke wrote that "revelation cannot be admitted against the clear evidence of reason". They did not at all mean to deny the reality of revelation, but they argued with Archbishop Tillotson that reason was the true guide in religion. Everything was plain and easy; Anglicanism was reasonable; there was no need for heat. Religion should be organised and seemly. Above all, it was necessary to avoid "enthusiasm", which was the eighteenth-century term for fanaticism. The deists, however, went farther. They believed that there was a God, belief in whom was necessary for morality, but they rejected revelation; all that was necessary was a natural religion based on reason. Such was the doctrine of John Toland and Anthony Collins. From this it was a short step to the sceptics and agnostics, such as David Hume, who denied the existence of God altogether. There thus spread, under the influence of the new science and scepticism, both a new latitudinarianism and a new irreligion.

How well equipped was the Anglican church to meet the new challenge? It was not without its saintly men, such as Sharp, Archbishop of York, and Fleetwood, Bishop of Ely. Some writers tried to meet their critics on their own ground by trying to provide proof for their religion. The greatest apologetic work of the time, however, was that of Bishop Butler, *The Analogy of the Christian Religion* (1736), in which he rested religion squarely upon divine mystery, and affirmed that Christianity could never rest on more than probability. It was one of the finest pieces of Anglican writing, but it was never widely read. Indeed, so far from the Anglican church closing its ranks against deism, it was deeply divided against itself. There was much hostility between the bishops, who tended to be whigs and men of latitude, and the great mass of the clergy who tended to look back to the controversies of the seventeenth century. This conflict was expressed in the Bangorian Controversy, which was begun when Bishop Hoadley of Bangor preached a famous sermon in 1717 in which he affirmed that the church had no outward and visible authority; that doctrine was of secondary importance, and that all that mattered was sincerity. The Lower House of Convocation demanded that Hoadley be silenced, and the controversy became so heated that Convocation itself was silenced, and did not meet again for a hundred and forty years. The views of Bishop Hoadley on the comparative unimportance of the Anglican church was to the taste of the whigs, and Hoadley went on an episcopal odyssey, being appointed successively Bishop of Bangor, Hereford, Salisbury and Winchester. His preferment was a scandal, for, as Professor Sykes wrote, "he reduced the visible church to ruin, and enthroned in its place the principle of unlimited private judgment".

After 1688 the Anglican church became too much the handmaiden of the state to fulfil its task properly. Bishops were too closely bound to what Bishop Gibson called "the maintenance of the Protestant Succession, the Church Establishment and the Toleration Act of 1689". True Christianity was placed second. Dr Johnson said in 1775 that: "no man can now be made a bishop for his learning and piety; his only chance of promotion is being connected with somebody who has parliamentary interest." By such means Shute Barrington proceeded rapidly via a royal chaplaincy to a canonry at Oxford, and then to the bishoprics of Llandaff, Salisbury and Durham. Bishop Watson, who said, "I happened to please a party, and they made me a Bishop", disliked his diocese of Llandaff, and preferred to live on Lake Windermere. Bishop Hoadley never once in six years stepped inside his diocese at Bangor. Many a country parson was like Parson Woodforde (whose diary makes interesting reading), and found solace in hunting rather than theology, in a good pie, tobacco and a jug of ale rather than in reading the classics.

> His talk was now of tithes and dues,
> He smoked his pipe and read the news.

At the end of the century it was calculated that over 7,000 out of 11,000 clergy were non-resident.

But we must not paint too dark a picture. Bishop Gibson, of London, who was "Walpole's Pope", and adviser on ecclesiastical appointments, was a conscientious man, and something of an authority on canon law. There were eminent theologians in the church, Warburton, Bishop of Gloucester, Butler, Bishop of Bristol, and Berkeley, Bishop of Cloyne. Thomas Wilson, Bishop of Sodor and Man, was a pastor of great saintliness. And from the diaries of the time, of Weston Longueville, John Skinner and Parson Woodforde, one has the impression of well-meaning pastors carrying out their duties as well as they are carried out by many parsons in any age. Dr Johnson was right when he commented:

> No, Sir, I do not envy a clergyman's life as an easy life, nor do I envy the clergyman who makes it an easy life.

There was, moreover, as the century progressed, a growing concern for moral and spiritual matters. As early as 1691 a Society for the Reformation of Manners was formed to combat the vices of the age. William III issued a Proclamation against immorality and profaneness in 1698, and Queen Anne issued one in 1702. Colley Cibber, the dramatist and theatrical manager, and Jeremy Collier led a campaign to purify the stage. Overseas missionary work was popular at this time, and the Society for the Propagation of Christian Knowledge (1698) and the Society for the Propagation of the Gospel (1701) were both founded by Thomas Bray to send books overseas. Charity schools were a noted feature of the period; the Grey Coat School, Westminster was founded in 1698, and by 1704 there were fifty charity schools in London. In 1739, after a labour of seventeen years, Captain Thomas Coram established his Foundling Hospital to save the lives of the waifs of London. The Bangorian Controversy called forth one of the supreme examples of devotional literature of the time in William Law's *Serious Call,* a book which had such an influence upon John Wesley.

John Wesley was himself a product of the great reaction from the cold rationalism and materialism of the age. Born in 1703 at the famous Epworth parsonage, he was the fifteenth child of Samuel and Susannah Wesley. The great influence of his early life was the stern puritanism of his mother. At Oxford he was a good deal more serious about his studies than was customary at the time, and in 1726 he became Fellow of Lincoln College, and was ordained two years later. Oxford was at one of the low-water marks in its history. A Fellow of St John's could write:

> We have had history professors who never read anything to qualify them for it. . . . We have had likewise numberless professors of Greek, Hebrew and Arabic who scarce understood their mother-tongue.

Wesley soon tired of it. In 1735 he met James Oglethorpe, a

philanthropist and soldier, who had established a colony in
Georgia as a home for debtors, and as a barrier against the
Spanish; and Wesley agreed to go out as a missionary at fifty
pounds a year. It was a disastrous failure, and Wesley returned home in 1737 with a deep sense of failure. He had,
however, been deeply attracted to the quiet religion of the
Moravians, a pious and puritan sect of German origin, and
under their influence he underwent a spiritual conversion in
1738. In 1739 there arose at Bristol a blazing youth of twenty-
five named George Whitefield, who began open-air preaching
to the colliers of Kingswood, and was soon preaching to
congregations of ten thousand. Whitefield wrote begging Wesley to join him. Wesley at first was much against preaching
in the open air, and there were always important differences
between himself and Whitefield, for Whitefield was a Calvinist, which Wesley never was. But he joined him in 1739,
and soon both were drawing vast crowds. The first Methodist Society was established in 1739, and the first chapel
was built in a disused foundry at Moorfields. Whitefield's
movement spread like wildfire through Wales; and Wesley
became an itinerant preacher, travelling more than a quarter
of a million miles in the course of his long life. The
physical effort of this alone was stupendous, for the roads
were appalling, and neither snow nor floods would deter
him. Sometimes he was stoned by hostile villagers. One
Methodist preacher, William Seward, in South Wales, was
first blinded and then killed in 1741. Perhaps Wesley's
greatest success was at Newcastle, where he aroused a flare
of enthusiasm, and founded the famous "Orphan House" in
1741. In the previous year he had started a school for poor
children at Kingswood, where, it must be admitted, his discipline was both strict and unimaginative. However, in many
parts of the country early Methodism seems to have made
little or no impact.

It had to encounter great hostility, both from the Anglican church and from the governing classes. The former
mistrusted the "enthusiasm and emotionalism which the
movement engendered". The upper classes resented the un-
couth character of some of the Methodist lay preachers, and
the abuse which they levelled against the Anglican clergy
and employers. The attitude of many of the upper classes is
shewn in this famous letter by the Duchess of Bucking-
ham.

Their (i.e. the Methodists) doctrines are most repulsive, strongly tinctured with Impertinence and Disrespect towards their Superiors, in perpetually endeavouring to level all Ranks, and do away with all Distinctions. It is monstrous to be told that you have a heart as *sinful* as the Common Wretches that crawl on the Earth. This is highly offensive and insulting.

In this respect Methodism's most important ally was Selina, Countess of Huntingdon (1707–91), who had undergone a religious conversion, and was present at the first Methodist meeting in London in 1738. She was a Calvinist, and always much preferred Whitefield to Wesley. Her great service to the movement was that she introduced Methodism to the upper classes, and it became the fashion for a number of society ladies to embrace the new faith; her sister-in-law, Lady Margaret Hastings, Lady Anne Frankland and Lady Betty Hastings for example. Even the Duchess of Marlborough was interested to hear Whitefield preach. For forty years Lady Huntingdon built her chapels up and down the country, and launched her preachers, celebrated names like William Romaine and Fletcher of Madeley. She made attendance at her chapels one of the social activities at Bath, Brighton and Tunbridge Wells, and she entertained the great names of the day, Lord Chesterfield, Horace Walpole, Lord North at her great house in Chelsea. When Cornwallis, Archbishop of Canterbury, gave a ball, Selina complained to George III, and the King wrote sternly to the Archbishop, and declared: "I wish there was a Lady Huntingdon in every diocese in the kingdom!"

John Wesley all his life regarded himself as a minister of the Anglican church, but in fact he was forced to begin the ordination of Methodist ministers (1784), and this involved a breach with the Established church. The first Methodist Conference was held in 1744, and thereafter the Methodists worked out their own organisation. Wesley's teaching was simple, and from the heart. He taught the religion of love; so long as one realised that God is Love there was little else in theology that was important. He cared little for theology. He preferred preaching to the lower and middle classes; the upper classes he regarded as "the Great Vulgar". This practice gave the movement a democratic veneer, and this has sometimes led to a misunderstanding of its character.

In all political matters Wesley was a staunch tory. He derived his political theory from the Old Testament; the ruler's power came from God, and was answerable only to God. He had no faith in the people's capacity in political affairs. He was opposed to Wilkes, and to the colonists in rebellion. He found no fault with the English Constitution. He was deeply concerned with the problems of poverty he saw around him, but he was more concerned with the holiness which would ensure a place in the next life, than with material conditions in this life. He did condemn the selfish materialism of the rich, and he did condemn the brutal treatment of Negro slaves, but it is impossible to say that Methodism as such advocated either political or social change. Methodists tended to be concentrated in certain areas, such as Wales, Yorkshire and Cornwall, and many of them were highly respectable middle-class who condemned every form of working-class agitation. In Yorkshire, however, the very areas where Methodism was strongest were also the areas where Luddite and radical activities were strongest in the early nineteenth century. By that time there had been a breakaway movement known as the Primitive Methodists, led by William Clowes (1780–1851) and this movement had strong radical tendencies.

It is important not to confuse Methodism with the whole dissenting activity of the eighteenth century. Dissent and Evangelicalism have made the very greatest contribution to the development of the eighteenth and nineteenth centuries. The dissenting Academies provided the very best education available in the eighteenth century. The best known was that of Dr Philip Doddridge at Northampton. Bishop Butler was educated in such a school, and later found Oriel College much inferior to it. The Quakers were a most active and prosperous sect, and were the first to raise their voice against the slave trade and slavery. The Unitarians were politically most wide awake, and Richard Price and Joseph Priestley were in favour of both the American and the French Revolutions. There was a clear connection between radicalism and dissent, but radicalism was a very different thing from revolution.

The same forces which gave rise to Wesley's movement gave rise to the Evangelical movement within the Anglican church, and the two movements often had much the same ideas. They both took a Fundamentalist view of the Scriptures; they both laid great emphasis on the need to be born again and on the doctrine of Grace. But the Evangelicals disliked open-air meetings, and the outward signs of "enthusiasm", and they were shocked at Wesley's ordination of ministers. They were strict sabbatarians, living constantly in the fear of hell-fire, and preferring texts from St Paul to those from the Gospels. Some were very favourable to Wesley, and Grimshaw and Berridge joined his movement as itinerant preachers. Some wrote best-selling works of devotion, like Venn's *Complete Duty of Man* and Milner's *History of the Church of Christ*. Some of them were great hymn-writers. Hymns had hitherto not been much used in church, but there is a crowd of noted writers in the eighteenth century among Methodists and Evangelicals, Charles Wesley ("Jesu, Lover of my soul"), Toplady ("Rock of Ages"), John Newton ("How sweet the name of Jesus sounds") and William Cowper ("God moves in a mysterious way"). William Cowper was the greatest literary genius among them, becoming a pathetic figure living on the edge of madness.

There was no lethargy about the Evangelical approach to religion. William Grimshaw, the curate of Haworth, was accustomed to chase tardy parishioners to church on Sundays with a whip, and when Wesley visited him in 1757 he noted that there were a thousand people at communion, and that they consumed thirty-five bottles of wine! John Berridge, vicar of Everton, was famous for his preaching all over East Anglia. The Evangelicals were the pioneers of Sunday Schools, the first of which was established by Robert Raikes of Gloucester in 1780. Fletcher went to an almost heathen parish of Madeley and turned it into a Christian one. Religion was certainly not asleep in later-eighteenth-century England.

The best-known activity of the Evangelicals was against the slave trade. In the eighteenth century British dealers were transporting some 50,000 Negro slaves a year from Africa to the colonies, in conditions of the most appalling suffering. George Fox, the Quaker, had condemned the trade as early as 1671, and Defoe, Adam Smith and Dr Johnson were all opposed to it. But it was argued that the trade was indispensable to the welfare of the colonies and an admirable training-ground for seamen. Moreover, as slaves were private property, the question of humanity did not arise. It was left to a little group of Evangelicals, known as the "Saints" to make a campaign. In 1772 the young Granville

Sharp won the famous Somersett's Case, which made slavery illegal in England. In 1787 he and Thomas Clarkson and the Quakers launched the Abolition Committee. They needed, however, a parliamentary spokesman, and were lucky to win over Pitt's close friend, William Wilberforce. In 1785 Wilberforce had undergone a sudden religious conversion, such as was frequent in the eighteenth century, and from being a brilliant society figure, he now took up the challenge to fight two important issues in the national life. Of these he wrote in his journal:

> God Almighty has set before me two great objects, the suppression of the Slave Trade and the reformation of manners.

In 1788 Pitt agreed to set up a committee of enquiry. Meanwhile Sir William Dolben, horrified at seeing for himself the contents of a slave-ship, introduced a Bill limiting the number of slaves which could be carried according to tonnage. Pitt supported the Bill, declaring that the trade, if unregulated, "is contrary to every humane, to every Christian principle, to every sentiment that ought to inspire the breast of man"; and it was carried. In 1791 Wilberforce introduced a Bill to abolish the trade altogether, but it was decisively defeated. The main argument against the Bill was that it was interference in the rights of the West Indians' private property. In the following year, however, a resolution was carried for the "gradual" abolition of the trade. What exactly this meant was uncertain, and in the ensuing years of fear of revolution, the subject was pushed into the background. Wilberforce had to wait another fifteen years for the achievement of his object.

The abolition of the slave trade and of slavery, although the best-known, was not the main task which Wilberforce set before himself. This was nothing less than the complete reformation of manners. The Evangelicals were deeply conscious of the sinfulness of their times, and were convinced that a terrible punishment would fall upon such a nation. They hated the violations of the Sabbath, the gambling, drinking, coarseness and cruelty of the times. In 1788 they formed the "Proclamation Society" to stamp out vice and immorality, and began by prosecuting Tom Paine's *Rights of Man* as an obscene book. One of Wilberforce's friends, Hannah More, once a celebrated Bluestocking, in 1789 opened a school for the poor in Cheddar, largely at Wilberforce's expense. The prime purpose was not to teach the poor to read and write, but to teach them Christian manners and frugality. She was also a celebrated writer of improving works, which taught the new morality at a halfpenny per copy, and were best-sellers. Thus began a movement which mostly lies beyond the limits of this book, but which had enormous importance in shaping the character of the nineteenth century. Many of the implications of "Victorianism" began, not with Queen Victoria, nor even Prince Albert, but with William Wilberforce and his friends.

Bibliography

Perhaps the books that the student will find most valuable for further reading are:

1. Sources

Bishop Burnet. *History of My Own Times*. London: W. Smith, 1833.
Lord Hervey's Memoirs. London: Eyre & Spottiswoode, Ltd., 1931.
Wesley's Journal. London: The Epworth Press.

2. Modern Works

Brooke, John. *The Chatham Administration, 1766–1768*. New York: St Martin's Press, Inc., London: Macmillan & Co., Ltd., 1956.

Carpenter, Spencer C. *Church and People*. London: The Society for the Promotion of Christian Knowledge, 1959.

Carswell, J. *The South Sea Bubble*. Stanford, Calif.: Stanford University Press; London: Cresset Press, Ltd., 1960.

Churchill, Winston. *Marlborough, His Life and Times*. 6 vols. New York: Charles Scribner's Sons; London: George G. Harrap & Co., Ltd., 1933–38.

Clapham, John H. *Economic History of Modern Britain*. 3 vols. New York: The Macmillan Company; London: Cambridge University Press, 1931–38.

Derry, John W. *The Younger Pitt*. London: B. T. Batsford, Ltd., 1962.

Feiling, Keith. *History of the Tory Party: 1640–1714*. New York and London: Oxford University Press, 1924.

Namier, L. B. *England in the Age of the American Revolution*. New York: St Martin's Press; London: Macmillan & Co., Ltd., 1961.

Ogg, David. *England in the Reigns of James II and William III*. New York and London: Oxford University Press, 1955.

Owen, J. B. *The Rise of the Pelhams*. London: Methuen & Company, Ltd., 1957.

Pares, Richard. *King George III and the Politicians*. New York and London: Oxford University Press, 1953.

Plumb, J. H. *Sir Robert Walpole*. 2 vols. Boston: Houghton Mifflin Company; London: Cresset Press, Ltd., 1956, 1961.

Trevelyan, G. *England Under Queen Anne*. 3 vols. New York and London: Longmans, Green & Company, 1930–34.

Watson, John S. *Reign of George III*. New York and London: Oxford University Press, 1960.

Whinney, M. D., and Millar, O. N. *English Art, 1625–1714*. New York and London: Oxford University Press, 1957.

Williams, Basil. *Life of William Pitt, Earl of Chatham*. 2 vols. New York and London: Longmans, Green & Company, 1913.

Index

233